Voices of Collective Remembering

Voices of Collective Remembering reviews various understandings of the term "collective memory" as it is used in the humanities and social sciences.

Drawing on this review, James V. Wertsch outlines a particular version of collective remembering grounded in the use of "textual resources," especially narratives. This takes him into the special properties of narrative that shape this process and how these textual resources are produced and consumed.

Professor Wertsch brings these ideas to life by examining the rapid, massive transformation of collective memory during the transition from Soviet Russia to post-Soviet Russia. This natural laboratory has many unique features, but it also provides general insights into processes of collective memory formation, especially as carried out by modern states.

James V. Wertsch is the Marshall S. Snow Professor of Arts and Sciences at Washington University in St. Louis. His books include *Vygotsky and the Social Formation of Mind* (1985); *Culture, Communication, and Cognition: Vygotskian Perspectives* (1985); *Voices of the Mind* (1991); *Sociocultural Studies of Mind* (edited with P. del Rio and A. Alvarez, 1995); and *Mind as Action* (1998). Professor Wertsch has been awarded honorary doctorates by the University of Linköping and the University of Oslo and is an honorary member of the Russian Academy of Education.

To my Russian friends and teachers

Voices of Collective Remembering

JAMES V. WERTSCH
Washington University in St. Louis

CAMBRIDGE
UNIVERSITY PRESS

PUBLISHED BY THE PRESS SYNDICATE OF THE UNIVERSITY OF CAMBRIDGE
The Pitt Building, Trumpington Street, Cambridge, United Kingdom

CAMBRIDGE UNIVERSITY PRESS
The Edinburgh Building, Cambridge CB2 2RU, UK
40 West 20th Street, New York, NY 10011-4211, USA
477 Williamstown Road, Port Melbourne, VIC 3207, Australia
Ruiz de Alarcón 13, 28014 Madrid, Spain
Dock House, The Waterfront, Cape Town 8001, South Africa

http://www.cambridge.org

First published 2002

Printed in the United States of America

Typeface Palatino 10/12 pt.   *System* LaTeX 2_ε [TB]

A catalog record for this book is available from the British Library.

Library of Congress Cataloging in Publication Data

Wertsch, James V.
Voices of collective remembering / James V. Wertsch.
     p.   cm.
Includes bibliographical references and index.
ISBN 0-521-81050-7 – ISBN 0-521-00880-8 (pbk.)
1. Memory – Social aspects.   2. History – Psychological aspects.   3. Memory – Social
aspects – Russia (Federation)   4. Historiography – Russia (Federation)   I. Title.
BF378.S65 W47 2002
901'.9–dc21   2001052866

ISBN 0 521 81050 7 hardback
ISBN 0 521 00880 8 paperback

Contents

Introduction and Acknowledgments

In this book, I take up three main tasks. First, I outline the meaning (rather meanings) of "collective memory." Because this term has almost as many interpretations as interpreters, I devote considerable attention to it, especially in Chapter 3. Second, in parts of Chapters 1, 2, and 3, I outline a particular approach to collective memory, one that focuses on how "cultural tools," especially narrative texts, mediate its functioning. From this perspective, collective memory is best understood as being "distributed" between active agents and the textual resources they employ. This amounts to narrowing the field of memory studies, but it remains an effort to harness ideas from a wide range of intellectual traditions. And third, in Chapters 4 through 7, I have sought to put these ideas to work in connection with a body of empirical evidence from Soviet and post-Soviet Russia. As will become clear, this is often not so much a matter of putting well-formulated ideas into practice as it is one of clarifying these ideas in the first place.

The general plan of the volume, then, starts out broadly and converges on a narrower set of concerns. It begins by opening up several issues that could, and eventually should, be addressed under the heading of collective memory, moves to outlining a particular way to proceed, and then to harnessing this particular approach to look at empirical examples. Any one of these topics could have taken up an entire book in its own right – and each almost did in various incarnations of this one. However, I have tried to weave them into a single discussion because I view the analysis of each as informing the others.

Nonetheless, it is possible to read sections of this book in relative isolation. Those interested primarily in the conceptual landscape that frames discussions of collective memory in general can turn to Chapter 3, and perhaps Chapter 2 as well. If the more specific issue of collective memory as a distributed phenomenon is one's interest, it is possible to focus on parts of Chapters 2 and 3 to get the overall argument. And if one's concern is with how the textual resources of collective memory have been produced and used in Soviet and post-Soviet Russia, then it may make sense to go directly to Chapters 4 through 7.

I hope, however, that the whole is greater than the sum of its parts. The glue that holds these parts together is the claim that collective remembering is a matter of agents using cultural tools, especially narratives. Drawing on others' ideas about the "multivoiced" nature of human consciousness, I emphasize that these cultural tools always have a history of being used by others, and as a result bring their own voices to the table. This line of reasoning provides a thread for tying together the pieces of the wide-ranging discussion in Chapter 3, and it is what lends coherence to the discussion of the empirical examples.

Regardless of how one reads the chapters that follow, it will undoubt-edly strike some that my treatment of each of the three issues I take up is incomplete, a charge to which I am undoubtedly guilty in more ways than I can imagine. One reason for this partial picture is my focus on one kind of collective, the modern state. And under this heading, I have nar-rowed things even further by examining Soviet and post-Soviet Russia. This setting is a "natural laboratory" capable of providing insights that would be hard to come by elsewhere. In particular, it provides insights into the central role that modern states play in forming collective mem-ory and what can happen when they lose their legitimacy. Hopefully, the insights that I glean from the Russian illustrations have implications for collective remembering in other settings as well.

Russia is also a significant site for me in a more personal way because it has been a major source of my intellectual inspiration over the past quarter century. Beginning in the 1970s with a post-doctoral year in Moscow, I have lived and worked there on numerous occasions to study with colleagues in psychology, semiotics, and other areas of the human sciences. My initial encounters in Moscow with figures such as A.R. Luria, A.N. Leont'ev, V.V. Davydov, and V.P. Zinchenko in the 1970s had a profound impact on me in all kinds of ways. After helping me overcome an early period of confusion and even resistance to radically new ideas, they, along with people in the United States such as Michael Cole, led me to appreciate the brilliance of the ideas of Lev Semënovich Vygotsky and others.

With this as a beginning, I went on to benefit from the intellectual guidance of friends and colleagues such as Michael Holquist, who intro-duced me, as well as so many others, to the ideas of Mikhail Mikhailovich Bakhtin. Along with Aleksandr Romanovich Luria and Vladimir Petrovich Zinchenko, I count Mike as one of my most important teachers. In re-cent years, my sources of instruction and inspiration have expanded to include colleagues such as Aleksandr Asmolov, Andrei Kvakin, and Irina Medvedeva in Moscow; Elena Ivanova in Kharkiv; and Martin Conway in Durham.

Closer to home, I have benefited immensely from my discussions with several people at Washington University in St. Louis. The list includes Wayne Fields, Roddy Roediger, Marc Raichle, Hillel Kieval, and Alison Wiley. Together we went through the process of searching for a candidate for the Henry R. Luce Foundation Professor of Collective and Individual Memory at Washington University, something that broadened my horizons immensely. The arrival of Pascal Boyer to fill this position has added to the discussion, while at the same time it is a discussion that has expanded beyond the borders of my own institution thanks to colleagues such as Cathy Caruth, James Young, Sam Wineburg, Jennifer Jenkins, and Peter Seixas. I am particularly indebted to Mike Holquist, Martin Conway, Roddy Roediger, and Elena Ivanova for their close readings and detailed commentaries on this manuscript.

Finally, I am indebted to several other actors whose support made this work possible. These include The National Council for Eurasian and Eastern European Research (Contract No. 811–07), which funded some of the early empirical work outlined in what follows, and the Swedish Collegium for Advanced Study in the Social Sciences, where I spent a wonderful semester in 1998 writing a draft of much of this book. The Spencer Foundation occupies a special position in this regard since it has provided the bulk of the funding for the theoretical and empirical research I report here. I thank the Foundation for making this book possible.

1

An Encounter with Collective Memory

While on a trip to Moscow in 1997, I spent a day at a high school known for its strong students and excellent instruction. In addition to observing several classes, I had the opportunity to engage some eleventh grade students in a discussion about World War II, and in this context I asked about the role that the United States had played in this conflict. In response, "Sasha," a sixteen-year-old boy, turned to me and said something like the following:

The United States made a lot of money from selling arms and other things to countries during the early years of the war, but it did not really contribute as an ally. In fact, along with Great Britain it refused to open a second front in 1942 and again in 1943. It was only after the U.S. and Britain began to think that the Soviet Union might win the war by itself and dominate post-war Europe that they became concerned enough to enter the war in earnest by opening a second front in 1944.

Sasha's comments left me with an impression as well as a question. The impression had to do with the way he spoke about these events. He made his presentation in a straightforward, confident manner, displaying little doubt or hesitation. It was almost as if he was providing an eye-witness account of what had happened. The idea that a competing account might exist seemed not to have been an option in his mind. Furthermore, based on the nods of Sasha's classmates and other evidence to be outlined in later chapters, it is an account that has some currency among his generation in Russia.

The question I had was tied to this impression of certainty. I wondered: Where did Sasha and other members of his generation in Russia get this account of the past? After all, neither he nor anyone else in his generation actually witnessed the events – indeed, they were not even born until nearly four decades after World War II was over. The obvious answer is that they had learned about World War II at school, at home, from the media, and so forth. Such learning invariably takes the form of mastering narrative texts about who did what to whom, for what reasons, and in what context,

4

and there is little reason to doubt that this is how Sasha had developed his account.

Instead of being grounded in direct, immediate experience of events, the sort of collective memory at issue in this case is what I shall term "textually mediated." Specifically, it is based on "textual resources" provided by others – narratives that stand in, or mediate, between the events and our understanding of them. Some may view this as being memory only in an unusual sense since it is not memory for events that have actually been experienced. From such a perspective, memory for a text may be involved, but this is not memory proper – that is, memory for the events themselves.

But the fact remains that what Sasha presented often *is* discussed under the heading of collective memory, a fact that raises the question of what we mean when we use the term. As I shall outline in Chapter 3, the unfortunate answer is that "collective memory" can mean any number of things depending on the conversation in which it is embedded. Furthermore, even when speakers assume they have one meaning in mind, this meaning often turns out to be fuzzy and not clearly differentiated from others. This unfortunate state of affairs is what motivates one of my major aims in the chapters that follow – sorting through and categorizing the various meanings of "collective memory."

Returning to my encounter with Sasha, the fact that he relied so totally on textual mediation makes the impression of certainty all the more striking. I was almost tempted to ask him, "How can you, a person who was not even alive at the time, be so sure of what you are saying?" As far as Sasha was concerned, however, he was recounting the events themselves, not some narrative about them. He seemed not to be the least bit tempted to qualify what he said with something like "What our textbooks tell us is . . . " or "The version provided in our movies is . . . ."

But it is of course not only Sasha or his generation in Russia who displays this lack of awareness of the textually mediated nature of much of collective memory. It is characteristic of collective memory more generally, and is an instance of what can be called the "transparency" of language. It was as if Sasha were "looking through" the narrative text he was employing and could not see it or appreciate the way it shaped what he was saying. It may be possible for people whose collective memories of World War II are quite different from Sasha's to detect the mediating texts shaping his account, but this clearly seems to have been something that escaped his attention. In reality, however, one can ask how often any of us recognizes such mediation in our accounts of the past.

These points came into sharper focus when I related my encounter with Sasha to American colleagues and friends. In this context, I have often encountered comments such as, "Where did he get that story?" or "That's the kind of thing you would expect them to say." And reactions sometimes shade over into indignation, giving rise to responses such as, "That's just not true! He doesn't know what he's talking about!" Conversely, Russians are surprised – if not dismissive or even deeply offended – when they hear accounts of World War II based on U.S. textbooks or on Hollywood movies such as *Saving Private Ryan*.

What all this suggests is the need to make visible and to understand the role of textual mediation in collective memory. Among other things, this means analyzing the specific forms that mediation takes in this case, especially narratives, and it calls on us to understand how such narrative texts are produced by the state, the media, and so forth, and how they are consumed, or used, by individuals and groups.

I shall approach these issues as part of a story about the more general category of "mediated action" (Wertsch, 1998). From this perspective, speaking, thinking, and other forms of human action are taken to involve an inherent, irreducible tension between agent and "cultural tools" such as language and narrative texts. This does not mean that such tools mechanistically determine how we act, but it is to say that their influence is powerful and needs to be recognized and examined. From this perspective, memory – both individual and collective – is viewed as "distributed" between agent and texts, and the task becomes one of listening for the texts and the voices behind them as well as the voices of the particular individuals using these texts in particular settings. In this approach, performances such as Sasha's are inherently "multivoiced" (Wertsch, 1991) rather than the product of an isolated speaker or cognitive agent. We implicitly recognize this when we respond to what he said by asking, "Where did he get that story?" In such instances, we are asking about the general perspective, or "speaking consciousness" (Holquist & Emerson, 1981, p. 434) that Bakhtin (1981) defined as "voice." Similarly, when we respond to Sasha's account by saying, "That's the kind of thing you would expect them to say," we are commenting on the speaking consciousness or general ideological perspective of the members of a collective (i.e., "them"), a collective that provides the narrative texts employed by Sasha to formulate his account of the past.

By implication, this approach identifies two things that Sasha was *not* doing. First, despite any impressions he might have had to the contrary, he was not simply relaying "what really happened." For this to be possible, we would have to presuppose a single, universally accepted, exhaustive, and true account of these events, one that would not allow for the sharp differences between his account and that of others. Second, the version of the past that Sasha provided was not the product of independent research. In principle, of course, it would have been possible for him to consult primary and secondary sources and arrive at his own formulation of what happened. It was not entirely surprising, however, to hear from his teacher and others familiar with his and his friends' ideas about World War II that this was not the case. Instead, Sasha was doing what most of us do most of the time when we produce collective memory accounts of the past – especially the past that occurred before our lifetime. Namely, he was employing an item from the "stock of stories" (MacIntyre, 1984) that exist in his sociocultural context.

This is not to say that Sasha was unable or unwilling to defend what he said. I did not go into a detailed discussion with him, but in countless discussions over the years with people like Sasha, I discovered that they are quite capable of backing up their own accounts with additional information. For example, if he were challenged about the motives his narrative attributed to the United States, he would be likely to point out that America emerged from World War II in a vastly more powerful economic position than it had in 1941. If we were to agree, but argue that this was not because the U.S. tried to improve its economic standing, he would be likely to say this is quite naive, and even might be able to point to documents or political decisions to support his interpretation.

Or in response to the argument that any attempt to open a second front earlier than 1944 would have resulted in an unacceptable level of casualties, Sasha might argue that the losses involved in D-Day were quite small compared with those experienced by the Soviets. Using even the more conservative estimate of war dead accepted during the Soviet years, the USSR lost *on average* 14,000 people every day between 1941 and 1945. This compares with 6,603 American deaths on D-Day in 1944 (The National D-Day Memorial Foundation homepage, June 10, 2000). Of course, using statistics to compare levels of pain and suffering is not a very satisfactory way to discuss such matters, but in fact, American claims about huge losses on June 6, 1944, and Russian claims about their relatively small size are often encountered in discussions about what happened in World War II. In short, Sasha was quite capable of supporting and defending his account and was not simply repeating it mindlessly.

Such observations highlight the fact that an active agent is involved in textually mediated collective memory. This requires us to keep a focus on how active agent and cultural tool operate in tandem rather than on how either element functions alone. Among other things, this means that textual resources used in collective memory usually do not take the form of isolated, hermetically sealed units that are either used in unmodified form and in their entirety or not used at all. Instead, they constitute a much more flexible kind of instrument that can be harnessed in combination with others in novel ways.

This line of reasoning is consistent with the past several decades of research in the psychology of memory. Such research has shown time and again that memory is more a matter of reorganizing, or reconstructing, bits of information into a general scheme than it is a matter of accurate recall of the isolated bits themselves. As Neisser (1967) argued decades ago, memory is not so much a matter of "reappearance" as it is a matter of active construction based on traces from earlier experiences. In this view, humans are often quite good at recalling the gist of what happened, a process that involves selectively using, and often distorting or deleting, pieces of information that do not contribute to the overall picture they are reconstructing. These are general points that apply to the resources of textual mediation as much as to any other kind of information.

Extending this line of argument, one can say that the narrative texts used in collective memory are best viewed as tools, or raw materials to be employed in organizing or reconstructing an account of the past. Instead of serving as containers of precise, unchanging information, these texts seem to play a role in memory by serving as indicators of "the sort of thing" an individual or group would say. Instead of remembering the precise words that someone uttered, we are much more likely to remember the gist of what he said, and in this effort we are likely to rely heavily on a sort of "implicit theory" (Ross, 1989) of what that voice, or type of voice, would utter.

A concrete illustration of these points can be found in how I remembered what Sasha had said on that morning in 1997. After relating this encounter from memory several times to others, I decided to write about it, and this took me back to the tape recording I had made of that discussion. At first, I thought I had been unable to find the right segment of conversation since I did not recognize what Sasha had said. But then I realized that what he said differed in some very significant ways from my recollection of it. I had remembered some bits of what he had said, but I had done a lot of "editing" to make them consistent with what I apparently believed he, or a person like him, would have said. A transcription from the tape of what said Sasha yielded the following:

Well, I think the United States benefited from that war. And Great Britain, too. They agreed to help other countries but won much more afterward. For example, when Germany began the war, England and France promised to help Eastern Europe but did nothing, and Hitler realized that they would not even come to the aid of Poland.

As any contemporary psychologist of memory would point out, my account of this incident had distorted it in some very predictable ways. To be generous, I got the gist of what Sasha had said, but I had also introduced, distorted, and deleted some important bits of information. Instead of remembering his precise words, or even his precise ideas, I apparently used pieces of what he had said as a basis for generating a text that I thought he would have produced. In short, what I remembered had more to do with the voice, or type of voice, I assumed was doing the talking than with what he actually had said.

Among other things, this little experiment reflects one final point I would like to make about the textual resources used in collective memory. In most cases, these resources are not neutral cognitive instruments that simply assist us in our efforts to remember. Instead, we are often committed to believing, or not believing them, sometimes in deeply emotional ways having to do with fundamental issues of identity. In my encounter with Sasha, this is reflected in the motivated way in which my recall was distorted. In retrospect, I found a level of defensiveness about historical accounts that surprised me.

It surprised me because over the past twenty-five years, I have had extensive exposure to Soviet and Russian accounts of World War II and have conscientiously tried to sort out what can be supported on rational, objective grounds and what cannot. In the process, I have come to believe very strongly that we in the West often vastly underestimate the Russian contribution to the war effort and overestimate our own. On countless occasions when speaking to Western friends and colleagues, I have recognized that massive blunders, self-inflicted loss, and monumental stupidity were part of the story of the Soviet war effort, but I have always made a point of emphasizing that the Soviets nonetheless deserve the lions' share of credit for winning the war against Hitler. In short, I had thought that after years of trying to understand the Russian account of World War II, I was fairly sensitive, and even sympathetic to their perspective.

Nevertheless, it appears that I had reacted with a good deal of defensiveness to what Sasha said. This defensiveness undoubtedly arose in response to being harangued by Soviet publications and the occasional individual about the pernicious tendencies of American capitalist cliques, and so on, and so on. Over the years, I had recognized that such statements were often best understood as public displays for the audience at hand rather than reflections of the core beliefs of the performers. Nonetheless, it appears that what I had been saying in public to Western colleagues differed from what at least some part of me believed in private. The result was that I had reconstructed Sasha's statement on the basis of more pernicious, Soviet-sounding motives to Allied actions than had appeared in what he actually said.

Put together with the shocked, and sometimes angry, response I hear from other Westerners when they encounter Sasha's account, my systematic distortion provides a reminder of something about the narrative texts used in the textual mediation of collective memory: They are important to us. Such accounts do not simply reflect different objective viewpoints to be accepted or not in a dispassionate way. Instead, they reflect strongly held commitments to a particular narrative account, commitments that are often masked by the tendency to think that our account simply relates what happened.

2

Methodological Preliminaries to the Study of Collective Remembering

The purpose of this chapter is to situate my perspective on collective memory, both in terms of theoretical and methodological commitments and in terms of broader historical context. The approach I shall outline does not fall neatly within any single academic discipline, a fact that I take to be an asset when studying this complex topic. Many research traditions have contributed to the study of this topic, and I believe it is important to draw on them as flexibly as possible. In this connection, I owe a great deal to studies in history, sociology, semiotics, psychology, and anthropology in particular, and the list does not stop there.

In developing my claims about collective remembering, I shall employ a set of illustrations. Indeed, several of the chapters that follow are almost entirely organized around such illustrations. These come primarily from a contemporary natural laboratory of collective memory: Russia as it makes the transition from Soviet to post-Soviet times. In particular, I shall be concerned with how state authorities in these two settings have played a role in shaping collective memory of an official sort. States are certainly not the only entities that try to purvey collective memory in the modern world, but they are unrivaled in the power and resources they have devoted to this effort. Indeed, their efforts constitute the most important experiment in collective memory in the world today, and hence make an obvious focus of study.

Sociocultural Analysis

The general theoretical framework I shall employ to hold the various strands of research on collective remembering together is what I term "sociocultural analysis" (Wertsch, 1991, 1998). My use of the term "sociocultural" reflects an intellectual heritage grounded largely in the writings of Russian scholars such as Vygotsky (1978, 1987), Luria (1928, 1979), and Bakhtin (1981, 1986). It is a heritage that has also been discussed by Cole

(1996) in connection with "cultural psychology" and by Asmolov (1998) in connection with "non-classical psychology."

A starting point for the sort of sociocultural analysis I have in mind is the notion that it takes "mediated action" as a unit of analysis. From this perspective, to be human is to use the cultural tools, or mediational means, that are provided by a particular sociocultural setting. The concrete use of these cultural tools involves an "irreducible tension" (Wertsch, 1998) between active agents, on the one hand, and items such as computers, maps, and narratives, on the other. From this perspective, remembering is an active process that involves both sides of this tension. And because it involves socioculturally situated mediational means, remembering and the parties who carry it out are inherently situated in a cultural and social context.

As an illustration, consider the following episode. A colleague recently asked me to recommend a book on a particular topic. I knew the book I wanted to suggest, and could even "see" it in my mind's eye in the sense that I could tell the colleague its color and approximate size. Furthermore, I could name the author. I was unable, however, to recall the book's title. I therefore used a cultural tool that has only emerged in a full-fledged form over the past few years, the Internet. I used my office computer to go to the bookseller Amazon.com, where I looked up the author of the book in question. Her list of books appeared on the screen, and I was able to recognize the correct title and recommend to my colleague the book I had intended.

Viewed in terms of mediated action, the question that arises here is, "Who did the remembering?" On the one hand, I had to be involved as an active agent who had mastered the relevant cultural tool sufficiently well to conduct the appropriate search. On the other hand, this active agent, at least at that moment, was quite incapable of remembering the title of the book in question when operating in isolation – that is, without additional help from an external cultural tool. If I could have done so, I would not have turned to Amazon.com in the first place, an observation suggesting that perhaps Amazon.com should get the credit for remembering. But Amazon.com is not an agent in its own right – at least the same kind of active agent that I am (hopefully); it did not somehow speak up on its own to tell my colleague or me what we wanted to know.

From the perspective of mediated action there are good reasons for saying that neither I nor Amazon.com did the remembering in isolation. Instead, both of us were involved in a system of distributed memory and both were needed to get the job done. In short, an irreducible tension between active agent and cultural tool was involved. The nature of the cultural tool and the specific use made of it by the active agent may vary greatly, but both contribute to human action understood from this perspective.

The use of Amazon.com to remember a book title involves the kind of "search strategies, new storage strategies, new memory access routes" and so forth outlined by Malcolm Donald (1991, p. 19) in his account of how memory has evolved in human history. The strategies are new in that they are situated in a unique historical, cultural, and institutional context. I could not have carried out this form of remembering a century, or even a decade, ago because Amazon.com, the Internet, and indeed computers in their present form did not then exist. Furthermore, even today I (Amazon.com and I – "we"?) could not have carried out this form of remembering if I had not had the cultural and institutional resources that make the Internet available and relatively inexpensive. In short, cultural tools are neither independent inventions of the agents using them nor are they universally available – two facts that remind us of how sociocultural situatedness is imposed by the use of mediational means.

As is the case for any cultural tool for remembering, Amazon.com has "constraints" as well as "affordances" (Wertsch, 1998), and its particular profile in this regard distinguishes it from other cultural tools. It is relatively easy to use Amazon.com, given the software and hardware I have in my office, and hence it affords the possibility of remembering a book title. It has constraints attached to it as well, however, constraints that could be pointed out by those who are more sophisticated than I in the use of such cultural tools. For example, others might know another on-line search strategy that provides faster responses or provides them without putting undue demands on the computer I have that sometimes cause it to crash when using Amazon.com. Such information might lead me to recognize the superior affordances of another way of searching for book titles, as well as the constraints introduced by the particular cultural tool I was using.

Another aspect of mediated action that comes to light in this illustration has to do with the relationship between agents and cultural tools – namely, the "mastery" (Wertsch, 1998) of these tools. No matter how powerful, fast, or efficient Amazon.com is, it cannot do the remembering by itself. An active agent is also required, and this agent must have mastered, at least minimally, the cultural tool in question. I do not claim a high degree of mastery in this case, but I do know how to do at least the minimum required. I know how to turn on my computer, how to get on to the Internet, how to use the "bookmark" menu to take me back to Amazon.com quickly, and so forth. The focus throughout all this is on "knowing how" rather than "knowing that" (Bechtel & Abrahamsen, 1991; Ryle, 1949) in the sense that such action is a matter of knowing how to use (i.e., mastering) relevant cultural tools.

A final implication of this illustration is that the cultural tool involved must be understood from the perspective of its "production" as well as "consumption." Up to now, I have focused on the ways that a particular consumer of Amazon.com – namely, me – uses this cultural tool. But a moment's reflection leads one to recognize the forces of production involved as well. When I turn to the Internet, I find it difficult to do very much at all without encountering an advertisement for Amazon.com. This is just the tip of the iceberg of a massive set of production processes that have given rise to this cultural tool. Like many commercially produced cultural tools, it is not just available; it is pushed on us in all kinds of ways in daily life. Of course, much more than advertising is involved. Massive resources have gone into producing the software, the access to stocks of books, and so forth, and those providing such resources often shape the cultural tool in ways that may have little to do with my wishes.

The point I wish to make in all this is not limited to Amazon.com, computers, the Internet, and so forth. Instead, the point is that most, if not all, forms of human memory can be understood from the perspective of mediated action. The resources available to agents as they engage in remembering range from Amazon.com to knotted ropes in ancient Peru (Cole & Scribner, 1974) to literacy (Olson, 1994), but I shall be particularly interested in narrative textual resources such as those employed by Sasha in the illustration in Chapter 1.

As in the case of Amazon.com, a key fact about the textual resources Sasha used is that they were not independently invented by the individual using them. Instead, they came from a "tool kit" (Wertsch, 1991) provided by a particular sociocultural setting. As Jerome Bruner (1990) puts it, such tools are "in place, already 'there,' deeply entrenched in culture and language" (p. 11). Sasha had mastered these textual resources in that he knew how to use them to respond to my question and to defend his answer, and it is possible to speculate on ways these resources constrained as well as afforded his memory performance. In short, all the basic properties of mediated action I outlined with regard to computer mediated remembering apply to Sasha's case of text mediated remembering.

To sum up, my commitment to sociocultural analysis reflects a commitment to ideas about mediated action deriving from the writings of Vygotsky, Bakhtin, and others. From this perspective, remembering is a form of mediated action, which entails the involvement of active agents and cultural tools. It is not something done by an isolated agent, but it is also not something that is somehow carried out solely by a cultural tool. Both must be involved in an irreducible tension. This has several implications, perhaps the most important being that because cultural tools reflect particular sociocultural settings, mediated remembering is also inherently situated in a sociocultural context.

Basic Terms in the Study of Collective Remembering as a Form of Mediated Action

Under the general heading of sociocultural analysis, I shall use several terms that imply methodological assumptions about how to study collective remembering, and hence deserve further comment. Indeed, I have already introduced these terms in my discussion in Chapter 1 of Sasha's account of World War II. The specific terms I have in mind are "text," "voice," and "remembering."

Text

The notion of text I shall be using derives from the writings of authors such as Yuri Lotman (1988, 1990) and Bakhtin (1986). In Bakhtin's view, "the text (written and oral) is the primary given" (p. 103) of linguistics, literary analysis, history, and other disciplines in the human sciences. From this perspective, text is viewed as a basic organizing unit that structures meaning, communication, and thought. In tracing out the implications of this line of reasoning for understanding history, Lotman wrote:

> The historian cannot observe events, but acquires narratives of them from the written sources. And even when the historian is an observer of the events described (examples of this rare occurrence are Herodotus and Julius Caesar) the observations still have to be mentally transformed into a verbal text, since the historian writes not of what was seen but a digest of what was seen in narrative form . . . The transformation of an event into a text involves, first, narrating it in the system of a particular language, i.e., subjecting it to a previously given structural organization. The event itself may seem to the viewer (or participant) to be disorganized (chaotic) or to have an organization which is beyond the field of interpretation, or indeed to be an accumulation of several discrete structures. But when an event is retold by means of a language then it inevitably acquires a structural unity. This unity, which in fact belongs only to the expression level, inevitably becomes transferred to the level of content too. So the very fact of transforming an event into a text raises the degree of its organization. (1990, pp. 221–222)

As a semiotician concerned with general problems of sign systems, Lotman tended to approach text and language as autonomous and as having their own structural principles. In his account, a text has "a separate, discrete, closed, final structure" (1988, p. 33), a point that led him to talk about the "structural unity" introduced by the "expression level."

Many points in Lotman's writings invite comparison with the claims of linguists such as Benjamin Lee Whorf (1956; Lucy, 1992) about the power of language to shape thought. For both Lotman and Whorf, the general line of reasoning is that the "expression level" shapes human perception, thought, and memory at the "level of content." In contrast to Whorf, however, who focused almost exclusively on the grammatical structure of language, Lotman considered a wider array of semiotic issues, including the uses and functions of texts. The figure from Russian semiotics and philosophy who perhaps had the most to say about how textual form and use are inextricably linked, however, is Bakhtin.

In an article entitled "The problem of the text in linguistics, philology, and the human sciences: An experiment in philosophical analysis" (1986b), Bakhtin insisted that focusing on the structure of a text tells only half the story. In his view, it was essential to go beyond this and recognize "two poles of the text" (1986b, p. 105). The first of these concerns the properties of structure or form. Bakhtin characterized this as "a generally understood (that is, conventional within a given collective) system of signs, a language" (Bakhtin, 1986b, p. 105). Without this pole, the text "is not a text, but a natural (not signifying) phenomenon, for example, a complex of natural cries and moans devoid of any linguistic (signifying) repeatability" (ibid.). The second, equally defining moment of text is its use by a concrete speaker in a concrete setting.

The overall picture is as follows:

And so behind each text stands a language system. Everything in the text that is repeated and reproduced, everything repeatable and reproducible, everything that can be given outside a given text (the given) conforms to this language system. But at the same time each text (as an utterance) is individual, unique, and unrepeatable, and herein lies its entire significance (its plan, the purpose for which it was created). This is the aspect of it that pertains to honesty, truth, goodness, beauty, history. With respect to this aspect, everything repeatable and reproducible proves to be material, a means to an end. This notion extends somewhat beyond the bounds of linguistics or philology. The second aspect (pole) inheres in the text itself, but is revealed only in a particular situation and in a chain of texts (in speech communication of a given area). This pole is linked not with elements (repeatable) in the system of the language (signs), but with other texts (unrepeatable) by special dialogue (and dialectical, when detached from the author) relations. (ibid.)

From the perspective of sociocultural analysis as outlined earlier in this chapter, the Bakhtinian notion of text constitutes a special case of mediated action. The repeatable aspect of text serves as "a means to an end" (Bakhtin, 1986b, p. 109) – that is, a cultural tool or resource, and this resource is used by a speaker in a unique, unrepeatable way in the production of any concrete utterance.

Both poles of text were in evidence in Sasha's account of World War II. There was a clear "language system" in the form of a narrative that gave rise to the "repeatable" aspect of the text. The fact that he was using a particular, socioculturally situated textual resource was not something that Sasha recognized, and as a result he assumed he was simply reporting truths about the level of content. There were also aspects of Sasha's performance that reflect the "individual, unique, unrepeatable" pole of text. Of course, no two uses of textual resources are ever completely identical, but more to the point for my purposes here, Sasha's performance reflected the unique setting provided by his teacher, fellow students, and me on that day in 1997.

Voice

An account of the irreducible tension between repeatable and unrepeatable moments of text provides only partial insight into why Sasha's account of

World War II may be so striking to readers who bring other perspectives to their understanding of World War II. It does little to explain why we might be surprised, or even take offense, at what he said. On this issue, it is useful to turn to Bakhtin's assertion that "every text has a subject or author (speaker or writer)" (1986b, p. 104). This is part of his line of reasoning about dialogicality, or multivoicedness in which "there are no voiceless words that belong to no one" (1986b, p. 124). From this perspective:

The word (or in general any sign) is interindividual. Everything that is said, expressed, is located outside the "soul" of the speaker and does not belong only to him. The word cannot be assigned to a single speaker. The author (speaker) has his own inalienable right to the word, but the listener also has his rights, and those whose voices are heard in the word before the author comes upon it also have their rights (after all, there are no words that belong to no one). The word is a drama in which three characters participate (it is not a duet, but a trio). It is performed outside the author, and it cannot be introjected into the author. (1986b, pp. 121–122)

With regard to the first of the "three characters" involved in the drama of an utterance, Bakhtin recognized that the meaning of a text obviously depends on speakers and their intentions, but he consistently warned against the pitfalls of "personalism" (Holquist, 1981) and emphasized that we must go beyond this character in the drama. Bakhtin discussed the second member of the trio, the listener, in several ways, most obviously under the heading of "addressivity" (1986a, p. 95). In the case of Sasha's account of World War II, the fact that his classmates, his teacher, and I were all listening undoubtedly made a difference in what he said. It is, after all, standard practice to formulate what we say in anticipation of who the listeners might be.

The third member of Bakhtin's trio is the voice, or voices "heard in the word before the author comes upon it," and it is the aspect of text and voice that will be of primary concern in what follows. Bakhtin outlined this claim in several ways. For example, he approached it from another angle in his claim that words and texts are always "half someone else's" (Bakhtin, 1981, p. 293).

It [the word or text] becomes "one's own" only when the speaker populates it with his own intention, his own accent, when he appropriates the word, adapting it to his own semantic and expressive intention. Prior to this moment of appropriation, the word does not exist in a neutral and impersonal language (it is not, after all, out of a dictionary that the speaker gets his words!), but rather it exists in other people's mouths, in other people's contexts, serving other people's intentions: it is from there that one must take the word, and make it one's own. (1981, pp. 293–294)

In this passage and elsewhere, Bakhtin was actually drawing on two notions of voice. First, there is the concrete voice producing a unique utterance or text with all its unrepeatable aspects. This is what I have elsewhere termed a "voice token" (Wertsch, 1991). Hence, when Sasha produced his text, the first sort of voice involved was that of a unique sixteen-year-old Russian boy speaking to a specific audience on a particular day in a particular school in Moscow, and so forth. This member of the "trio" – the speaker – had "his own inalienable right to the word."

As I noted in Chapter 1, however, the text Sasha produced about World War II did not derive solely from his own intention in that setting. Instead, he obviously utilized words that had existed "in other people's mouths, in other people's contexts, serving other people's intentions" (Bakhtin, 1981, p. 294). In some cases, the textual means he employed might have come from another unique voice token – say, an utterance by his grandfather – but in most such instances, the voices "heard in the word before the author comes upon it" (1986b, p. 122) are attributed to generalizations about a category or collective of speakers. The use of such a "voice type" (Wertsch, 1991) is what gives rise to the comments of some observers that Sasha was just saying what all the Russian kids in his generation would say about this topic.

Remembering

Employing Bakhtin's analysis of the "trio of characters" involved in any text or utterance has major implications for the study of collective remembering. Most important is the fact that the speaker or author producing concrete utterances about the past is not the only voice involved. It remains the case that Sasha had his "own inalienable rights" as a speaker when talking about World War II, but the voice of listeners and "the voices . . . heard in the word before the author comes upon it" played a role as well. Again, I shall be particularly interested in the latter. Specifically, I shall be concerned with the textual resources involved in speaking or writing about the past and how these textual resources reflect the perspective of others who have used them, and hence introduced their own voice. From this perspective, if we ask who was doing the speaking in the illustration in Chapter 1, the answer has to be at least two voices: Sasha's as the author of a unique speech utterance, or text, and the voice built into the textual means he employed. And if we take into account issues of addressivity, the voice of a third character can be detected as well.

This entire orientation puts a strong emphasis on process, or action, and hence my preference for the term "remembering" rather than "memory." Instead of talking about memories that we "have," the emphasis is on remembering as something we do. This is consistent with Bakhtin's understanding that voice is best understood in terms of a "*speaking* consciousness" (Holquist & Emerson, 1981, p. 434; emphasis added). It also reflects the general line of reasoning that gave rise to many of Vygotsky's claims. For example, the focus on remembering as a form of action ran throughout the writings of P.I. Zinchenko (1981) and can be found in more contemporary writings such as those by Ivanova (1994).

While not necessarily building their accounts on these theoretical foundations, other authors have made the point that it is important to speak of remembering rather than memory. Frederic Bartlett, considered by many to be the father of the modern psychology of memory, titled his classic work *Remembering* as a way of emphasizing the active processes of engagement in the "effort after meaning" (1995, p. 20) that lay at the core of his analysis. Similarly, David Middleton and Derek Edwards (1990b) used the term "remembering" in the title of their more recent edited volume as a way of emphasizing the active processes involved.

The Historically Laminated Meanings of "Collective Memory"

As noted earlier, a basic claim of sociocultural studies is that human action is inherently connected to the cultural, historical, and institutional contexts in which it occurs. This claim derives from the observation that humans think, speak, and otherwise act by using the cultural tools such as textual resources that are made available by their particular sociocultural settings. Hence the analytical category of cultural tools serves as a mediating link between sociocultural setting and agents.

This line of reasoning suggests the need to reflect on the present discussion – namely, the fact that those of us analyzing collective remembering and other forms of human action are just as socioculturally situated as the individuals and groups we examine. This calls on us to consider how the concepts and methods we employ as investigators reflect and reproduce the sociocultural setting in which we exist.

This point has major implications for the study of memory. The very nature of memory, and hence the interpretations we make of it, vary according to sociocultural context. In particular, it is essential to recognize that memory has undergone fundamental change over the history of its discussion. To those of us operating comfortably in today's setting, viewing it as natural and simply the "way it is," this may be difficult to accept. However, scholars such as Donald (1991), Kerwin Klein (2000), Pierre Nora (1989), and Frances Yates (1966) have amply documented the fundamental transformations that memory has undergone.

These scholars do not speak in a single voice, but a point on which they do generally agree is that the rise of mass literacy and the mental habits associated with it have had a profound impact on human memory. The most obvious impact of literacy on memory is that it allowed information to be off-loaded into written texts, a point I shall examine further in Chapter 3. For my purposes here, the crucial point is that the emergence of literacy – especially its widespread dissemination during the Enlightenment – was associated with privileging new forms of critical thought and discourse.

This in turn was associated with a new way of representing the past, one that contrasts with previous ways.

This new way of representing the past is usually termed "history," and is placed in opposition to memory. In the 1920s, the father of collective memory studies, Maurice Halbwachs (1980, 1992), formulated a version of this opposition, and it continues to be a part of the discussion. As will become evident in the chapters that follow, contemporary scholars are often uncomfortable in drawing this distinction too sharply, but it nonetheless continues to crop up. In the view of at least one observer, "much current historiography pits memory against history even though few authors openly claim to be engaged in building a world in which memory can serve as an alternative to history" (Klein, 2000, p. 128).

As a starting point for discussing this distinction, consider the following comments by the historian Peter Novick (1999). Building on the ideas of Halbwachs, he writes:

> To understand something historically is to be aware of its complexity, to have sufficient detachment to see it from multiple perspectives, to accept the ambiguities, including moral ambiguities, of protagonists' motives and behavior. Collective memory simplifies; sees events from a single, committed perspective; is impatient with ambiguities of any kind; reduces events to mythic archetypes. (pp. 3–4)

This constitutes a snapshot of a distinction between history and collective memory that is at the core of many contemporary discussions. In order to understand some of the assumptions and meanings that are woven into it, however, we need to trace its own history, something that has been of special concern to scholars such as Nora (1989). Nora argues that "real memory" has been largely pushed aside, if not eradicated, by the practices of creating critical historical accounts of the past. As a result, "we speak so much of memory because there is so little of it left" (p. 7), and we have a felt need to create *lieux de mémoire* [sites of memory] "because there are no longer *milieux de mémoire*, real environments of memory" (p. 7).

For Nora, the difference between collective memory and history is not just a distinction, but takes the form of a conflict: "far from being synonymous, [they] appear now to be in fundamental opposition" (p. 8). From this perspective, memory is "social [and] retained as the secret of so-called primitive or archaic societies . . . [It is] an integrated, dictatorial memory – unself-conscious . . . a memory without a past that ceaselessly reinvents tradition, linking the history of its ancestors to the undifferentiated time of heroes, origins, and myth" (p. 8). As formulated by Nora, memory "remains in permanent evolution" and is "unconscious of its successive deformations, vulnerable to manipulation" (p. 8). In contrast, "history, because it is an intellectual and secular production, calls for analysis and criticism . . . At the heart of history is a critical discourse that is antithetical to spontaneous memory" (pp. 8–9).

Nora's account suggests that memory existed in an undifferentiated state before the rise of analytical history. The emergence of the latter brought the "unself-conscious" nature of memory into question. It was no longer allowed to remain uncontested because "history is perpetually suspicious of memory, and its true mission is to suppress and destroy it" (p. 9). Nora's account does not entail the idea that analytical history simply supplanted memory. Instead, the implicit contrast with history resulted in a differentiation and redefinition of what memory could be, and the struggle over this issue continues in the renewed debates of the "memory industry" (Klein, 2000, p. 127) that has emerged over the past few decades.

This line of reasoning implies that the distinction between history and memory was not conceivable before the rise of the former. Instead of yielding a clear-cut distinction between the two notions, however, we have something like poles in dynamic opposition, poles that can be understood only in relationship to each other: "*History,* as with other key words, finds its meanings in large part through its counter-concepts and synonyms, and so the emergence of *memory* promises to rework *history's* boundaries" (Klein, 2000, p. 128).

This dynamic tension has yielded terms that come with various parts of their past laminated into a "complexive" rather than "genuine" concept (Vygotsky, 1987). This is reflected in discussions in the philosophy of history, which note that narrative tendencies associated with collective memory shape even the most assiduously analytical and critical efforts to write history. Conversely, the kind of truth claims now made so vehemently on behalf of collective memory came under a new kind of scrutiny with the emergence of analytical history.

The upshot of all of this is that it is often quite difficult to categorize an account of the past unequivocally as either memory or history. For example, official histories produced by the state and unofficial histories produced outside of its purview both include elements of collective remembering as well as history. Nonetheless, the analytical task I shall set out often calls for maintaining some kind of distinction, and I shall therefore examine that between history and collective memory in subsequent chapters. The empirical phenomena I shall examine usually do not fall neatly on either side of the history versus collective memory opposition, but this opposition nonetheless provides essential grounding for understanding the issues at hand.

Strong and Distributed Versions of Collective Memory

I now turn to another fundamental, but seldom examined, distinction lurking behind many discussions of collective memory. In reality, it may be more accurate to say that this distinction lurks behind disagreements – many of them bogus – in such discussions. In contrast to the incompletely differentiated opposition between history and collective memory, this is one that can be resolved, and hence will not reappear in subsequent chapters. The distinction I have in mind is between two basic notions of collective memory: what I shall term a "strong version" and a "distributed version."

The strong version of collective memory assumes that some sort of collective mind or consciousness exists above and beyond the minds of the individuals in a collective. In general, it has been difficult to defend this position. The distributed version of collective memory assumes that a representation of the past is distributed among members of a collective, but not because of the existence of a collective mind in any strong sense. In what follows, I shall outline different forms that this distribution may take. However, in accordance with my approach to collective remembering as a form of mediated action, I shall be particularly interested in analyses that assume that the key to this lies in the textual resources employed by the members of a group.

The Strong Version of Collective Memory

Strong versions of collective memory are typically based on assumptions about parallels between individual and collective processes. These usually rely on metaphorical extensions of assertions about individuals, and may reflect a general tendency in Western thinking about collective processes. Handler (1994), for example, warns that:

Western notions of collectivity are grounded in individualist metaphors. That is, collectivities in Western social theory are imagined as though they are human individuals writ large. The attributes of boundedness, continuity, uniqueness, and homogeneity that are ascribed to human persons are ascribed as well to social groups. (p. 33)

Such parallels and metaphorical extensions are widely, and sometimes productively, employed when discussing how remembering occurs in groups. However, to the degree that they are taken to suggest that collectives have some kind of mind of their own, they can be highly problematic. Doubts on this score have been raised for decades. For example, in his classic work *Remembering*, Bartlett criticized the "more or less absolute likeness [that] has been drawn between social groups and the human individual" (1995, p. 293) and the tendency to assume that "whatever is attributed to the latter has been ascribed to the former" (ibid.). In his view, assuming such parallels is highly questionable, and he warned that speculation grounded in this analogy is likely to be "incomplete and unconvincing" (ibid.).

Bartlett did not object to the claim that the memory of individuals is *influenced* by the social context in which they function. Indeed, a central point of his argument – one that has often been overlooked in contemporary psychology (Rosa, 1996) – is that "social organisation gives a persistent framework into which all detailed recall must fit, and it very power-fully influences both the manner and the matter of recall" (Bartlett, 1995, p. 296). Bartlett did, however, object to the notion that the collective, qua collective, can be usefully characterized as having some sort of memory in its own right. In his view, such an approach "ought to be able to demonstrate that a group, considered as a unit, itself actually does remember, and not merely that it provides either the stimulus or the conditions under which individuals belonging to the group recall the past" (p. 294).

Bartlett made these points in a critique of Halbwachs, the figure who is widely credited with introducing the term "collective memory" and hence deserves special attention in any discussion of this topic. According to Mary Douglas (1980), Bartlett was dismissive of Halbwachs for "reifying collective memory into a quasi-mystic soul with its own existence" (pp. 16–17). This charge seems to have some foundation when one considers statements by Halbwachs such as: "Often we deem ourselves the originators of thoughts and ideas, feelings and passions, actually inspired by some group. Our agreement with those about us is so complete that we vibrate in unison, ignorant of the real source of the vibrations" (Halbwachs, 1980, p. 44).

Other points in Halbwachs's writings, however, make Bartlett's assessment more controvertible. For example, Halbwachs argued that "While the collective memory endures and draws strength from its base in a coherent body of people, it is individuals as group members who remember" (p. 48). This formulation is actually quite consistent with Bartlett's observation that most investigators concerned with collective memory actually deal with "memory *in* the group, and not memory *of* the group" (p. 294).

The key to evaluating Bartlett's critique of Halbwachs is the latter's notion of "individuals as group members." On the one hand, "it is individuals" who remember, but on the other, these individuals must be understood as members of groups. In the end, it turns out that the positions of Bartlett and Halbwachs appear to be complementary rather than contradictory. Both focused on memory *in* and not *of* the group, but Bartlett was primarily concerned with how individuals' mental processes are influenced by socially organized associations and cues, whereas Halbwachs was primarily concerned with how these associations and cues are provided and organized by social groups. Even Halbwachs's comments about how the thoughts and ideas of the members of a collective may "vibrate in unison" (1980, p. 44) reflect a claim about how "collective frameworks" provide memory cues to individuals, cues that give rise to similar representations among the members of a group.

This is not to say that others who have used the term "collective memory" are not assuming a strong version. In some cases, they clearly are. The general point is whether it is legitimate to draw parallels between individual and collective memory, and if so, whether these parallels commit one to attributing questionable mental properties to groups per se. Such commitments often appear in the form of implicit theoretical or methodological assumptions rather than as explicit formulations, but even in this form, they introduce a strong version of collective memory with all its attendant problems.

The Distributed Version of Collective Memory

It is possible to distinguish several variants of the distributed version of collective memory. For my purposes they are similar in that (a) the representation of the past is distributed across members of a group, but (b) no commitment is made to a collective mind of the sort envisioned in a strong version of collective memory. The simplest version of distributed collective memory can be termed "homogeneous," and posits that all members of a group share the same representation of the past. In this view, there is little difference among the memories of group members. When pressed about such claims, most would agree that such a state of homogeneity seldom, if ever, really exists. However, some such notion of collective memory often can be found to underlie sweeping statements about the collective memory of groups, especially groups to which those making the statements do not belong.

A second form of distributed collective memory can be termed "complementary." In this case, it is assumed that different members of a group have different perspectives and remember different things, but these exist in a coordinated system of complementary pieces. This view is consistent with the notion of socially distributed cognition outlined by Edwin Hutchins (1994). He views groups such as crews on ships as systems that are composed of individuals with complementary skills and responsibilities. In this case, no member of the group has access to all the information or skills involved in the system. Instead, its operation depends on the smooth functioning of a set of reciprocally organized efforts. In terms of memory, the various partial representations involved may constitute a counterpart to what Donald Campbell (1988) termed a "fish scale" knowledge system in that there is partial, but not total, overlap of memories that forms a more general pattern.

Processes of complementary distribution occur in various ways depending on factors having to do with the social organization of the group involved. For example, groups vary in terms of the extent to which their members are acquainted with and interact with one another. It is possible for a group of people to operate as a closely-knit community in which everyone remembers something about an event from the past, and the overlap of knowledge is quite extensive. Such conditions can be found in small, traditionally organized communities where the density of social interaction is quite high and social mobility is low (Cole, 1998, 2001).

Conversely, in large, loosely organized groups, there may be little or no personal contact among members. Indeed, large post-industrial societies can be characterized in terms of the absence of the direct social contact that characterizes traditional societies, yet they are still often said to have collective memories. For example, political observers have argued that after the 1970s, the United States was reluctant to engage in military actions that could result in casualties to American troops because of the collective memory of the war in Vietnam. Even those individuals who participated directly in the event, let alone the rest of the U.S. population, are unlikely to know one another personally, yet there still seems to be a sense in which Americans can be said to have a collective memory of the war.

A third form of distributed collective memory involves what I shall call "contested distribution." As in the case of complementary distribution, different perspectives are inherent to this, but they do not function together in a cooperative or reciprocal fashion. Instead, they exist in a system of opposition and contestation. The sort of memory I have in mind in this case has many similarities to what John Bodnar (1991) has termed "public memory." Competition and conflict characterize this sort of representation of the past. Instead of involving multiple perspectives that overlap or complement one another, the focus is on how these perspectives compete with or contradict one another. Indeed, in some cases, one perspective is designed specifically to rebut another.

Much of the contemporary writing on collective memory, especially by historians and sociologists (Bodnar, 1991; Confino, 1997; Linenthal & Engelhardt, 1996; Schwartz, 1990), focuses on contested distribution. Collective memory from such a perspective may be envisioned more as a site of contestation than as a form of information storage – a viewpoint that differs quite strikingly from what one tends to find in psychological studies of individual memory. Of course, this is not to say that there is not a psychological moment in this or any other form of distributed memory. Instead, the point is that different forms of social distribution reflect what Halbwachs termed different "collective frameworks" and associated forms of socially organized memory cues. A complementarity of perspectives rather than an argument about phenomena at the same level of analysis is involved.

In what follows, much of my focus will be on the contested social distribution of collective memory. Homogeneous and complementary social distribution will emerge occasionally, but the empirical examples I analyze are steeped in processes that seem to characterize "[collective] history wars" (Linenthal & Engelhardt, 1996) in many places in the world today.

The Mediation of Collective Memory

Any discussion of differences among types of distributed collective memory begs the question of what generally makes this distribution possible in the first place. It is precisely at this point that one may be tempted to invoke assumptions about a strong version of collective memory. People often begin speaking of how collective memory is just "out there" somehow, and in the absence of a clear alternative, implicit notions about ephemeral mnemonic agents or essences begin to creep into the picture.

The simplest way to avoid going down this path is to posit that collective memory emerges because members of a group all have participated in the event being remembered and hence have memories of it based on their individual experience. The existence of similar memories across individuals in such cases is simply a reflection of the fact that everyone in the group happened to have had the same experience individually. The collective memory would be homogeneous, and there would be little reason to distinguish between its content and the content of any member's individual memory. This is the sort of account that Jeffrey Olick (1999) outlines in his account of "collected," as opposed to collective memory. Insofar as this account is based on "individualistic principles" (p. 338), it is susceptible to the critique of methodological individualism (Wertsch, 1998).

In most instances, however, the distribution of collective memory does not arise in this manner. Even if members of a group have experienced the events being remembered, they typically do not interpret or remember these events in the same way. In the case of Americans' collective memory of the Vietnam War noted earlier, for example, the collective includes many people who never experienced the conflict directly. Indeed, it includes people who were not even born at the time. And even for those who did experience the conflict directly, there are major differences in how the war is remembered. If the notion of collective memory can be legitimately applied in such cases, how does such memory come into existence? In particular, how can we address such issues without lapsing into a strong version of collective memory by invoking ideas about a central mnemonic agency?

A good answer to these questions, I shall argue, can be found by going beyond the categories of individual and collective narrowly defined. Specifically, it involves introducing notions such as mediated action and textual resources into the discussion. This amounts to positing a second sense in which memory can be said to be distributed. If the first sense has to do with how memory is distributed across the members of a collective, the second concerns distribution between agents and the texts they employ when representing the past – the basic issue of memory as mediated action.

The point I am making here is part of a more general set of claims about how "mind extends beyond the skin" (Wertsch, 1991, 1998) in two related, but analytically distinct senses. From this perspective, mental processes such as remembering and thinking are not viewed as being situated solely within the individual. Instead, they often are distributed across individuals, and they are nearly always distributed between agents and the cultural tools they employ to think, remember, and carry out other forms of action.

The specific form of distribution between agents and textual resources I shall consider is textual mediation. Textual mediation emerged as part of the last of three major transitions in human cognitive evolution that have been outlined by Donald (1991). It is grounded in "the emergence of visual symbolism and external memory as major factors in cognitive architecture" (p. 17). At this point in cognitive evolution, the primary engine of change was not within the individual. Instead, it was the emergence and widespread use of "external symbolic storage" such as written texts, financial records, and so forth. At the same time, however, Donald emphasizes that this transition does not leave the psychological or neural processes in the individual unchanged: "the external symbolic system imposes more than an interface structure on the brain. It imposes search strategies, new storage strategies, new memory access routes, new options in both the control of and analysis of one's own thinking" (p. 19).

A major reason for introducing the notion of textual mediation, then, is that it allows us to speak of collective memory without slipping into a strong version account. In this connection, it is worth noting that although Halbwachs did not give textual mediation the degree of importance that I do, he clearly did recognize it as a legitimate part of the story. In a striking parallel with Donald, he argued that "there is . . . no point in seeking where . . . [memories] are preserved in my brain or in some nook of my mind to which I alone have access: for they are recalled by me externally, and the groups of which I am a part at any given time give me the means to reconstruct them" (Halbwachs, 1992, p. 38). In describing the collective memory of musicians, Halbwachs fleshed this out in the following terms:

> With sufficient practice, musicians can recall the elementary commands [of written notations that guide their performance]. But most cannot memorize the complex commands encompassing very extensive sequences of sounds. Hence they need to have before them sheets of paper on which all the signs in proper succession are materially fixed. A major portion of their remembrances are conserved in this form – that is, outside themselves in the society of those who, like themselves, are interested exclusively in music. (1980, p. 183)

In analyzing such phenomena, Halbwachs focused primarily on the role of social groups in organizing memory and memory cues, and said relatively little about the semiotic means employed. What I am proposing amounts to placing these semiotic means front and center. It is precisely this step that makes it possible to talk about collective memory without presupposing a strong version of it. Instead of positing the vague mnemonic agency that is a thread running through the members of a group, the idea is that they share a representation of the past because they share textual resources. The use of this text may result in homogeneous, complementary, or contested collective memory, but in all cases, it is the key to understanding how distribution is possible.

As noted earlier, one response to this line of reasoning might be that what I am proposing is not really a form of memory at all, but instead a type of knowledge – namely, knowledge of texts. Such a claim is consistent with the distinction between remembering and knowing that psychologists such as John Gardiner (2001) have discussed. According to Gardiner & Richardson-Klavehn (2000), remembering involves "intensely personal experiences of the past – those in which we seem to recreate previous events and experiences," whereas experiences of knowing are "those in which we are aware of knowledge that we possess but in a more impersonal way" (p. 229). The distinction they have in mind is manifested not only in subjective experience, but in how memory is affected in various populations with amnesia and other forms of memory impairment, and it is a distinction that is worth considering when trying to avoid slipping into a strong version of collective memory.

Because so many discussions in disciplines other than psychology employ "collective memory" rather than a term such as "collective knowledge," I shall continue using it as well. However, the distinction between remembering and knowing outlined by Gardiner and others is one that makes sense in my view, and much of what I shall say could be discussed under the heading of knowledge rather than memory. Indeed, my point is that a coherent account of collective memory can be based on notions of knowledge of texts, a line of reasoning behind the notion of "textual communities" as outlined by Brian Stock (1983, 1990).

Stock describes textual communities as part of his analysis of the reemergence of literacy in eleventh- and twelfth-century Europe. In his account, these communities were "microsocieties organized around the common understanding of a script" (1990, p. 23). The sort of collective involved is "an interpretive community, but it is also a social entity" (p. 150), suggesting that it involves psychological and cultural, as well as social dimensions.

Wherever there are texts that are read aloud or silently, there are groups of listeners that can potentially profit from them. A natural process of education takes place within the group, and, if the force of the word is strong enough, it can supercede the differing economic and social backgrounds of the participants, welding them, for a time at least, into a unit. In other words the people who enter the group are not precisely the same as those who come out. Something has happened, and this experience affects their relations both with other members and with those in the outside world. Among the members, solidarity prevails; with the outside, separation. The members may disperse, but they can also institutionalize their new relations, for instance, by forming a religious order or a sectarian movement that meets on regular occasions. If they take this course, the community acquires the ability to perpetuate itself. An aspect of the social lives of the group's members will from that moment be determined by the rules of membership in the community. (1990, p. 150)

Throughout his analysis, Stock emphasizes that the simple existence of a text guarantees nothing about the existence of a textual community. Interpretive and social processes surrounding the text are also required. In his view, "What was essential to a textual community was not a written version of a text, although that was sometimes present, but an individual, who, having mastered it, then utilized it for reforming a group's thought and action" (1983, p. 90). Thus a textual community is a collective whose thought and action are grounded in written texts, but for at least some members this grounding may be indirect. Some members of a textual community may not have even read the text, but by participating in the activities of a textual community, they can have the access to the textual material around which the group is organized.

In contrast to Stock, who developed his account of textual communities by studying the use of religious texts in the Middle Ages, I shall focus on official histories produced by modern states. Such official histories are usually viewed as being quite different from religious texts, not only because of the institutions that produce them, but because they make claims about historical accuracy grounded in documentation and rational argument.

To say that texts of this sort can provide the foundation for a textual community is not to assume that all texts grounded in documentation and rational argument can play this role. For example, logical or scientific proofs often differ from official history texts in this respect. The former might convince various parties of their correctness, and have a set of adherents, but they usually do not provide the foundation for creating strong collective identity, something that state-sponsored histories are intended to do.

Official history texts can be said to occupy a middle ground between religious texts, on the one hand, and other sorts of texts grounded in documentation and rational argument, on the other. In the chapters that follow, I shall be particularly concerned with ways in which they bear important similarities to the sorts of religious texts examined by Stock, something that reflects my concern with collective memory, rather than analytical history. For example, some of the points Stock makes about issues of indoctrination and heresy apply quite readily to the official histories promulgated by states. Like religious collectives, states often seek to produce texts in which "the force of the word is strong enough" to "supercede the differing economic and social backgrounds of the participants, welding them, for a time at least, into a unit" (Stock, 1990, p. 150).

In sum, I shall borrow from Vygotsky, Bakhtin, Lotman, Stock, and several other figures to explore topics usually discussed under the heading of collective memory. I shall approach these issues by examining both the "production" and the "consumption" of the texts. Given the importance of texts in organizing what Stock calls "microsocieties," it is essential to understand who has a vested interest in creating and promulgating these texts – that is, their production. Equally important, however, is an understanding of how textual resources are used, or consumed by individuals as members of a collective. I shall argue that this requires an analysis not only of what these individuals know about a text, but what they believe – the two need not be the same. Furthermore, it requires an analysis of the various contexts in which textual consumers display their knowledge and belief.

3

Collective Memory: A Term in Search of a Meaning

In this chapter, I outline the meaning of several key terms that surface repeatedly in discussions of collective remembering. By beginning with how others have treated these terms, I hope to clarify my own line of reasoning and its relationship to a broader conceptual framework. I shall organize this review around the broad categories of "memory," "collective memory," "narratives as cultural tools," and "textual community."

Memory

Nora's dictum that "we speak so much of memory because there is so little of it left" (1989, p. 7) seems quite apropos when trying to account for today's widespread concern, if not anxiety, about the issue. Whatever the motivation, memory is a major topic of discussion both in the public sphere and in specialized academic disciplines such as psychology, neuroscience, sociology, anthropology, and history. Indeed, in today's world, we have what Klein (2000) has called a "memory industry" (p. 127).

One upshot of being at the center of myriad debates is that the term "memory" has come to be understood in many different ways. The elasticity, if not fragmentation, of its meaning has been exacerbated by the rhetorical uses to which it has been put, a point that led John Gillis (1994b) to argue that it may be "losing precise meaning in proportion to its growing rhetorical power" (p. 3).

It is not obvious how to catalogue all the interpretations of memory that now clutter the conceptual landscape, especially since these interpretations often exist in the form of implicit assumptions rather than explicit formulation. Differences there are, however, and they have a profound effect on how memory is discussed and how participants in this discussion understand – and misunderstand – one another. I shall go into detail on several of these disparities, especially in my consideration of collective memory,

30

but I begin by addressing a distinction that constitutes a major divide in memory studies in general.

The divide I have in mind stems from the fact that memory has been viewed from the perspective of two separate functions. On the one hand, we often approach memory in terms of how it can provide an accurate account of the past and hence how it can be assessed in terms of what might be called an "accuracy criterion." On the other hand, memory is often called upon to provide a "usable past" (Zamora, 1998), an account of events and actors that can be harnessed for some purpose in the present. The most common reasons for developing a usable past have to do with individual or collective identity claims (e.g., Sacks, 1990; Novick, 1999). These claims appear in debates that can become quite heated and sometimes escalate into "history wars" (Linenthal & Engelhardt, 1996). Identity claims take many forms and are tied, among other things, to the need to mourn (Winter, 1995), the desire to foster patriotism (Kammen, 1993), and the need to erase the sting of defeat and redeem a lost cause (Sherry, 1996).

Differentiating accurate representation from the creation of a usable past runs the risk of suggesting that these two functions can be neatly separated and can exist in isolation. In fact, they tend to operate in tandem, vying for position in any particular instance of remembering. As will become clear in what follows, the tendency to present the two functions in opposition is more a reflection of contrasting disciplinary perspectives than of some inherent property of memory itself.

In the approach I shall be taking, memory typically involves a complex mix of meeting the needs of accurate representation and providing a usable past. Taking a cue from the semiotician Lotman (1988), I shall formulate this issue in terms of a "functional dualism." On the one hand, we judge memory by its accuracy, and we raise objections when inaccurate representations of the past are put forth as truthful. On the other hand, memory functions to provide a usable past for the creation of coherent individual and group identities. Gillis, for example, emphasizes this second function when he argues, "The core meaning of any individual or group identity, namely, a sense of sameness over time and space, is sustained by remembering" (1994b, p. 3).

To argue that memory serves both of these functions is not to say that one cannot differentiate one form from another. The role of the two tendencies in this functional dualism may vary greatly. In some cases, the focus may be on accuracy no matter how threatening it is to identity commitments, and in others the motivation of presenting a coherent identity may lead to sacrificing objectivity and accuracy. Approaching these orientations in terms of a functional dualism provides a means for avoiding the temptation to place the two functions in simple opposition.

Understanding which of these two functions is taken as foundational is the key to understanding some important disciplinary differences in the study of memory. For example, contemporary studies of memory in cognitive psychology tend to focus on accuracy as the basic function and hence to privilege the accuracy criterion. This is not to say that memory is viewed as some sort of simple copy, or picture, of reality. Indeed, the history of psychology is filled with warnings against such a view. William James (1890) made this point over a century ago; it was elaborated a few decades later by Bartlett (1995, first published in 1932), who emphasized the reconstructive nature of memory; and contemporary researchers such as Neisser (1967) have criticized it as the "reappearance hypothesis." Memory is now widely recognized in psychology as involving an active "effort after meaning" (Bartlett, 1995) that is, to be sure, grounded in traces from the past, but an effort that actively reshapes them in the present (Schacter, 1996).

Theoretical formulations that emphasize active reconstruction, however, do not change the fact that there is a reliance on the accuracy criterion in the concrete methodological practices of cognitive psychology. Hundreds, if not thousands, of studies have demonstrated that memory can be accurate or inaccurate in a variety of ways for a variety of reasons, hence presupposing that accuracy is to be taken as the standard against which empirical results are to be measured. This is apparent in studies of memory where the focus is on the accuracy of subjects' recall or recognition, as well as in studies of "memory distortion" (Roediger & McDermott, 2000; Schacter, 1995). In general, the terms and claims of these debates make sense only against background presuppositions about an accuracy criterion.

Any critique of the tendency in cognitive psychology to focus on the accuracy criterion should not be taken to suggest that accurate representation is somehow bogus or should be ignored. Instead, my point is that accurate representation is not the sole function of memory, and hence should not be the only criterion used to assess it. This is a point that is often recognized even by those who generally privilege this criterion. For example, Daniel Schacter, a psychologist and neuroscientist who generally presupposes an accuracy criterion, also makes a point of noting that "our sense of ourselves depends crucially on the subjective experience of remembering our pasts" (1996, p. 34).

In contrast to the reliance on an accuracy criterion in psychology and cognitive science, discussions in history, anthropology, and sociology often begin with the assumption – again, usually implicit – that another function of memory is paramount. They begin with the assumption that memory is to be understood in terms of its role in rhetorical and political processes concerned with identity and a usable past. Negotiation and contestation are assumed to be a natural part of the "memory politics" (Confino, 1997, p. 1393) and "identity politics" (Calhoun, 1994) involved. This does not mean that analysts of collective memory believe that accuracy is unimportant. It does mean that they view memory as being sufficiently committed to an identity project that the notion of accuracy may be downplayed or sacrificed in the service of producing a usable past.

The kind of focus on identity politics that characterizes analyses of collective memory is reflected in Bodnar's definition of "public memory."

Public memory is a body of beliefs and ideas about the past that help a public or society understand both its past, present, and by implication, its future. It is fashioned ideally in a public sphere in which various parts of the social structure exchange views. The major focus of this communicative and cognitive process is not the past, however, but serious matters in the present such as the nature of power and the question of loyalty to both official and vernacular cultures. (p. 15)

In this passage, Bodnar goes out of his way to note that the driving force behind public memory is not accurate representation of the past. Instead, it has to do with the present and future. This might strike some as strange, given that the discussion is about memory, and for others it will sound like rampant presentism – the creation of an account of the past to serve interests in the present. From the perspective being outlined here, however, the point remains that the function of creating a usable past is privileged in such a formulation. This means that Bodnar and others concerned with collective memory typically do not start with the assumption that the analysis of memory should focus exclusively or even primarily on accuracy. Instead, memory is assessed from the perspective of how effective it is in creating a usable past.

The functional dualism inherent in memory is reflected in discussions from a wide range of disciplines. One of the two poles of this dualism tends to be privileged in particular discussions, but the other can usually be found to be lurking somewhere in the background. In the end, it is important in my view to understand how these two forces operate in tandem to create particular representations of the past, realizing that both are usually at work.

Collective Memory

Up to this point, I have outlined some general properties of memory: the need to consider it as an active process – more specifically, a form of mediated action – and its functional dualism. These points apply to both individual and collective forms of remembering, but the latter has several unique properties and has been the topic of a distinct literature.

Collective memory has been examined by scholars from anthropology (Cole, 1998, 2001), sociology (Halbwachs, 1992; Schudson, 1990, 1995; Schwartz, 1990), communication and rhetoric (Billig, 1990; Middleton & Edwards, 1990b; Schudson, 1992), and history (Bodnar, 1992; Crane, 1997; Confino, 1997; Novick, 1999). The fact that names of psychologists seldom surface when reviewing the research on collective memory (for exceptions, see Pennebaker, Paez, & Rimé, 1997 and Weldon, 2001) is no accident since there has been an implicit division of labor between those who study individual memory and those who study collective memory. To the extent that psychology has staked out the study of the individual – whereas disciplines such as sociology focus on collective phenomena – this makes sense. However, this division also contributes to the isolation of perspectives and repeated calls from both sides to develop a larger, more inclusive picture of memory.

The amount of research devoted to individual memory is many times greater than that devoted to collective memory. Countless journals, conferences, funded research projects, and other such activities are dedicated to the former, whereas no comparable organized effort has been devoted to the latter. The fact that a large research community has emerged to study individual memory might lead one to expect this field to be fragmented into a range of isolated schools of thought, and to some extent this is the case. However, the research community that has evolved in this case has arrived at a broad consensus on some basic terms and methods. This is attested to by the fact that authors such as Schacter (1996) and Roediger and Goff (1998) can provide a summary of basic categories of individual memory and memory experiments that is widely recognized among the community of cognitive psychologists.

This picture stands in marked contrast to what exists in collective memory studies. It is striking that nearly a century after Halbwachs, the founder of this field, began his work, authors feel compelled to warn that "[collective] memory, more practiced than theorized, has been used to denote very different things" (Confino, 1997, p. 1386). Such comments reflect a continuing lack of agreement about what the basic categories of collective memory are or how they should be studied.

In what follows, I shall outline some of the basic issues that have emerged in collective memory studies. There is little overall coherence or agreement in this research literature, so my aim is not to identify how various strands of research fit into a well-defined framework. Instead, I shall be concerned with providing the outlines of a conceptual landscape on which these issues can be discussed. Understanding at least the basic dimensions of this landscape is essential if we are to avoid bogus disagreements. As things currently stand, we are all too likely to be talking at cross-purposes in discussions of collective memory because different participants begin with different sets of implicit assumptions.

I shall proceed by laying out several conceptual oppositions that provide the background for a discussion of collective memory. As is the case with most of the other oppositions that I employ in this book, these are neither simple nor neat. Instead, they designate contrasting tendencies that usually operate in tension such as that outlined earlier under the heading of functional dualism.

Collective Memory vs. Individual Memory

One of the most important dividing lines in the conceptual landscape of memory studies is that between individual and collective memory. There are several criteria one can use to distinguish them. For example, in my earlier comments about functional dualism I noted that collective memory studies tend to focus on how efforts to create a usable past serve political and identity needs, whereas individual memory studies tend to take the criterion of accuracy as a basic standard. Investigators of collective memory often approach their subject more as a site of active contestation and negotiation than as a means for accurately representing the past.

Of course, the processes of contestation and negotiation that characterize collective memory do not operate without regard to accurate representation of the past, but any agreement on such representation is viewed as tenuous and likely to be subject to further challenge. In his discussion of "public memory," for example, Bodnar (1992) recognizes issues of representation – even accuracy – when talking about "a body of beliefs and ideas about the past" (p. 15), but the bulk of his discussion concerns the contestation out of which such representations emerge. It is a discussion of how "public memory emerges from the intersection of official and vernacular cultural expressions" (p. 13) and how public memory's function is to "mediate the competing restatements of reality these antinomies express" (p. 14).

A danger in drawing stark distinctions between individual and collective processes is that it can encourage the tendency to isolate the work of one discipline from that of another. Instead of trying to set off individual from collective processes, it is often worth trying to understand how they are related. The relationship involved here can be envisioned in several ways – some of which are more rigorously formulated than others. In what follows, I shall outline three ways of approaching this issue. The first is to invoke metaphors about individual memory in discussions of collective memory, something that I discussed briefly in Chapter 2. This practice often introduces unrecognized and unwanted conceptual baggage, and hence can be quite misleading. The other two ways of forging connections are based on explicitly formulated claims and are more likely to provide useful insight. Specifically, one involves examining how individual memory processes may derive from social interaction, and the other involves exploring the relationship between autobiographical and collective memory.

As already noted in Chapter 2, there is a strong temptation to use metaphors from individual memory when discussing collective memory. This underlies the use of terms such as "collective amnesia" (Chang, 1997), terms that often occur in analyses of how national groups and other collectives represent the past. In some cases, employing such metaphors can be the source of productive hypotheses. However, it can also lead to confusion, and for this reason it is useful to reflect on what parallels can, and cannot, be legitimately posed in each case.

Novick (1999) has outlined a position that occupies a middle ground on this issue, suggesting that drawing parallels between individual and collective memory may be more or less appropriate depending on the sort of collective involved.

When we speak of collective memory, we often forget that we're employing a metaphor – an organic metaphor – that makes an analogy between the memory of an individual and that of a community. The metaphor works best when we're speaking of an organic (traditional, stable, homogeneous) community in which consciousness, like social reality, changes slowly ... How appropriate the metaphor is for the very inorganic societies of the late twentieth century (fragmented rather than homogeneous, rapidly changing rather than stable, the principal modes of communication electronic rather than face to face) seems to me questionable. (pp. 267–268)

Even in cases where an "organic community" is involved, however, there are reasons for being cautious about drawing too heavily on individual processes as a model for collective memory. Among these is the fact that studies of individual memory are often based on specific psychological and brain mechanisms, and it may be quite misleading to assume that counterparts in collective memory exist. Indeed, in some cases it is clear that no such counterparts exist.

As an example of this, consider one of the most interesting and important phenomena analyzed in the study of individual memory over the past half-century, the "encoding specificity principle" as formulated by Endel Tulving and his colleagues (Tulving & Thompson, 1973; Tulving, 1983). Schacter (1996) summarizes this principle as follows:

According to this principle ..., the specific way a person thinks about, or encodes, an event determines what "gets into" the engram, and the likelihood of later recalling the event depends on the extent to which a retrieval cue reinstates or matches the original encoding. Explicit remembering always depends on the similarity or affinity between encoding and retrieval processes. (p. 60)

The encoding specificity principle has spawned a host of studies in psychology, and many of the findings have been quite unanticipated. For example, Eich (1989) outlines studies of "state-dependent retrieval" in which it has been demonstrated that subjects' state of mind at the time of encoding information can influence how they remember this information. To the extent that their state of mind at the time of retrieval matches that at the time of encoding, their retrieval is likely to be more accurate. This includes intoxicated states of mind, and means that subjects may actually be more accurate in their memory of information encoded in a state of intoxication if they are similarly intoxicated at the time of retrieval.

This is an example of a phenomenon in individual memory that would seem to differ quite clearly from the workings of collective memory. Whereas the former can be shown to be heavily influenced by the conditions in which a memory is originally formed, the opposite tendency seems to operate in collective remembering. If anything, it seems to be shaped more heavily by the conditions in which it is "retrieved" (a term that reflects the accuracy criterion) than by the conditions of its original formulation. This tendency in collective memory encourages the propensity to sacrifice accuracy in the service of providing a usable past. Such comparisons reveal the sort of dangers one can encounter when using metaphors about individual memory in discussions of collective memory. The conceptual baggage of such metaphors is often misleading, yet powerfully seductive.

A second, more conceptually sound way to approach the connection between individual and collective memory begins with an attempt to formulate this relationship explicitly rather than relying on unexamined metaphors. Among other things, this formulation provides a foundation for considering how specific aspects of social processes might give rise to individual processes of memory. It builds on the notion I introduced in Chapter 2 about how mind extends beyond the skin in two senses. One of these is at the center of my argument about mediated action and concerns the relationship between cultural tools and agents. The second sense concerns ways in which mental processes such as remembering can be distributed among members of a group – that is, the "social distribution" of remembering mentioned in Chapter 2. From this perspective, the group is conceived "as the cognitive system, and therefore as a necessary unit of analysis" (Weldon, 2001, p. 81).

A study by Hinsz, Tindale, and Vollrath (1997) provides an illustration of research based on this line of reasoning. In their analysis of how small groups can be treated as information-processing systems, they employ as a starting point a generic information-processing model that has been used to study individuals. From this perspective, they focus on how groups have goals, direct their attention to objects, learn, retain, retrieve, and integrate information, and so forth. Similarly, in their studies of "collaborative remembering," Mary Weldon and her colleagues (Weldon, 2001; Weldon & Bellinger, 1997) have investigated a set of issues having to do with remembering in social groups.

Studies such as those by Hinsz et al. (1997) and Weldon (2001) focus primarily on remembering in groups, but they also have implications for how such functioning might be tied to individual remembering. Weldon makes this point explicitly when she notes "the individual's own mental processes are transformed as the interpsychological processes and mediational tools are internalized" (2000, p. 74). She borrows this line of reasoning from Vygotsky (1978, 1981) and Leont'ev (1981), who viewed individual mental functioning as deriving largely from the internalization of social discourse.

This line of reasoning involves a formulation of the relationship between individual and collective memory that tends to be overlooked in contemporary, discipline-bound discussions. Specifically, it proceeds on the assumption that the distinction between individual and collective memory may not be as ironclad as current disciplinary divisions would suggest. From this perspective, processes at the two levels may be objects of different lines of inquiry simply because different disciplines and traditions have examined them. Instead of leaving it at that, this perspective suggests that individual, or what Vygotsky (1981) termed "intramental," memory processes often emerge through internalizing "intermental" processes of the sort envisioned by Weldon (2001). Such an approach makes the relationship between social and individual processes the focus of explicit study and holds the promise of a principled understanding of the relationship between individual and collective memory.

Yet a third possibility for building a connection between individual and collective memory grows out of the study of autobiographical memory. One of the most obvious reasons why many collective memories are deeply subjective and involve what Novick (1999, p. 4) calls a "single, committed perspective" is that they concern events that have been experienced in one's lifetime. This clearly may have a powerful impact on the way it is remembered, a point recognized by Halbwachs, among others. Several contemporary studies in psychology and sociology indicate that the nature and power of these memories may depend on the point in an individuals' life span at which they occurred. For example, in a study of the collective memories of different generations, Schuman and Scott (1989) found that events occurring in a generation's early adulthood seem to have a particularly powerful impact on their collective memory and political outlook for the rest of their lives.

Martin Conway (1997) has extended and expanded upon this line of reasoning by documenting the way a "reminiscence bump" exists for members of a generation for events occurring when they are between fifteen and twenty-five years of age. More generally, Conway has developed a line of inquiry that suggests that memory is powerfully linked with the goal structure and concerns of identity as it emerges over a life span, especially during young adulthood. For example, Conway and Pleydell-Pearce (2000) have discussed autobiographical memory in such a way that its function in providing a usable past comes more clearly into focus. In their view, autobiographical knowledge is linked to goals in a self-system, and narrative memories about the self are accessible and take on affective force as a function of their role in forming goals of the self or personality. While they do not formulate it in such terms, this can be expected to result in tensions with the accuracy criterion that has been at the heart of many studies of individual memory.

All of these findings provide a foundation for examining the relationship between collective and individual memory in new ways. Reviewing them also leads to new questions about the precise nature of autobiographical experience. This is so first of all because even one's "direct" autobiographical experience of events must be considered from the perspective of how it plays a role in the goals of self-system if one follows the line of reasoning outlined by Conway and Pleydell-Pearce. Perhaps even more problematic is the fact that "direct" autobiographical experience can now be seen to be mediated by linguistic and cultural categories. For example, how does my experience of the Apollo 13 mission (something I experienced only through the media even though it occurred during my lifetime) differ from my experience of World War II (something that I also experienced primarily through media but that occurred before I was born)? If anything, there is a sense in which it would seem that I have more direct experience of World War II than of Apollo 13 since I know individuals who were directly involved in the former event but not in the latter.

Such observations provide an indication of the sort of problems one may expect to encounter when trying to draw a neat distinction between collective memory for lived experiences and historical memory for events from earlier times. Nevertheless, psychological studies such as those conducted by Conway suggest that events occurring in one's lifetime, regardless of the degree of their mediation, have a unique impact both on individual memory and on the collective memory of a generation.

It is worth taking special note of the privileged position that autobiographical memory occupies in our understanding of the past, something that is reflected in political and cultural disputes. Consider, for example, the highly emotional debate in the mid-1990s over an exhibit at the National Air and Space Museum (NASM) in Washington, D.C. about the decision to drop atomic bombs on Hiroshima and Nagasaki in 1945. In preparing this exhibit, the staff of the museum gathered a set of materials and consulted with a range of professional historians. When the NASM made its plans public, however, it ran into a firestorm of public criticism, largely from American World War II veterans and their supporters, who objected to what was being proposed. Specifically, this criticism was aimed at statements suggesting that America had prodded Japan into attacking the United States Pacific Fleet at Pearl Harbor and hence bore some responsibility for the beginning of hostilities. Furthermore, veterans' groups and others strongly objected to statements suggesting that using the atomic bombs might have been unnecessary because Japan was already preparing to surrender at the time they were used.

After a great deal of heated discussion in the media, in the United States Congress, and in the public at large, it was decided that a smaller, much different version of the exhibit would be used. This exhibit included only the "facts" and avoided any mention of issues such as how Japan may have been pushed into the war and how it may have been preparing to surrender even before the atomic bombs had been used.

There are several dimensions to this dispute (e.g., Linenthall & Engelhardt, 1996; White, 1997), but for my purposes I shall focus on one.

This has to do with claims made by veterans of World War II about the nature of events in 1945 and why it was that their arguments prevailed over those of professional historians. At first glance it might appear that the veterans prevailed for straightforward political reasons; they were simply able to muster the appropriate allies in the U.S. Congress and elsewhere. There is certainly no reason to doubt the role of politics in this case, but if one goes further and asks what underlay them, additional factors emerge. The most important of these was that the veterans' groups were able to appeal to autobiographical memory to trump claims put forth by professional historians. In doing so, these groups spoke in a voice that reverberated much more strongly with the public than some of the parties involved in this debate had anticipated.

The highly emotional tenor of this struggle over representing the past suggests the importance of recognizing a distinction between collective memory for events falling within one's lifetime and events occurring earlier. To some degree, this distinction may be based on whether or not people actually participated in the events being remembered. Even when such participation is at a remove and highly mediated, however, the fact that the events occurred during one's lifetime, especially during young adulthood, seems to have a powerful impact. Furthermore, this experience often seems to give those who lived through the events a particular status in cultural and political debates.

In sum, there are differences as well as parallels to be explored between individual and collective memory. The study of individual memory has tended to focus on issues of representation and has taken accuracy as its basic criterion. In contrast, studies of collective memory have tended to assume that remembering is a highly contested and negotiated process in the public sphere and that it is driven by the need to create a usable past. These two orientations have given rise to distinct bodies of research that often have little to do with one another. There are various ways of linking the two sorts of memory, three of which I have reviewed.

Collective Memory vs. History

As outlined in Chapter 2, a complex relationship between collective memory and analytical history has emerged over time. There are several dimensions of this relationship that suggest the need to maintain a distinction, but at the same time others make it difficult to do so. On the one hand, most contemporary analyses of collective memory in fact draw some distinction, either implicit or explicit, between subjective representations of the past grounded in the committed perspective of a group and distanced, objective representations that seek not to be tied to a perspective. On the other hand, discussions such as those by Mink (1978) and White (1987) have raised questions about whether any representation of the past, including those generated by academic historians, can be genuinely distanced and objective and hence whether this distinction can be maintained.

Like many other claims about collective memory, a useful starting point when trying to understand this issue can be found in the writings of Halbwachs (1980). In his view, collective memory differs from history on several counts. For example, the former tends to focus on the stability and continuity of a group and often resists the idea that it has changed over time: "What strikes us about [collective] memory . . . is that resemblances are paramount. When it considers its own past, the group feels strongly that it has remained the same and becomes conscious of its identity through time" (p. 85). As elaborated by Nora (1989), this is "memory without a past that ceaselessly reinvents tradition, linking the history of its ancestors to the undifferentiated time of heroes, origins, and myth" (p. 8).

In contrast, history according to Halbwachs is a "record of changes" (p. 86). It divides the past into discrete periods, each with its own defining project.

Situated external to and above groups, history readily introduces into the stream of facts simple demarcations . . . Each period is apparently considered as a whole, independent for the most part of those preceding and following, and having some task – good, bad, or indifferent – to accomplish. . . . Viewed as a whole from afar and, especially, viewed from without by the spectator who never belonged to the groups he observes, the facts may allow such an arrangement into successive and distinct configurations, each period having a beginning, middle, and end. (p. 81)

The prototype of what Halbwachs had in mind is universal history produced from an objective perspective capable of integrating all partial viewpoints into a coherent whole. It "can be represented as the universal memory of the human species" (p. 84), it "is unitary [and] it can be said that there is only one history" (p. 83). By way of contrast, "there is no universal collective memory [because] every collective memory requires the support of a group delimited in space and time" (p. 84). Indeed, a group "retains from the past only what still lives or is capable of living in the consciousness of the groups keeping the memory alive. By definition it does not exceed the boundaries of this group" (p. 80), and for this reason "there are as many memories as there are groups" (Nora, 1989, p. 9).

Today, many scholars have grave doubts about the possibility of producing a universal history, but this does not obviate the need to maintain some distinction between collective memory and history. For example, Novick (1988), a figure who has produced a major critique of the "noble dream" of objectivity in history, begins his account of the Holocaust in American life by outlining the distinction between collective memory and history. As noted in Chapter 2, he contrasts history's willingness to deal with complexity and multiple perspectives with the tendency of collective memory to simplify, to see events from a "single committed perspective," and to be "impatient with ambiguities of any kind" (1999, pp. 3–4).

In developing his version of the distinction between history and collective memory Novick goes so far as to assert that the latter "is in crucial senses ahistorical, even anti-historical" (p. 3). This is so because:

Historical consciousness, by its nature, focuses on the *historicity* of events – that they took place then and not now, that they grew out of circumstances different from those that now obtain. Memory, by contrast, has no sense of the passage of time; it denies the "pastness" of its objects and insists on their continuing presence. Typically a collective memory, at least a significant collective memory, is understood to express some eternal or essential truth about the group – usually tragic. A memory, once established, comes to define that eternal truth, and, along with it, an eternal identity, for the members of the group. (p. 4)

Novick agrees with Halbwachs about the simplifying tendencies of collective memory. Its tendency to see things from a "single, committed perspective," its impatience with ambiguities, and its tendency to reduce "events to mythic archetypes" (1999, pp. 3–4) all stand in contrast to what professional historians strive to do, at least in principle. Nora (1989) likewise argues that in place of the "dictatorial . . . unself-conscious, commanding" tendencies of memory, "at the heart of history is a critical discourse that is antithetical to spontaneous memory" (pp. 8–9).

Recent studies of commemoration, a practice closely tied to collective memory, have made similar points about the tendency to eschew ambiguity and to present the past from a single committed perspective. In his discussion of the distinction between the commemorative voice and the historical voice in history museum exhibits, for example, Linenthal (1996) touches on this point. He does so in connection with the dispute over the 1995 exhibit at the NASM discussed earlier, a case that escalated into a "history war" (Linenthal & Engelhardt, 1996). His analysis led Linenthal to argue that accepting what I am calling a single committed perspective results in taking the museum to be a "temple" (p. 23), whereas encouraging the exploration of ambiguity presupposes that the museum is a "forum." In the museum as a forum, there is a tendency to take into consideration the "complicated motives of actions and consequences often hardly considered at the moment of the event itself" (pp. 9–10). Instead of being a "reverently held story," it should involve "later reappraisal" (p. 10) of these complicated motives, actions, and consequences.

In another analysis of the forces that gave rise to the history wars around this exhibit at the NASM, the historian John Dower (1996) provides additional insight into how history differs from commemoration. Specifically, he discusses "two notions that most historians take for granted: that controversy is inherent in any ongoing process of historical interpretation, and that policymaking is driven by multiple considerations and imperatives"

(p. 80). In formulating ways in which commemoration (and collective memory) stand in opposition to history, Dower outlines a notion of heroic narratives as inherently hostile to the assumptions guiding the historian.

Heroic narratives demand a simple, unilinear story line. In popular retellings, that simple line often takes the form of an intimate human-interest story . . . In the case of the atomic bombs, the American narrative almost invariably gravitates to Colonel Paul W. Tibbets, Jr., who piloted the famous plane, and his crew – brave and loyal men, as they surely were. And the pilot and his crew tell us, truthfully, what we know they will: that they carried out their mission without a second thought in order to save their comrades and help end the war. Such accounts . . . tell us little if anything about how top-level decisions were made – about who moved these men, who gave them their orders, and why. To seriously ask these questions is to enter the realm of multiple imperatives. (pp. 80–81)

In sum, what emerges is a set of oppositions that can be used to distinguish "collective memory" from "history." At the risk of reinforcing the mistaken impression that the two can be neatly separated, I offer the tabulation that follows (Table 1, p. 44). It is essential to keep in mind that the oppositions I provide are *tendencies* and *aspirations* of collective memory and history rather than *ironclad attributes*, and that the opposing tendencies often operate in tension with one another.

Change in Collective Memory and History

Having outlined some of the oppositions that have been used to distinguish collective memory from history, I turn to issues of whether and how each can change. The first point to make is that both do in fact undergo transformation. Given that controversy and change in ongoing historical interpretation are part of its self-image, this comes as no surprise in its case. Collective memory, however, typically assumes that it reflects the unchanging essence of a group, and it is therefore less likely to recognize any transitions it has undergone.

A review of specific cases reveals that the most interesting difference between collective memory and history may not concern whether they undergo change, but why. At least in their idealized versions, historical accounts undergo change because the ongoing process of critical reflection reveals that one version of the past should be revised or replaced by another. In some cases, the need for such change may stem from the discovery of new evidence or archives, and in others it may stem from the use of new analytical tools or theoretical perspectives. In all cases, however, the basic argument for why one account should replace another will be grounded in some notion of objective accuracy, completeness, and so forth.

Despite its claims to the contrary, collective memory also undergoes change over time, but the motivation behind such change often differs from that in historical analysis. Given that collective memory emerges in

TABLE 1. *Collective memory and history*

Collective memory	History
"Subjective" • single committed perspective	"Objective" • distanced from any particular perspective
• reflects a particular group's social framework	• reflects no particular social framework
• unself-conscious	• critical, reflective stance
• impatient with ambiguity about motives and the interpretation of events	• recognizes ambiguity
Focus on stable, unchanging group essence	Focus on transformation
Denial of "pastness" of events • links the past with the present	Focus on historicity • differentiates the past from the present
• ahistorical, antihistorical	• views past events as taking place "then and not now"
Commemorative voice • museum as a temple	Historical voice • museum as a forum
• unquestionable heroic narratives	• disagreement, change, and controversy as part of ongoing historical interpretation

response to the need to create a usable past, and this need varies over time, this is to be expected. What constitutes a usable past in one sociocultural setting is often quite different from what is needed in another.

Studies by historians provide some insight into this issue. For example, Novick (1999) has outlined some of the ways that the collective memory of the Holocaust in the United States has changed during the latter half of the twentieth century. In his view, the concerns of the present "have, in one period, made Holocaust memory seem inappropriate, useless, or even harmful; in another period, appropriate and desirable. As we examine the changing fortunes of Holocaust memory, we'll be struck by how they relate to changing circumstances and, particularly among American Jews, changing decisions about collective self-understanding and self-representation" (p. 5).

Bodnar (1992) has made a related argument about other transitions in American public memory during the twentieth century. He views these transitions as part of an ongoing struggle that takes many twists and turns, depending on the needs of the moment. In his view:

The essential contest that shaped commemoration and the interpretation of the past and present has been waged between the advocates of centralized power and those who were unwilling to completely relinquish the autonomy of their small worlds. Cultural leaders, usually grounded in institutional and professional structures, envisioned a nation of dutiful and united citizens which undertook only orderly change. These officials saw the past as a device that could help them attain these goals and never tired of using commemorations to restate what they thought the social order and citizen behavior should be.

Defenders of vernacular cultures, however, had misgivings about centralized authorities and their interpretations of the past and the present. Their cultural expressions and public memory were not always grounded in the interests of large institutions but in the interests of small structures and associations that they had known, felt, or experienced directly. These attachments could change from time to time and include interests that served the needs of leaders as well. (pp. 245–246)

From Bodnar's perspective, the twentieth century has seen the rise and subsequent diminution of central governmental control of public memory in the United States. The domination of official culture shifted from the business and cultural elite to the U.S. government over the course of the first half of the twentieth century, but "the political culture of our own times is no longer dominated by a central symbol as powerful as the nation-state" (p. 252). Again, the negotiation of a usable past is seen to change with the demands of the present.

Shifting back to collective memory for the Holocaust, it is interesting to note that some authors argue not only that it does change, but that it *should.* This point is often made by those concerned with insuring that memory for the Holocaust continues to be the focus of active engagement.

In this view, it is important for each generation to negotiate a usable past of its own about this event. This claim is reflected in James Young's (2000) fascinating analysis of the political and cultural travails of deciding on a national memorial in Berlin to the European Jews killed in World War II. In outlining the pluses and minuses of one of the finalists who had competed to provide a design for this memorial, he writes:

Rather than pretending to answer Germany's memorial problem in a single, reassuring form, this design proposed multiple, collected forms arranged so that visitors have to find their own path to the memory of Europe's murdered Jews. As such, this memorial provided not an answer to memory but an ongoing process, a continuing question without a certain solution. (p. 206)

Despite its claims for stability and constancy, then, it appears that one of the few genuinely constant attributes of collective memory is that it is likely to undergo change. In reviewing the reasons for such change, I have contrasted them with the transformations that occur in historical analysis. In case it is required, a reminder of the difficulty of maintaining this contrast can be found in writings by authors such as Joyce Appleby, Lynn Hunt, and Margaret Jacob (1994). In looking at the scholarly pursuit of historical interpretation, these authors argue that at least in some instances, such interpretation changes not because of newly available information or an ongoing, disinterested quest for accuracy, but because of the identity of who is doing the speaking. In their case, they have focused on how the writing of American history has changed as a function of increased representation among the ranks of professional historians by women and minorities, but the point they make obviously has wider implications as well.

Remembering vs. Re-experiencing

As is apparent from the preceding sections, the distinction between collective memory and history is a multifaceted one. In delving into it further, I shall introduce yet another opposition – namely, that between "remembering" and "re-experiencing." This distinction concerns the distance, or separation that an individual or group experiences between itself and an event from the past. Remembering presupposes such a separation. While the textual mediation involved may be somewhat difficult to detect, its functioning is present in this case and creates a degree of separation. Re-experiencing, in contrast, assumes that the individual or group merges with, or is a part of the past event. In its extreme form, this may be a way of representing the past that seems to involve no textual mediation at all, the result being that the distance between observer and event dissolves. It is as if the individual is actually there, re-experiencing and participating in the event. This is sometimes discussed in terms of a memory being "experience-far" or "experience-near" (Conway, 2001).

By its very nature, re-experiencing is highly subjective and hence not readily available for observation or corroboration by others. Nonetheless, it has been widely discussed in analyses of individual and collective memory and hence provides part of the conceptual framework within which many issues are considered. Some version of re-experiencing has been contemplated in fields ranging from neurology to history to literature.

Perhaps the most powerful version of re-experiencing is trauma. At least since early discussions of "war neuroses" in World War I, the study of trauma has been a part of the study of memory. Sigmund Freud (1955) discussed this phenomenon under the heading of "traumatic neuroses," where he wrote about how powerful dreams "have the characteristic of repeatedly bringing the patient back into the situation of his accident" (1955, vol. 18, p. 13), and these reflections draw on even earlier observations by figures such as Pierre Janet (Ellenburger, 1970).

Several contemporary lines of research have built on and extended these early ideas in psychology. For example, scholars from literary studies (Caruth, 1995a), psychiatry (van der Kolk & van der Hart, 1995), and sociology (Erikson, 1995) have addressed a range of issues concerned with trauma. In outlining these, Caruth describes trauma in terms of "the literal return of the event against the will of the one it inhabits" (p. 5). In a discussion of Post-Traumatic Stress Disorder (PTSD), she outlines how "overwhelming events of the past repeatedly possess, in intrusive images and thoughts, the one who has lived through them" (1995b, p. 151). And as the psychologists Ehlers and Steihl (1995) note:

Even months and years after a traumatic event, patients with Posttraumatic Stress Disorder (PTSD) continue to involuntarily reexperience aspects of the trauma. Re-experiencing can take the form of images, thoughts, perceptions, flashbacks, or dreams of the trauma. (pp. 217–218)

The comments of Caruth as well as other contemporary writers on trauma (e.g., van der Kolk & van der Hart, 1995) reflect an important point about its characterization – namely, it is viewed as experience that is not integrated into understanding because it has not been placed in a narrative. As a result, individuals do not have the agency normally associated with remembering. Instead of individuals having memories, it is as if memories have agency over individuals. This characterization of where agency lies in trauma can be found all the way from Janet and Freud to the present, and it lies behind the paradox that "recall of the actual trauma may often be impaired, whereas patients may reexperience aspects of the trauma in the form of intrusive thoughts, nightmares, or flashbacks" (Krystal, 1990, p. 6).

Whereas re-experiencing takes on particularly powerful form in the case of trauma, it has been presented in other guises as well. For example, in his monumental work *Remembrance of Things Past* (1982), Marcel Proust presented a famous depiction of this phenomenon. He was concerned throughout this work with recalling the past, but he was particularly impressed with episodes of what I am calling re-experiencing. He warned that remembering, as an effort of the "intellect," is at best capable of providing only a pale reflection of the past compared with re-experiencing.

And so it is with our own past. It is a labour in vain to attempt to recapture it: all the efforts of our intellect must prove futile. The past is hidden somewhere outside the realm, beyond the reach of intellect, in some material object (in which sensation with that material object will give us) of which we have no inkling. And it depends on change whether or not we come upon this object before we ourselves must die. (pp. 47–48)

In Proust's account, the "material object" involved serves in the role of what psychologists of memory would call a "cue," but in his view, cuing episodes of re-experiencing is fundamentally different from what occurs in remembering. This is clear from his description of an instance of re-experiencing.

Many years had elapsed during which nothing of Combray, save what was comprised in the theatre and the drama of my going to bed there, had any existence for me, when one day in winter, on my return home, my mother, seeing that I was cold, offered me some tea, a thing I did not ordinarily take. I declined at first, and then, for no particular reason, changed my mind. She sent for one of those squat, plump little cakes called "petites madeleines," which look as though they had been moulded in the fluted valve of a scallop shell. And soon, mechanically, dispirited after a dreary day with the prospect of a depressing morrow, I raised to my lips a spoonful of the tea in which I had soaked a morsel of the cake. No sooner had the warm liquid mixed with the crumbs touched my palate than a shudder ran through me and I stopped, intent upon the extraordinary thing that was happening to me. An exquisite pleasure had invaded my senses, something isolated, detached, with no suggestion of its origin. And at once the vicissitudes of life had become indifferent to me, its disasters innocuous, its brevity illusory – this new sensation having had on me the effect which love has of filling me with a precious essence; or rather this essence was not in me, it *was* me. (p. 48)

Like scholars of trauma, Proust emphasized the distinction between such episodes of re-experiencing and episodes of remembering. He termed this encounter with re-experiencing as an "unremembered state which brought with it no logical proof, but the indisputable evidence, of its felicity, its reality" (p. 49). It was only subsequently and separately that the event reached "the clear surface of my consciousness" where "suddenly the memory revealed itself" (p. 50). At that point Proust realized intellectually that "the taste was that of the little piece of madeleine which on Sunday mornings at Combray . . . when I went to say good morning to her in her bedroom, my aunt Léonie used to give me, dipping it first in her own cup of tea or tisane" (p. 50).

In his account of re-experiencing and remembering, Proust stressed that the latter involves some form of conscious, voluntary control, whereas the former does not. Remembering is something that a person does, whereas re-experiencing, as in the case of trauma, is something that happens *to* a person. Proust emphasized the importance of the senses of taste and smell in episodes of re-experiencing – senses associated with primitive, less consciously controlled functioning than sight or hearing.

But when from a long-distant past nothing subsists, after the people are dead, after the things are broken and scattered, taste and smell alone, more the fragile but more enduring, more unsubstantial, more persistent, more faithful, remained poised a long time, like souls, remembering, waiting, hoping, amid the ruins of all the rest; and bear unflinchingly, in the tiny and almost impalpable drop of their essence, the vast structure of recollection. (pp. 50–51)

In their account of re-experiencing, analysts of trauma share with Proust a concern with phenomena that occur at the level of the individual. For all of these authors, re-experiencing is unusual, if not somewhat exotic, and is elicited only in exceptional circumstances. Furthermore, "is elicited" is the operative phrase here since re-experiencing is viewed as something that happens to people rather than being subject to their conscious control. Finally, although not all of these authors formulate it as such, the distinction between re-experiencing and remembering concerns mediation. Specifically, re-experiencing is viewed as an unmediated process – and for that very reason not subject to voluntary control – whereas remembering is viewed as involving some form of intellectual or conceptual mediation usually associated with language as a cultural tool, especially language in the form of narrative.

Turning to accounts of re-experiencing in anthropology and sociology, the focus shifts to collective, as opposed to individual, memory. Furthermore, the distinction between re-experiencing and remembering is not so clear or stark as it was for Proust and for scholars of trauma, the reason being that mediation is involved in both phenomena. Instead of assuming that some experience can be revisited in its relatively "raw," unmediated form, anthropological and sociological accounts tend to focus on re-experiencing through the use of cultural tools like spoken language and enacted rituals.

For example, in *The Myth of the Eternal Return*, Mircea Eliade (1954) argued that members of "archaic societies" are characterized by a tendency to re-experience the past rather than remember it from a distance. They do so through the repeated use of collective ritual performances, the result being that "although they are conscious of a certain form of 'history,' [they] make every effort to disregard it" (p. ix). They are characterized by a "revolt against concrete, historical time . . . [and a] nostalgia for a periodical return to the mythical time of the beginning of things, to the 'Great Time'" (p. ix). In this "primitive" ontological conception, "an object or an act becomes real only insofar as it imitates or repeats an archetype. Thus, reality is acquired solely through repetition or participation . . . the man of traditional culture sees himself as real only to the extent that he ceases to be himself (for a modern observer) and is satisfied with imitating and repeating the gestures of another" (p. 34).

This emphasis on repeating or participating in the words and gestures of others led Eliade to ask: "to what extent does collective memory preserve the [accurate] recollection of a historical event?" (p. 37). He argued that instead of a form of historical representation that retains ambiguity and complexity, what is involved is the "transfiguration of history into myth" (p. 37). From this perspective, processes of "imitating and repeating the gestures of another" (p. 34) yield a simplified, schematized account of the past.

The recollection of a historical event or a real personage survives in popular memory for two or three centuries at the utmost. This is because popular memory finds difficulty in retaining individual events and real figures. The structures by means of which it functions are different: categories instead of events, archetypes instead of historical personages. The historical personage is assimilated to his mythical model (hero, etc.), while the event is identified with the category of mythical actions (fight with a monster, enemy brothers, etc.). (p. 43)

In Eliade's account, mediational means associated with "categories," "archetypes," "mythical models," and so forth play an essential role. The re-experiencing that is involved in these cases comes through the repeated use of cultural tools such as ritual texts, and this leads to the differentiation of "collective" or "popular" memory from history.

In his account *How Societies Remember* (1989), the sociologist and social theorist Paul Connerton has developed a line of reasoning that extends some of Eliade's ideas. Connerton argues for the importance of "habit-memory," which consists in "having the capacity to reproduce a certain performance" (p. 22). In his view, "we frequently do not recall how or when or where we have acquired the knowledge in question; often it is only by the fact of performance that we are able to recognise and demonstrate to others that we do in fact remember. The memory of how to read or write or ride a bicycle is like the meaning of a lesson thoroughly learned; it has all the marks of a habit" (pp. 22–23).

Connerton's interest in habit memory grows out of his concern with how hierarchies of power are created and maintained in society. Beginning with the assertions that "it is surely the case that control of a society's memory largely conditions the hierarchy of power" (p. 1) and "our experience of the present largely depends upon our knowledge of the past, and . . . our images of the past commonly serve to legitimate a present social order" (p. 3), he proceeds to focus on how collective memory is inculcated in citizens of a society. As was the case with Sasha as described in Chapter 1, the assumption is that accounts of the past are not devised through independent research by individuals or groups. Instead, these accounts come into existence through being exposed to the textual resources provided by others.

In sum, the distinction between remembering and re-experiencing surfaces in a variety of ways in accounts of memory. As outlined by authors concerned with trauma and by Proust, the purest forms of re-experiencing involve little or no textual mediation in individual memory. Such re-experiencing allows for little voluntary control by the individuals involved and is viewed as a form of direct participation in archaic events. Accounts of re-experiencing on the collective plane do involve textual mediation, but it is textual mediation heavily oriented toward embodied, ritualistic performance. The mythic schematization involved in such cases resonates with many characterizations of collective memory and is suggestive of how groups of individuals may be socialized into accepting a view of the past.

In the chapters that follow, my primary concern will be with remembering, as opposed to re-experiencing. In the case of several issues I shall raise, however, re-experiencing lurks in the background, and for this reason it is useful to formulate it explicitly and to understand how it stands in opposition to remembering.

Episodic vs. Instrumental Collective Memory

Viewing memory as a form of mediated action makes it possible to clarify strands of discussion that often remain confused. One point on which such clarification is useful involves the basic elements of mediated action: agents and cultural tools. Most discussions of collective memory focus on the content to be remembered, but some are also concerned with the cultural tools used to do the remembering. Examples of the former orientation involve the "episodic" memory of events such as the American Civil War or the atomic bombing of Hiroshima. Examples of the latter involve what I shall term "instrumental" memory, and are reflected in claims about how collectives share knowledge about how to use cultural tools such as language, literacy, and particular forms of explanation. Although one or the other of these orientations underlies most analyses of collective memory, the fact that they are seldom clearly distinguished means that misunderstanding and spurious disagreements can easily arise.

A starting point for disentangling such issues is the notion of "episodic memory" introduced by Tulving (1972) in the psychological study of individual memory. This form of memory involves "the remembering of episodes of our lives and is contextually bound; that is, the time and place of occurrence are inextricable parts of memory for episodes. This type of memory enables the mental time travel in which we engage when we think back to an earlier occasion" (Roediger & Goff, 1998, p. 250).

A problem with importing ideas from the study of individual memory into the analysis of collective memory comes immediately into focus here. It is not readily apparent what the counterpart in collective memory is for notions such as "episodes in our lives." At a more general level, however, the contrast provided by cognitive psychology between episodic and other forms of memory has some important implications for developing a set of analytical constructs for the study of collective memory. Specifically, the difference between remembering particular episodes, on the one hand, and remembering the "semantic knowledge" and "procedural knowledge" that underlie it, on the other, is important in this regard.

Most psychological studies of memory in the individual focus on episodic memory, and this has been the main focus of my comments so far on collective memory as well. However, behind any analysis of episodic collective memory there is typically some assumption about how this memory occurs, and this raises the issue of "instrumental memory." Instrumental memory is memory or knowledge about a cultural tool and the procedures for using it. The cultural tools used by one collective may differ from those employed by another, and this can be expected to lead to different memory processes and products. This point is reflected in claims about how cultural tools such as a language shape, or even "contain," the memory of a group.

Introducing the notion of instrumental memory makes it possible to address the issue of how different collectives may form different accounts of the past as a result of employing different cultural tools. David Lowenthal (1994) makes this point in his review of forms of "textual heritage." Such heritage "comprises not only tragic and triumphal tales but uniquely national modes of explanation – the Whig interpretation of English history, the American mystique of Manifest Destiny, the grandeur of an eternal France, one and indivisible" (p. 53).

Returning to the case of the atomic bombing of Hiroshima, it is possible to provide an extensive list of instruments, or cultural tools, that have shaped collective memories. Along with one or another textual heritage, various parties have employed cultural tools such as documentary films about the aftermath of the bombing, museum exhibits that include artifacts from the bomb site (Linenthal & Engelhardt, 1996), and statistical reports on the effects of the atomic bomb. The fact that it is possible to use such a range of forms of semiotic mediation suggests that there is no single cultural tool that captures the essence or "truth" of the episode. Instead, one must recognize important differences in collective episodic memory that result from employing different cultural tools. From the perspective of mediated action, these cultural tools are not simply different means for forming the same representation of the past. Instead, they yield episodic memories that differ essentially in their content.

Among those who have been particularly sensitive to this fact are literary scholars. For example, in *The Great War and Modern Memory*, Paul Fussell (1975) outlines how literary conventions affect the ways in which different generations have remembered the events of World War I. He argues that the experience of this war was so disillusioning and traumatic for its participants that it was impossible to represent or remember it using the cultural tools then in existence. Instead, it called for the creation of new means for remembering, especially irony, and this gave rise to the "mechanism of irony-assisted recall" (p. 30).

In reading memoirs of the war, one notices the same phenomenon over and over. By applying to the past a paradigm of ironic action, a rememberer is enabled to locate, draw forth, and finally shape into significance an event or a moment which otherwise would emerge without meaning into the general undifferentiated stream. (Fussell, 1975, p. 30)

Although irony provided an important new means for remembering World War I, Fussell argues that it was not sufficient in the long run to remember an event that was so traumatic and senseless. It was only with the much later writings of authors such as Norman Mailer, Thomas Pynchon, and James Jones that cultural tools that are really up to the job began to be employed.

It is the virtual disappearance during the sixties and seventies of the concept of prohibitive obscenity, a concept which has acted as a censor on earlier memories of "war," that has given the ritual of military memory a new dimension. And that new dimension is capable of revealing for the first time the full obscenity of the Great War. The greatest irony is that it is only now, when those who remember the events are almost all dead, that the literary means for adequate remembering and interpreting are finally publicly accessible. (p. 334)

Hence there is a sense in which the individuals or groups who had actual autobiographical memory for some event can be said to have less adequate episodic memories of it than others who had not because they had less adequate instruments for remembering. This is a line of reasoning that has much in common with points made by analysts of trauma. In both cases, the concern is with the use of a cultural tool such as an appropriate narrative that will allow people to bring an experience into understanding.

A figure whose ideas are particularly powerful when formulating the notion of instrumental memory at a general level is Ernst Cassirer (1944, 1946, 1955), someone who had an important impact on Vygotsky, Bakhtin, and many others concerned with mediated action. Beginning with the observation that "all symbolism harbors the curse of mediacy" in that "it is bound to obscure what seeks to reveal" (1946, p. 7), Cassirer argued that human cognition and action are basically beholden to "symbolic forms." Furthermore, he viewed the emergence of particular symbolic forms such as myth, art, and science as holding the key to the emergence and current state of human cognition, memory, and other aspects of mental life. One of Cassirer's most insightful interpreters, Susanne Langer (1949), has summarized his ideas on this point in the following terms:

...the history of thought consists chiefly in the gradual achievement of factual, literal, and logical conception and expression. Obviously the only means to this end is language. But this instrument, it must be remembered, has a double nature.

Its syntactical tendencies bestow the laws of logic on us; yet the primacy of *names* in its make-up holds it to the hypostatic way of thinking which belongs to its twin-phenomenon, myth. Consequently it led us beyond the sphere of mythic and emotive thoughts, yet always pulls us back into it again; it is both the diffuse and tempered light that shows us the external world of "fact," and the array of spiritual lamps, light-centers of intensive meaning, that throw the gleams and shadows of the dream world wherein our earliest experiences lay. (pp. 391–392)

In the terminology I have been employing, Langer's comments amount to saying that different historical epochs can be characterized in terms of different forms of instrumental memory. Her statement also touches on the important point that with the emergence of a new symbolic instrument such as science, we retain certain remnants of earlier symbolic forms. This is an argument that echoes the line of reasoning I outlined in Chapter 2 on the relationship between collective memory and history. Recognizing that the idea and ideals of history emerged in a context populated by collective memory means that those pursuing history are likely to be "pulled back" occasionally into ways of thinking tied to collective memory. As a result, analytical history remains incompletely differentiated from collective memory, and forms of symbolic and mental functioning that reflect earlier epochs may be expected to continue to exert their influence.

Such claims have obvious implications for how the notion of instrumental memory is to be understood. Without our being fully aware of it, the cultural tools we employ to remember something like the bombing of Hiroshima or World War I themselves have a sort of memory, or at least memory potential, built into them. Furthermore, these cultural tools and the affordances and constraints built into them are unequally distributed among various collectives, and as a result these collectives may be expected to remember the "same" event differently. This is Fussell's point in his analysis of the Great War and modern memory. At a more general level, it has been made in connection with the impact of literacy (Goody & Watt, 1963; Yates, 1966), and if Cassirer was right, it is something that is pervasive in collective memory in general.

Before leaving the issue of how differences in instrumental memory may shape episodic memory, it is worth noting that the possible range of variation of the former is not unlimited. Instead, evidence from fields such as cognitive and developmental psychology and cognitive anthropology suggests that the emergence and intergenerational transmission of representations of the past may be shaped by universal cognitive constraints. This is a claim that has been explored by scholars such as Pascal Boyer (1992, 1993, 1999). Boyer argues that "human minds are predisposed, by virtue of early developed intuitive understandings, to acquire a specific range of cultural concepts" (1999, p. 216), and he goes on to outline the implication that "cognitive capacities make certain types of concepts more likely than others to be acquired and transmitted in human groups" (p. 206).

Boyer's perspective does not deny that cultural variability exists, but it does argue that in the end such variability consists of "an enrichment, never a revision of . . . intuitive principles" (p. 209). He outlines several forms of evidence that support the claim that intuitive categories and principles are strikingly similar across cultures, and argues that "there is no evidence for major cultural differences in categorical distinctions or inferential engines. Take intuitive biology: there are, to be sure, cultural differences in the way biological phenomena are explained. However, the major features of biological essentialism, as described here, are stable across cultures" (p. 209).

The implications of Boyer's ideas for instrumental memory derive from the fact that "intuitive ontology imposes some constraints on the range of concepts likely to be 'culturally successful' [in transmission across generations], because it makes some concepts much easier than others to acquire, store and communicate" (p. 210). Such claims have been the topic of research on natural kinds and other categories and principles usually considered to be part of natural science, but Boyer suggests that they apply to religious concepts and their transmission as well.

Despite obvious cultural diversity, recurrent patterns show that religious concepts are constrained by a small number of principles that are not specifically religious . . . This is true in particular of religious *ontologies*, that is, culturally specific assumptions about the existence and causal powers of unobservable entities. (p. 213)

In sum, the line of inquiry outlined by Boyer suggests that the range of possible items to be found in instrumental memory, and hence episodic memory, may be limited by universal cognitive constraints. Given that my focus tends to be on differences rather than similarities among collective memories and textual communities, I shall not pursue these universals in detail, but Boyer's research provides a reminder of the need to take this into account in a more comprehensive picture.

Narratives as Cultural Tools

Having laid out several oppositions that shape our understanding of collective memory in general, I narrow the focus by turning to the workings of textually mediated collective memory in particular. This leads to a consideration of the function and organization of the cultural tools involved. My earlier example of remembering with the help of Amazon.com dealt with a specialized cultural tool and focused on retrieving an isolated piece of information. In what follows, I shall focus on a form of mediational means that plays a much broader role in human life – namely narrative – and I shall be concerned with its role in remembering settings, actors, and events.

As I have outlined elsewhere (Wertsch, 1998), narrative is one of a few different instruments we have for representing settings, actors, and events of the past. Other semiotic means such as chronicles and annals may also be employed, means that are likely to yield different sorts of memory (White, 1983). However, narrative is widely recognized as playing a central role in human consciousness in general (Bruner, 1986, 1990) and history and collective memory in particular (Mink, 1978; White, 1987; Young, 1988).

The past several decades have witnessed continuous interest in narrativity and its relationship to human consciousness. The discussion of these issues has ranged across the disciplines of history (White, 1987), literature (Scholes & Kellogg, 1966), psychoanalysis (Schafer, 1981), philosophy (MacIntyre, 1984; Ricouer, 1984–1986), and psychology (Bruner, 1990). Many of these efforts are thoroughly interdisciplinary. For example, in cultural psychology, Bruner (1986) has mapped out an account of "narrative cognition" and how it contrasts with the more typical focus of cognitive psychology, "paradigmatic cognition." A central point in this line of inquiry has been the importance of narrative in human consciousness. Indeed, Bruner argues that the "narrative mode for construing reality" (1996, p. 130) is central to being human.

Alasdair MacIntyre (1984) has developed a similar set of claims about the ubiquity of narrative in human consciousness.

[M]an is in his actions and practice, as well as in his fictions, essentially a storytelling animal. He is not essentially, but becomes through his history, a teller of stories that aspire to truth. But the key question for men is not about their own authorship; I can only answer the question 'What am I to do?' if I can answer the prior question 'Of what story or stories do I find myself a part?' We enter human society, that is, with one or more imputed characters – roles into which we have been drafted – and we have to learn what they are in order to be able to understand how others respond to us and how our responses to them are apt to be construed. It is through hearing stories about wicked stepmothers, lost children, good but misguided kings, wolves that suckle twin boys, youngest sons who receive no inheritance but must make their own way in the world and eldest sons who waste their inheritance on riotous living and go into exile to live with the swine, that children learn or mislearn both what a child and what a parent is, what the cast of characters may be in the drama into which they have been born and what the ways of the world are . . . Hence there is no way to give us an understanding of any society, including our own, except through the stock of stories which constitute its initial dramatic resources. (p. 216)

MacIntyre's line of reasoning has several implications when thinking about the narrative organization of collective memory. The first of these has to do with the omnipresence and importance of narrative in human activity. Like Bruner, MacIntyre stresses that a great deal of thinking, speaking, and other forms of action are fundamentally shaped by narratives. We are especially "story-telling animals" when it comes to recounting and interpreting our own and others' actions – the motives that lie behind them, the settings in which they occur, the outcomes they produce, and so forth.

Second, MacIntyre stresses that the narrative tools we employ in this connection are provided by the particular cultural, historical, and institutional settings in which we live. Just as Bruner claims that "symbolic systems...[are] already in place, already 'there,' deeply entrenched in culture and language" (1990, p. 11), MacIntyre sees the narratives we use to make sense of human action to come from a "stock of stories" from which any particular individual may draw. Rather than being part of some universal human essence, they are part of the "cultural tool kit" (Bruner, 1990; Wertsch, 1998) that characterizes a sociocultural setting.

The literature on narrative in general, or even the narrative organization of memory in particular, is so vast as to defy any neat summary. In keeping with my emphasis on collective memory as a form of mediated action, I shall therefore focus more narrowly on how narratives serve as cultural tools for remembering. As a way of organizing this still extensive topic, I shall approach it in terms of two distinctions that will play a role in the chapters that follow. The first of these has to do with two general functions of narratives: a "referential" function and a "dialogic" function; the second distinction has to do with whether concrete, particular narratives or more abstract "schematic narrative templates" are at issue.

The Referential and Dialogic Functions of Narratives

The referential function of narratives concerns their potential to refer to settings, characters, and events. The basic relationship involved in this function is between narratives and the objects they represent. These may be either real or imagined, giving rise to the distinction Robert Scholes and Robert Kellogg (1966) develop between "empirical" or "fictional" narratives, respectively. My focus will be on the former – that is, on events that are assumed to have actually occurred. In contrast, the dialogic function concerns the relationship one narrative may have to another. From this perspective, narratives are viewed as responding to one another, something that can affect anything from the motivation to tell a particular story in the first place to the particular form it takes. As was the case for the functional dualism of memory, my point will not be that we should view narratives in either/or terms. Instead of considering the referential or dialogic function in isolation, the point is to recognize how these two tendencies operate in tandem and how one or the other may predominate in any particular instance.

The referential function of narratives involves more than simply referring to settings, actors, and events. A crucial fact about narratives as cultural tools is that they make it possible to carry out the "configurational act" required to "grasp together" (Ricouer, 1981, p. 174) sets of temporally distributed events into interpretable wholes or plots. As Mink (1978) has argued, they serve as "cognitive instruments" for organizing our understanding of the past. This configurational act is often discussed under the heading of "emplotment" by narrative theorists.

As is the case with any cultural tool, the affordances of narratives are accompanied by constraints. In particular, an unavoidable narrowing of perspective is the other side of the coin of the cognitive efficiency and power afforded by emplotment. In order to include some information in a well-configured story, one is forced to neglect other information that is clearly available and indeed might be included in another narrative account. In short, the construction of an account of historical events is inherently constrained by "radically selective narrativizations of events" (Novick, 1996, p. 28).

A crucial factor in shaping the affordances and constraints of emplotment is the "sense of an ending" (Kermode, 1967) around which narratives are organized. In this connection, consider William Cronon's (1992) observations about the power of a conclusion to shape historical narrative. These observations were made in the course of analyzing two accounts by professional historians of the Dust Bowl in the American Southwest in the 1930s. One account takes the form of a "progressive" story of improvement and human victory over adversity, and the other takes a "tragic" form that reflects "romantic and antimodernist reactions against progress" (p. 1352). In this instance, the resulting narratives are so different that they

... make us wonder how two competent authors looking at identical materials drawn from the same past can reach such divergent conclusions. But it is not merely their *conclusions* that differ. Although both narrate the same broad series of events with an essentially similar cast of characters, they tell two entirely different *stories*. In both texts, the story is inextricably bound to its conclusion, and the historical analysis derives much of its force from the upward or downward sweep of the plot. (p. 1348)

Of course, narratives produced by academic historians involve a great deal of careful reflection and hence may be somewhat different from other accounts of the past not grounded primarily in analytical reflection. However, the processes of emplotment, organized around a sense of an ending, shape the way that narratives grasp events together in general, and hence the affordances and constraints they provide characterize both analytical history and collective memory.

In the course of making his point about how endings shape the process of grasping events together into a plot, Cronon also touches on the issue of how narratives are socioculturally situated. In his view, the distinction between "the upward or downward sweep of the plot" (p. 1348) is associated with the struggle between "eighteenth-century Enlightenment notions of progress" and "romantic and antimodernist reactions against progress" (p. 1352). The two types of plots are not universal and ahistorical, nor are they independently invented by individuals. Instead, they are part of a particular "stock of stories" (MacIntyre, p. 216) made available by a particular sociocultural setting.

In contrast to the referential function, which concerns the relationship between narratives and the settings, actors, and events they depict, the dialogic function concerns the relationship between one narrative and another. From this perspective, it is essential to recognize that narratives do not exist in isolation and do not serve as neutral cognitive instruments. Instead, they are embedded in concrete discourse characterized by dialogic and rhetorical opposition.

The sort of dialogic processes I have in mind have been outlined by Barbara Hernstein Smith (1981) in her critique of the "lingering strain of naive Platonism" she sees in narrative theory. Her starting point is that "no narrative version can be independent of a particular teller and occasion of telling" (p. 215). Instead, it "has been constructed in accord with some set of purposes or interests" (ibid.).

Smith makes these points in her critique of the tendency to analyze narratives primarily, if not solely, from the perspective of what I am calling their referential function. Such a view reflects a "conception of discourse as consisting of sets of discrete signs which, in some way, correspond to (depict, encode, denote, refer to, and so forth) sets of discrete and specific ideas, objects, or events" (p. 221). According to Smith, "This model of language has . . . been the major one in Western intellectual history and, in spite of some epistemological doubts and technical modifications introduced recently by various linguists and philosophers of language, it continues to be the model that dominates not only narratology but literary studies generally" (p. 221).

In contrast to a single-minded focus on the referential function of narratives, Smith argues for the need to incorporate an analysis of what I am calling their dialogic function.

An alternative conception of language views utterances not as strings of discrete signifiers that represent corresponding sets of discrete signifieds but as *verbal responses* – that is, as *acts* which, like any acts, are *performed in response to various sets of conditions.* These conditions consist of all those circumstantial and psychological variables of which every utterance is a function. (pp. 221–22)

In Chapter 5, I shall examine the sort of responsive discourse Smith envisions in the case of collective memory, but it is worth noting that it also shapes the writings of professional historians striving to provide objective accounts of the past. As noted by David Thelen (1989), the "historian's narrative tradition" introduces an inherent constructive moment, and hence history "is not made in isolation but in conversation with others that occur in the contexts of community, broader politics, and social dynamics" (p. 1119).

In Smith's account, narratives may respond to a variety of contextual forces, but I shall focus in particular on one: other narratives. Following the lead of Bakhtin (1981, 1984, 1986a) and Lotman (1988, 1990), my concern will be with how narratives exist in dialogic relationships with one another. As such, the key to understanding the meaning and form of one narrative is how it provides a dialogic response to previous narratives or anticipates subsequent ones. And the nature of the response can range from hostile retort to friendly elaboration, from a studied attempt to ignore another narrative to its celebration.

Specific Narratives and Schematic Narrative Templates

Up to this point, I have been talking about narratives in a fairly generic way, as if they always exist at one level. In order to appreciate the richness of how they function as cultural tools, however, it is important to make some additional distinctions. In particular, it is useful to distinguish between specific narratives and what I shall term "schematic narrative templates." Under the heading of specific narratives, I have in mind items such as those MacIntyre (1984) lists when he alludes to "stories about wicked stepmothers, lost children, good but misguided kings, wolves that suckle twin boys, youngest sons who receive no inheritance but must make their own way in the world and eldest sons who waste their inheritance on riotous living and go into exile to live with the swine" (p. 216). These are narratives in the Western tradition that have specific settings, characters, and events.

When addressing issues of the role of narrative as a cultural tool in collective remembering, however, it will turn out to be useful to contrast this sort of specific narrative with more generalized, abstract forms, the latter being schematic narrative templates. The notion of a schematic narrative template that I shall use can be traced to several sources. One of the most important of these is the Russian folklorist Vladimir Propp (1968). In developing his line of reasoning about Russian folk tales, Propp argued for the need to focus on the generalized "functions" that characterize a broad range of narratives, as opposed to the particular events and actors that occur in specific ones. From this perspective, "recurrent constants" or functions "of dramatis personae are basic components of the tale" (p. 21). This focus on abstract function means that several specific events and individuals may qualify as a particular function in a narrative. In this view, *"Functions of characters serve as stable, constant elements of a tale, independent of how and by whom they are fulfilled "* (p. 21, italics in the original).

Propp identified an extensive network of generalized functions, including items such as "THE VILLAIN RECEIVES INFORMATION ABOUT HIS VICTIM" (p. 28) and "THE VILLAIN IS DEFEATED" (p. 53). From my perspective, the primary value of Propp's ideas about narrative functions concerns his general line of reasoning rather than his detailed claims about particular functions, claims that were developed in connection with Russian folk tales. Specifically, I am concerned with the notion that a generalized narrative form may underlie a range of narratives in a cultural tradition. This changes the focus from analyzing a list of specific narratives to analyzing an underlying pattern that is instantiated in many of them.

Switching from folklore to psychology, an analogous line of reasoning may be found in the writings of Bartlett (1995). His classic book *Remembering* spawned a host of research efforts that continue to this day in the psychology of memory. Although there is no reason to assume that he was familiar with Propp's writings, Bartlett did develop some similar claims. In his view, human cognitive functioning is usually more of a "constructive" process (p. 312) than a product of stimuli, and this led him to examine the generalized patterns or "schemata" brought to this process by the agent doing the constructing.

Bartlett took as a starting point for his inquiry the assumption that one can "speak of every human cognitive reaction – perceiving, imagining, remembering, thinking and reasoning – as an *effort after meaning*" (p. 44). This effort is grounded in "tendencies which the subject brings with him into the situation with which he is called upon to deal" (p. 44). Bartlett discussed these tendencies in terms of "schemes" that "are utilised so as to make [the subject's] reaction the 'easiest', or the least disagreeable, or the quickest and least obstructed that is at the time possible" (p. 44). He also noted that these schemes are often used in a "completely unreflective, unanalytical and unwitting manner" (p. 45).

Bartlett's general line of reasoning continues to have a powerful impact on memory research in psychology to this day. An example of this can be seen in the writings of Ross (1989) on "implicit theories." Ross is concerned with the construction of personal histories, or autobiography, which is "depicted as an active, constructive, schema-guided process" (pp. 341–342). Like many psychologists of memory, Ross assumes that remembering is typically not very accurate with regard to details. He sees the construction of personal histories as being shaped by a host of biasing factors, including implicit theories. In this account, "Implicit theories are schemalike knowledge structures that include specific beliefs" (p. 342). Furthermore, "These theories are implicit in that they encompass rarely discussed, but strongly held beliefs" (p. 342).

The writings of Propp, Bartlett, and Ross contribute different points to an understanding of schematic narrative templates. Drawing on all of them, the point is that narrative templates are schematic in the sense that they concern abstract, generalized functions of the sort that Propp discussed in his structural analysis of folk tales or that Bartlett and Ross discuss under the heading of "schemalike knowledge structures." They are concerned with narrative, a point that is explicit in Propp's writings and consistent with what Bartlett and Ross propose. And as will become apparent, the notion of template is involved because these abstract structures can underlie several different specific narratives, each of which has a particular setting, cast of characters, dates, and so forth.

The picture that emerges here is one in which collective remembering is grounded in a generalized narrative tradition defined in terms of schematic narrative templates. A particular set of these narrative templates form what Lowenthal (1994) terms a "textual heritage" with its "uniquely national modes of explanation" (p. 53). This suggests that rather than learning a long list of specific narratives about the past as separate items, there may be a tendency to construct the means used in textual mediation out of a few basic building blocks.

The writings of Propp, Bartlett, and Ross suggest a few additional properties worth keeping in mind when dealing with these narrative templates. First, they are not some sort of universal archetypes. Instead, they belong to particular narrative traditions that can be expected to differ from one cultural setting to another. Second, narrative templates are not readily available to consciousness. As Bartlett noted, they are used in an "unreflective, unanalytical and unwitting manner" (1985, p. 45), and Ross notes that they are "rarely discussed" (1989, p. 342). These are precisely the sorts of properties that make textual resources "transparent," just as they were in the illustration involving Sasha in Chapter 1.

In sum, when considering the textual mediation of collective memory, I begin with the notion of narratives as cultural tools and memory as a form of mediated action. This calls on us to recognize the affordances and constraints of narratives in terms of their referential and dialogic functions. It is precisely this functional dualism inherent in cultural tools that gives rise to the functional dualism of memory outlined in Chapter 2. Specifically, the referential function of narratives tends to provide the foundation for discussions about accuracy in memory, and the dialogic function of narratives is associated with the contestation and negotiation involved in creating a usable past. In examining the role of narratives as cultural tools for collective remembering, it is also useful to distinguish between the way that specific narratives and schematic narrative templates play this role.

Textual Community

The final term that I shall examine in this chapter is "textual community." My use of this term reflects a concern with a specific type of community – namely, one grounded in the use of a shared set of texts. In contrast to Stock (1983, 1990), who focuses on religious texts in formulating the notion of a textual community, I am concerned with texts about history. The notion of community in this discussion is not a simple or obvious one. In trying to explicate it, I shall be concerned with a distinction between communities that seem to spring effortlessly into existence around a particular text and others that require a great deal of effort to create and maintain.

Implicit and Imagined Communities

A starting point for my analysis of textual community is a distinction I shall draw between communities that are "implicit" and those that are "imagined." Both share the attribute of being grounded in the use of cultural tools, but they differ in how these tools function in the formation and reproduction of a collective. The distinction I have in mind is not one of unchanging essence. A group that may appear to be one sort of community in one setting may take on the attributes of the other under other circumstances. Furthermore, the nature and degree of an individual's membership in either sort of community may vary. Nonetheless, differentiating implicit from imagined groups is crucial when trying to understand the notion of a textual community.

An implicit community is a group of individuals who use a common set of cultural tools even though they may be unaware of this fact and may make no effort to create or reproduce their collectivity. As an example, consider the set of people who use Microsoft Word:mac 2001, the word processing program I am using as I write this. I know that other people use this program, but I have no idea how many do or who they are, and furthermore, I have little interest in finding out. In short, I generally do not view myself as a member of this community, and I have little interest in creating or reproducing it.

To be sure, I am not totally disinterested. I might wish to know who at least one or two expert members of this implicit community are since I can turn to them for help when I have problems in using this cultural tool. From my perspective, however, the existence of the implicit community of Word:mac 2001 users is largely an accident rather than the outcome of an intentional effort to create and reproduce a collectivity. I am inclined to do very little to maintain it (although I may object strenuously if someone were to deprive me from using the cultural tool that underlies it).

This is not to deny that there are devoted members of this group who consider it to be something more than an implicit community. Indeed, institutions such as the Microsoft Corporation often expend significant effort to encourage such community building through publications, conventions, and so forth. Individuals who consider themselves to be members of an active collective, as opposed to an implicit community, may make a point of knowing who the other members are, they may celebrate the group and try to strengthen it, and they may view people who switch to other word processing software as "traitors."

Such phenomena suggest that implicit communities may become imagined communities, an issue to which I shall return later. The major point I wish to emphasize at present is that there is a sense in which it is misleading to say of most users of Word:mac 2001 that they "joined" a group. Instead, they became members in the process of pursuing an individual, instrumental course of action – namely, selecting a software package. In their view, this software is simply a means to an end, and any talk about group membership is superfluous. One indication of this is that if members find another word processing program that proves to be a better means to their ends, they are often quite willing to switch to it with no thought given to leaving one group or joining another. And even if some individuals of this group do consider themselves to be members of an imagined community, the fact remains that many do not – and *need* not in order to use this software.

Standing in contrast to implicit communities are "imagined communities." Prototypical – or perhaps extreme examples of imagined communities – are secret societies that use special handshakes, passwords, or other semiotic means to indicate membership. As in the case of implicit communities, membership in such communities requires the use of a shared sign system. However, in contrast to implicit communities, there is an emphasis given to recognizing or imagining the collectivity and to creating or reproducing it. For this reason, elaborate initiation procedures and rites of passage may be employed to induct individuals into the community and equip them with the cultural tools requisite for membership. In such cases, at least part of the function of cultural tools is to produce, reproduce, and mark the community.

The notion of imagined communities I am outlining is based on Benedict Anderson's (1991) analysis of nations and nationalism. For Anderson, a nation is "an imagined political community" (p. 6). Specifically, "It is *imagined* because the members of even the smallest nation will never know most of their fellow-members, meet them, or even hear of them, yet in the minds of each lives the image of their communion" (p. 6, italics in original). He views nations and nationality as "cultural artifacts of a particular kind" (p. 4), and he argues that their emergence requires what I am calling cultural tools, or mediational means such as newspapers, maps, and historical narratives.

A major difference between implicit and imagined communities, then, is in the role and function of the cultural tools involved. In the case of implicit communities, cultural tools typically serve an instrumental purpose for individuals, and have little, if any, impact on the formation of a community that is imagined or recognized by its members. For them it is purely a secondary concern as to whether any collectivity emerges out of using a particular set of cultural tools. Because these cultural tools are not employed in order to create a community, implicit communities tend to have little organization, and their very existence may not be recognized. In contrast, the cultural tools that lie behind imagined communities are typically employed in order to create a collective that can be clearly recognized.

Sociologists have long recognized distinctions that are related to the one I envision between implicit and imagined communities. For example, Karl Mannheim (1952) discussed this issue when addressing social class.

Class position is an objective fact, whether the individual in question knows his class position or not, and whether he acknowledges it or not. Class-consciousness does not necessarily accompany a class position, although in certain social conditions the latter can give rise to the former, lending it certain features, and resulting in the formation of a 'conscious class.' (pp. 289–290)

As I mentioned at the beginning of this section, the distinction between implicit and imagined communities is often not hard and fast. One indication of this is that implicit communities may be transformed into imagined communities. Indeed, one could think of implicit communities as "*un*imagined communities," or as potential candidates for undergoing the transformation to imagined ones. This transformation does not occur in all cases, but in certain instances implicit communities may be taken as a kind of "raw material" to be mobilized in constructing a conscious, or imagined, community.

The implicit community of Word:mac 2001 users I outlined earlier could be transformed into an imagined community if someone succeeded in mobilizing members into an active collective. Thus, if members of this implicit community became convinced that someone was trying to deprive them of the use of their beloved software and that the best way to resist this would be to become active in a political movement of Word:mac 2001 users, then they might transform themselves into a group that clearly qualified as an imagined community ("Word:mac 2001 Users of the World, Unite!").

Summary

In this chapter, I have reviewed several key terms that provide the background for my approach to collective memory. In addition to outlining the basics of sociocultural analysis, I have discussed issues falling under the headings of memory, collective memory, narratives as cultural tools, and textual community. My purpose in doing this has been to outline a conceptual space within which we can understand and compare claims about collective memory. As things currently stand, the discussion of collective memory is all too often characterized by isolated perspectives and bogus disagreements, problems that stem from not realizing where we and others stand on basic assumptions that frame the debate.

At several points in my discussion, I have employed conceptual oppositions as a way of laying out the issues. I have emphasized that the actual empirical phenomena of collective memory seldom fall neatly on one or the other side of an analytical distinction. Instead, these distinctions need to be viewed as tensions between two poles. For example, I am primarily interested in collective memory, as opposed to history, but elements of both sides of this opposition are typically found in many actual representations of the past. Similarly, my primary interest is in collective, as opposed to individual, memory; remembering, as opposed to re-experiencing; and episodic, as opposed to instrumental, memory. But in examining empirical phenomena in the chapters that follow, elements of the second item in each opposition will often come into play. Hence the need to remember that these are analytic distinctions for guiding inquiry, not ironclad categories into which instances of memory can be neatly sorted.

Following in the tradition of figures such as Vygotsky and Bakhtin, the starting point in this inquiry is that memory, both individual and collective, is usually mediated. This is the basic tenet of the sociocultural analysis of mediated action that underlies the account of collective memory I shall outline. In analyzing collective memory from this perspective, I pay particular attention to the role of narrative texts as cultural tools. The functional dualism of these tools means that memory can be used to provide accurate accounts of the past as well as accounts that are "usable" in the present for various political and cultural purposes.

The analytical distinctions I employ in my discussion of collective memory are intended to provide a conceptual framework for understanding a very broad and often very confused topic. In an attempt to sort this out, I argue that in contrast to history, collective memory reflects a committed perspective, and belongs to one group, and not others. Consistent with this is the notion that an effective way to socialize members of a collective into having a particular view of the past is to provide them with the appropriate textual resources. Collective memory tends to be impatient with ambiguity and to represent itself as representing an unchanging reality, so it provides a particular textual resource for creating a particular kind of community.

Approaching collective memory from the perspective of these basic claims leads naturally to some idea of a textual community. The basic dynamics of such communities involve the production and consumption of texts, processes that are carried out in such a way as to give rise to imagined as well as implicit communities. In the chapters that follow, I shall apply these points in connection with the production and consumption of texts in the context of a particular kind of collective, the modern state.

4

State Production of Official Historical Narratives

Maurice Halbwachs took as his starting point the idea that human memory presupposes a social framework. In this chapter, I shall be concerned with the inverse claim – that social groups presuppose memory. By this I mean that collective remembering typically provides an essential basis for the creation and maintenance of groups – specifically, imagined communities. In what follows, I shall examine how a particular type of collective – the modern state – pursues this agenda by providing its citizens with official accounts of the past. My line of reasoning begins with the notion of distributed collective memory outlined in Chapter 2. From this perspective, remembering is an active process involving agents and cultural tools, especially narrative texts. Modern states have implicitly recognized the two basic elements in this form of mediated action in that they have sought to control both the textual resources involved in remembering and the particular uses made of them. When successful, the result may be the kind of transparent textual mediation that characterized Sasha's account of World War II outlined in Chapter 1. But even when citizens are more reflective about the forms of textual mediation they employ, states are often successful in controlling their uses of narratives about the past.

In what follows, I shall be concerned with issues such as the peculiarities of the state as a promulgator of collective remembering and the role of formal education in this effort. In the process, I shall also revisit the distinction between history and collective memory. Much of what I have to say involves going into the particular case of the Soviet Union, a context in which state control over the production and use of textual resources took on extreme form.

State Production of Official Texts about the Past

Many points that I shall make in my analysis of how states seek to control collective remembering apply to other kinds of collectives as well.

Members of all sorts of groups recognize the inherent link between memory and identity and make special efforts to promulgate their account of the past. The modern state stands apart, however, in the level of resources and authority it can muster when creating a usable past and restricting competing efforts. In many respects, its efforts outweigh others, past or present, and as such serve as a natural arena for studying collective remembering.

A central institution involved in the state control of collective memory is education. Indeed, some analysts have come to view education as a defining function of the state. Ernest Gellner (1983) has proposed that Max Weber's classic definition of the state as the agency within society that possesses the monopoly of legitimate violence needs to be revised in light of how central education has become. "At the base of the modern social order stands not the executioner but the professor. Not the guillotine, but the (aptly named) *doctorate d'état* is the main tool and symbol of state power. The monopoly of legitimate education is now more important, more central than the monopoly of legitimate violence" (Gellner, 1983, p. 34).

In Gellner's view, this monopoly of legitimate education is important first of all because of the "generic" education that states must provide in order to ensure the productive functioning of their citizens. It also plays a central role, however, in creating citizens whose loyalty to a particular state's community outweighs that to other groups.

The task with which [the educational] system is entrusted is to turn out worthy, loyal and competent members of the total society whose occupancy of posts within it will not be hampered by factional loyalties to sub-groups within the total community; and if some part of the educational system, by default or from surreptitious design, actually produces internal cultural differences and thereby permits or encourages discrimination, this is counted as something of a scandal. (p. 64)

States typically possess several means for carrying out these tasks, the most obvious being mandatory universal education. More specifically with regard to the formation of collective memory, they have means such as national examinations in history to ensure that their citizens are conversant, at least to some degree, with official history. State institutions such as museums, media, and commemorative organizations that coordinate the observation of national holidays also play a role in this effort.

Modern states differ from many other collectives in the importance they attach to assumptions about natural characteristics, or essences, that bind their members together. Such assumptions are often widely shared and strongly defended by the members of a nation-state. A common language, history, religion, genetic make-up, or some other characteristic has been variously proposed as the essence that binds people together into a natural national community. Claims about these matters are often accompanied by assertions about the purity of the essence, and hence the group, and about how ancient this essence and group are.

The temptation for states to inculcate such views is very strong, and such practices can be found the world over. For example, in analyzing "the history of the history of Xinjiang," Bovingdon (2001) has analyzed how authorities in the Chinese Communist Party have sought to integrate this region and its Turkic people (the Uyghurs) into the Chinese state's imagined community.

After 1949, the pasts of the Uyghurs and of Xinjiang were rewritten in the PRC. Historical accounts provided an increasingly simplified, flattened, and distorted narrative favorable to the needs of the Chinese state. Uyghur history was rewritten to obscure the existence of a number of independent Turkic states ... The new histories substituted for these inconvenient historical realities a seamless story in which the Uyghurs had been a member of the "great family of the Chinese nation ... ," and Xinjiang had been party of China, "since ancient times." (p. 97)

Over the past several decades, scholars from a variety of perspectives have made such assertions and strategies the object of criticism, noting that the essences that supposedly underlie a group are often more "imagined" (Anderson, 1991) or "invented" (Hobsbawm & Ranger, 1993) than real. From this perspective, nations are not natural or spontaneous formations. Instead, they are imagined communities, and their creation and maintenance require major effort and unceasing vigilance. In this vein, Gellner (1983) made the following widely known observation:

Nations as a natural, God-given way of classifying men, as an inherent though long-delayed political destiny, are a myth; nationalism, which sometimes takes pre-existing cultures and turns them into nations, sometimes invents them, and often obliterates pre-existing cultures: *that* is a reality, for better or worse, and in general an inescapable one. (p. 49)

From this perspective, one of the fundamental problems for the nation-state is how to construct national identity and loyalty. In contrast to a picture in which nation-states are natural communities that awaken or spring into existence because they reflect pre-existing essences, the reality is that massive efforts must go into their formation and preservation. One of the best settings to observe these processes at work is in the emergence of new nations. Miroslav Hroch (1985) has documented the multiple stages of concerted effort in this process, effort that is required because "The nation is made up of individuals whose patriotism is not an unalterable datum, but undergoes a long formative period, proceeding initially from an elemental awareness of belonging to a greater whole" (p. 13).

These are concerns that are never settled once and for all. Instead, they typically reemerge from time to time, especially during periods of uncertainty, as the "politics of identity" (Calhoun, 1997) continue to be negotiated. In the United States, for example, they have recently been the focus of renewed fears over the "disuniting of America" (Schlesinger, 1992) and claims about the need for a common "cultural literacy" (Hirsch, 1988).

As analysts such as Anthony Smith (1991) have noted, of crucial importance to efforts to build and maintain national identity are "compulsory, standardized, public mass education systems, through which state authorities hope to inculcate national devotion and a distinctive, homogeneous culture" (p. 16). Many aspects of formal education undoubtedly contribute to this socialization effort. For example, the study of geography typically plays a role by introducing ideas about the "natural" boundaries of nation-states, and routines such as singing a national anthem or raising a flag contribute to the formation of "banal nationalism" (Billig, 1995). My particular focus, however, will be on the production of the materials used in history instruction.

Education in History or Collective Memory?

History instruction plays a role in the formation of national identity and state loyalty just about everywhere, but how this occurs varies with sociocultural context. The process often goes relatively unnoticed, but during times of transition and turmoil, the importance of history instruction in the formation of national identity snaps into focus. A recent episode of this in the United States occurred in the early 1990s when "culture wars" (Nash, Crabtree, & Dunn, 1997) broke out over the writing of new standards for schools. Among the participants in this heated debate was the historian Arthur J. Schlesinger, Jr., who provided an explicit formulation of the rationale for teaching history:

[H]istory is to the nation rather as memory is to the individual. As an individual deprived of memory becomes disoriented and lost, not knowing where he has been or where he is going, so a nation denied a conception of its past will be disabled in dealing with its present and its future. As the means for defining national identity, history becomes a means for shaping history. (pp. 45–46)

Such claims make the difference between history and other areas of instruction in education quite clear. In contrast to mathematics, for example, one of the goals of history instruction is to help students become knowledgeable and loyal members of a nation-state. It is because the political stakes are so high that disputes can break out over the appropriateness and accuracy of various accounts of the past. But this raises the question as to whether the instruction involved is really about history or collective memory.

Although he was writing about history instruction, Schlesinger's statement focuses on how history can serve as a means for dealing with the present and future. This in turn sounds like a concern for creating a usable past, which is a hallmark of collective memory. Schlesinger's statement reflects a longstanding debate and continuing ambivalence in the United States and elsewhere about this issue. This debate concerns whether the goal of history instruction is to promote critical thought and reflection on texts – that is, to engage in the practice of analytical history – or to inculcate collective memory grounded in "state-approved civic truth" (Tyack, 1999). If it is the former, then there should be a tendency to maintain a critical perspective on how the past is portrayed and an openness to revising existing accounts. This is the sort of approach favored by scholars such as Peter Seixas (2000) who are concerned with history instruction. If it is the latter, then the kind of committed perspective, impatience with ambiguities, and resistance to change outlined in Chapter 3 should be expected to prevail. According to Seixas, this amounts to "'enhancing collective memory,' since it does not engage students in the historical disciplines' modes of inquiry" (p. 20).

In his discussion of the "noble dream" of objectivity in the American history profession, Novick (1988) traces the history of this ambivalence between teaching history and enhancing collective memory in the United States. He points out that for over a century, professional historians have struggled with "the seemingly contradictory demands of history for moral and patriotic indoctrination, and history as objective science" (p. 70). Arguing for the former in 1892, Woodrow Wilson asserted that "we must avoid introducing what is called scientific history in the schools, for it is a 'history of doubt,' criticism, examination of evidence. It tends to confuse young pupils . . . . What we need to study in schools is the united effort, the common thought, of bodies of men; of the men who make public opinion, that is of the uncritical and conservative rather than the educated classes" (from Novick, 1988, p. 71).

Novick goes on to document the changing role of academic historians in the United States in this regard. They have always had a part in the production of state histories, but their influence in public education has varied, not always being at the level they would like.

In the late nineteenth century newly professionalized historians had expected that they would, in short order, be able to establish their hegemony over the production and consumption of history at every level – in the schools, in the colleges, and in the literary marketplace. In the interwar period it became clear that only the second of these professional aspirations was to be realized: control of history in the schools slipped through their fingers, and professional historians failed to displace amateurs with the book-buying public. (Novick, 1988, p. 185)

David Tyack (1999, 2000) has pursued this line of argument further by examining the history of textbooks in the United States. This has involved tracing the rise and fall of various versions of "school history," a genre involving "a peculiar mix of inspirational heroes and the flat facts that young citizens are supposed to believe in" (2000, p. 3).

According to Tyack, the nineteenth-century version of school history took as its overarching theme "the Providential progress of the 'land of the Pilgrim's pride'," and its goal was to provide a "template of worthy

Americans" (p. 3). In contrast, the focus of the "textbook truth police" had shifted by the early twentieth century to "how to use school histories to 'Americanize' immigrants" (p. 17).

An underlying issue for all such discussions is whether accounts of the past should be a form of history or textual resources for collective remembering. On the one hand, authors such as Novick and Tyack clearly see elements of collective memory in school history, elements such as a single committed perspective and impatience with ambiguity. In this connection, it is worth noting that part of Tyack's characterization of the genre includes the point that "the tone of most textbooks was authoritative – it did not invite debate" (p. 11). On the other hand, claims about truth of the sort associated with analytical history are typically employed in these debates. Tyack, for one, takes a sardonic view of such claims, mentioning actors such as the "truth police." However, the fact that the very notion of truth is invoked and that appeal is made to scientific methods for substantiating it reflect an appeal to history that would not be expected in any pure form of collective memory.

This tendency for the genre of school history to reflect a combination of collective memory and analytic history is a version of the functional dualism outlined in Chapter 3 and seems to be a part of all state-sponsored official collective memories. Indeed, it is often difficult to know whether one should speak of official history or official collective memory in such cases. To recognize that this conflation is pervasive is not to assert that all official collective memories are the same, however. In the rest of this chapter, I shall focus on how the production of official collective memory is shaped by particular aspects of sociocultural context. Specifically, I shall examine how this has occurred in the context of Soviet society.

The Production of a Univocal Official Collective Memory in the Soviet Union

Few states have tried to control collective memory more assiduously than the Soviet Union. Mikhail Heller and Aleksandr Nekrich (1986) argue that "history was placed at the service of the [Soviet] state to the greatest possible extent and in the most conscious, systematic way. After the October [1917] revolution not only the means of production were nationalized but all spheres of existence, and above all, memory, history" (p. 9). As will become apparent in what follows, this control took on different forms during different periods, but it was at work in one way or another throughout.

The extent to which Soviet efforts at controlling collective memory were successful is still open to question, and is a topic I shall take up in my discussion of textual consumption in later chapters. In the view of many observers, however, it was all too effective. Heller and Nekrich (1986) assert that "In the decades after the Bolshevik revolution an unparalleled expertise was developed in manipulating the past and controlling history" and as a result "the Soviet people were successfully deprived of their social memory" (p. 10). And writing after the Soviet Union's disintegration, David Remnick (1993) concluded, "It's as if the regime were guilty of two crimes on a massive scale: murder and the unending assault against memory. In making a secret of history, the Kremlin made its subjects just a little more insane, a little more desperate" (p. 101).

The efforts of the Soviet state to control what was remembered, as well as forgotten, were topics of debate in the late Soviet period both within the USSR and elsewhere. For example, the Soviet author Chingiz Aitmatov published a widely read novel in 1980 titled *The Day Lasts More than a Hundred Years* (1988). This work included an account of fictional characters called "mankurts" who were enslaved after having been deprived of their memory through a terrible torture involving headgear that gradually shrank their skulls.

The parallels between this procedure and the efforts of a totalitarian state were clear to Soviet readers. For example, the term "mankurtization" (mankurtizatsia) was widely known in that context, and passages such as the following provided grist for reflection in countless private conversations.

Deprived of any understanding of his own ego, the *mankurt* was, from his master's point of view, possessed of a whole range of advantages. He was the equivalent of a dumb animal and therefore absolutely obedient and safe . . . This most cruel form of barbarism . . . had discovered the means of removing from slaves their living memory, in this way causing to a human being the most dreadful of all imaginable or unimaginable evils. (pp. 126–127)

The ideological underpinning for official history in the USSR was provided by Soviet Marxist-Leninist claims about the inevitable march of progress toward the shining heights of communism. The implications of these claims were obvious in that "the teleological nature of ideology makes history a legitimizing factor. History validates the firm hand that leads men toward the great goal" (Heller & Nekrich, 1986, p. 292). From this perspective, any account of the past that questioned Marxist claims about progress in general or the leading role of the Communist Party in particular was problematic and would merit critical attention.

Throughout the Soviet period, political and cultural figures were quite open about the ideological dictates that lay behind their production of history. For them, discussions about the distinction between analytical history and collective memory had little relevance, and this had as correlates the assumptions that the production of history must be closely controlled by the state and that alternative accounts should be vigorously criticized, if not suppressed. A single, state-produced version of the past was the only one allowed.

The Emergence of a Unitary Voice in the Production of
Official Collective Memory

There are several phases one can identify in the development of official collective memory in the Soviet Union. The first of these extended for a decade or so after the 1917 Revolution and was marked by relatively open debate and coexistence between Marxist and non-Marxist camps of historians. This was part of a general trend in Soviet society at the time, and stemmed from several sources. For example, it was in part the result of Bolshevik preoccupation with political consolidation and economic reconstruction in the aftermath of almost a decade of international and internal war. It also reflected the relatively optimistic and humanistic reading of Marx's theories of culture that were advanced by the reigning ideologists of the early Soviet period (Billington, 1966, p. 521).

This early period in Soviet history was followed by one in which the range of competing voices was sharply reduced. Again, this reflected more general trends. For example, "whereas about two fifths of all publishing was outside of government hands at the time of Lenin's death early in 1924, only one tenth had survived three years later" (Billington, 1966, p. 521). Once this and other aspects of what I shall call "state univocality" had emerged, they continued to characterize Soviet society in general and the production of official collective memory in particular for the remaining decades of the USSR's existence, albeit in various degrees and forms.

An essential ingredient in the drive toward state univocality was the heavy-handed influence of the Communist Party. However, analysts such as George Enteen (1984) have documented the way local institutional and personal rivalries within the community of historians played an important role as well. The Bolshevik historian Mikhail Pokrovskii (1868–1932) and his associates were particularly important in this regard. After participating for a decade or so of the Soviet period as one of several competing voices in the debate over history, Pokrovskii launched a successful assault on the ideas and institutional bases of non-Marxist historians in 1929. The debates were often quite heated, and involved attacks and counterattacks, but by the end of the 1920s, the "Pokrovskii School" had come to dominate the Marxist perspective, which in turn dominated the profession through its command of institutions and journals.

This reign proved to be shaky, however, and was destined to end a few years later. The major event that marked the beginning of the demise of the Pokrovskii School was a 1931 letter by Josef Stalin to the editors of *Proletarskaya Revolutsiya*. In this letter, Stalin did not assail Pokrovskii personally, but he expressed a lack of patience with the analyses that Marxist historians (i.e., the group dominated by Pokrovskii) had been conducting. This attack has been interpreted as part of an orchestrated effort in which the state initially allowed Pokrovskii, who had been motivated by his own concerns, to carry out his work, and then pushed him aside. In the words of Billington (1966), "Figures like . . . Pokrovsky in history were used in this first 'proletarian' phase of Stalinist terror to discredit others before being rejected themselves" (p. 523).

Stalin's 1931 attack was written in the highly polemical style of the time and included strong criticisms of the historians' questions about "whether Lenin was or was not a real Bolshevik" (Enteen, 1984, p. 164), questions that had arisen in inquiries about whether or not some of Lenin's actions were in accord with the dictates of Marxist theory. The fact that the letter was written by Stalin resulted in its having consequences difficult to imagine in other settings. The events that followed reveal just how powerful Stalin was, but more interesting for my purposes, they revealed how seriously he and the rest of the Soviet leadership took accounts of the past to be in the formation of collective identity. Clearly, in their view, "history-writing was too important a weapon in the arsenal of culture and ideology to be left outside party control" (Suny, 1998, p. 281).

The highly polemical and public manner of Stalin's critique may appear to have some parallels with disputes that have occurred in the West. For example, it would seem to have something in common with Tyack's notions of "state approved civic truth" as enforced by the "history police." These parallels come into different perspective, however, when one considers the impact of Stalin's contribution in the charged political atmosphere of the Soviet Union of the 1930s.

The effect of Stalin's letter was to send the historians (and indeed all other Marxist scholars) into a flurry of self-criticism. A host of meetings was convoked immediately; in time Stalin's letter was discussed in every institute of the Communist Academy and every Party organization in the country. The Society of Marxist Historians demanded a review of all existing historical literature, and students of the Institute of Red Professors were formed into brigades preparing assessments of large portions of the existing literature for publication in the press. More than one hundred thirty speakers were dispatched throughout Moscow to deliver reports, and even more were later sent to outlying Republics. According to I.I. Mints . . . "extermination of cadres of historians began. Many historians were slandered, then repressed. Many were compelled to admit 'errors'." (Enteen, 1984, p. 165)

This was just the first episode of what proved to be a series of interventions by Stalin and other Soviet leaders in the production of official collective memory. Indeed, the extent and nature of their involvement increased to the point that Stalin himself took a personal hand in writing history texts. For example, in 1934 he "read the drafts of textbooks and pronounced them failures . . . [and he] approved the team-produced text that became the standard history of the USSR for the next twenty years, the *Short Course in the History of the Soviet Union* (Suny, 1998, p. 282).

An interesting and paradoxical aspect of these events is that the rewriting of history that took place under Stalin involved a dilution of the theoretical dictates of Soviet Marxism. Instead of remaining committed to an approach that was "deterministic, cosmopolitan in spirit, and indisposed to stress the importance of exceptional individuals" (Enteen, 1984, p. 155), the new orientation reintroduced a nationalistic perspective in the form of claims about Russian exceptionalism and the importance of great Russian individuals.

The outcome of this struggle was that official collective memory in the Soviet Union continued to be formulated ostensibly in Marxist-Leninist terms, but in a somewhat inconsistent manner, one that also made room for the glorification of Russia. In the view of Heller and Nekrich (1986), "Soviet history, as cooked to taste by Stalin, took the form of a monstrous mixture of nationalism and Marxism" (p. 295).

This general line – criticizing pre-Revolutionary leaders while at the same time giving them credit for laying the foundations for the Russian, and then Soviet, state – was characteristic of official Soviet history for decades to come. Summarizing the trajectory of this discussion as it related to Ukraine, Heller and Nekrich (1986) write:

Reconsidering the main thesis of the Pokrovsky school, that annexation of other nations by the Russian empire had been an absolute evil, [a jury in the 1930s] recommended that such annexation be viewed as "a lesser evil." A few years later historians were advised to regard unification with Russia as an absolute good. To this day, Soviet historians invariably refer to the incorporation of the Ukraine (under Bogdan Khmelnitsky) into Russia as the "unification of two great sister peoples." (p. 300)

The internally contradictory mixture of Marxism-Leninism and nationalism that resulted from this process did not prevent Soviet authorities from claiming that the official history they produced was unified and coherent. The simplification and impatience for ambiguity and complexity that are characteristic of collective memory ran throughout these texts. As will become evident in Chapter 5, the characters in these texts had straightforward, transparent motives, and the plots were rigidly organized in such a way that alternative accounts were almost impossible to formulate if one accepted the basic story line.

Successive Sole Truths about the Past

As noted in the last chapter, one of the hallmarks of collective memory is that despite its claims to the contrary, it changes over time. While this is true to some extent in any context, the Soviet case was unique in the vehemence with which the state denied that such changes had occurred and in the consequences of publicly raising the possibility that they had. The result was a kind of bizarre fantasy world in which the participants knew that official history had changed, knew that others knew this, and knew that others knew that they knew this, and yet everyone pretended in the public sphere that nothing of the sort had occurred.

The certainty and vehemence with which Soviet authorities argued that their account of the past was the only acceptable one were striking. In a 1936 article from *Pravda*, the official newspaper of the Communist Party, for instance, it was proclaimed that "'Marxist-Leninist history' was the sole 'truth about the past'" (from Heller & Nekrich, 1986, p. 295), and such claims pervaded public discourse to such an extent that they seldom had to be made explicit.

A major problem for claims about this sole truth, however, was that it clearly did change from time to time. These changes took many forms, but many of them had to do with the individuals and groups involved in various historical events. In a volume titled *The Commissar Vanishes: The Falsification of Photographs and Art in Stalin's Russia*, for example, David King (1997) provides striking illustrations of how individuals were literally airbrushed or cut out of history during the Soviet years. In many cases, this was a stepwise process. First one individual then another would disappear as state history changed over time, in some instances yielding only Stalin where an entire group had formerly been. King writes:

Like their counterparts in Hollywood, photographic retouchers in Soviet Russia spent long hours smoothing out the blemishes of imperfect complexions, helping the camera to falsify reality. Joseph Stalin's pockmarked face, in particular, demanded exceptional skills with the airbrush. But it was during the Great Purges, which raged in the late 1930s, that a new form of falsification emerged. The physical eradication of Stalin's political opponents at the hands of the secret police was swiftly followed by their obliteration from all forms of pictorial existence. (p. 9)

Analogous processes were going on in the rewriting of narrative accounts of the past. Individuals and events that had played a major role in one version were cut out of the next. In some cases, this amounted to "cropping" the narrative picture in a slightly different way, but in others it amounted to leaving obvious blank spots in the middle of a text. For ordinary citizens as well as major actors on the Soviet scene, keeping track of which truth was current was a deadly serious task, but it also gave rise to bits of Soviet humor such as the aphorism that "Nothing is so unpredictable as Russia's past."

The fact that my concern is with narratives as textual resources means that I shall touch on a somewhat different set of issues than I would were I to focus on photographs. Indeed, the same notion of falsification may not apply, or it may apply in a different way than when dealing with photographs. For example, it is widely accepted that one narrative may present an account of the past that leaves out something included in others, even something that the other narratives view as central. In such cases, one might speak of bias, but the charge of falsification is more difficult to make. Instead, it is understood that the nature of narrative is such that any account is inherently perspective bound and partial and must leave out, as well as include information (Uspenskii, 1973).

This is not to say that photographs provide fewer opportunities for misrepresentation than do narratives, but it is to say that the nature and range of possibilities differ. A general point where they share some similarities, however, concerns the difference between inserting, as opposed to deleting, information. While some may quibble about whether all cases of cutting something out of a photograph amount to falsification, it seems clear that introducing something that was not part of the original picture does qualify. Similarly, leaving out information is always involved in creating a narrative account, and hence may be difficult to call falsification, but asserting that something happened when one knows it did not clearly qualifies as falsification.

Soviet authorities recognized this point about how narratives provide different possibilities for leaving out and adding information. Many efforts at rewriting history involved deleting a character or an event that had been included in previous versions, but claims to the effect that someone was at a place on a particular date when she was not or that an event occurred when it did not were rare. In contrast to the kind of rewriting of history envisioned by George Orwell (1949) in *Nineteen Eighty-Four*, there were few outright falsifications of this sort. However, there were many "blank spots" in official narratives, as well as photographs, and these blank spots changed over the years of official Soviet history production.

A more concrete picture of how some of these changes in the sole official collective memory occurred can be gleaned from reviewing guidelines published by Soviet authorities on what was to be taught in schools. For example, a comparison of guidelines from various years on what was to be taught about World War II reveals some quite different pictures of the central actors in the Soviet effort. The first item I shall outline in this regard was published during Stalin's lifetime – namely, a 1949 pamphlet titled "The Great Patriotic War of the Soviet Union." The official status of this guideline is reflected by the fact that it was published by *Pravda*, the newspaper of the Communist Party. This forty-page pamphlet was intended to serve as a guide for teachers as they prepared for the 1949–50 school year.

In this account, Stalin is given a central role in the war effort. "Comrade Stalin" is mentioned numerous times as a major, if not *the* major, figure in the narrative. In addition to comments about his speeches and decisions, he is presented as the mastermind behind the successful Soviet war effort. For example, on page 15, the pamphlet claims that it was Stalin alone, with his superior insight and genius, who was able to identify the real aim of one of the major German offensives of the war – the attack on Stalingrad.

Having gained a preponderance of strength in this sector, the German-Fascist forces occupied the eastern part of Ukraine, moved to Voronezh, crossed the Don River, and broke out to the Kuban. The Germans broke out to Stalingrad and to the Caucasus.... In the Soviet Union it was comrade Stalin who exposed the perfidious plans of the enemy. He divined that the German advance toward the Caucasus in reality had an ancillary character, that its main goal was the same as in 1941 – taking Moscow. Only this time the Germans were trying to do this by another path: going around impregnable Moscow far to the east, cutting it off from the rear in the Volga and Urals, and then striking Moscow itself. (p. 15)

In this pamphlet, Stalin's presence outweighs that of the Communist Party and the Soviet people, let alone that of any Soviet allies. A sense of the overall orientation of this narrative can be obtained from its final paragraph, where the authors (who remained anonymous) wrote:

Comrade Stalin played the leading role in the rout of the German-Fascist aggressors. During the years of the war the greatness of I.V. Stalin emerged with new force as a wise leader of the people, a leader of the party and the Soviet government, and a brilliant military commander. (p. 40)

A comparison of this pamphlet with one published in 1955, just two years after Stalin's death, reveals striking differences. This later pamphlet was published by the Main Directorate of Higher and Middle Pedagogical Student Institutes of the USSR Ministry of Education and was titled "The Great Patriotic War of the Soviet Union: 1941–1945. Special Seminar on the History of the USSR." As opposed to the earlier publication, which listed no author and hence seemed to come from the faceless state, this publication was authored by M.I. Stishov, a writer and editor of one of the official textbooks of the time.

The structure of this publication differs markedly from that of the 1949 pamphlet. Among other things, it contains an extensive bibliography (the 1949 pamphlet had none). This bibliography includes several items by Stalin, but it has many more items by other authors, including several whose views differed from Stalin's, though they were by no means unofficial. What is most striking about this publication compared with the earlier one, however, is that the name of Stalin is noticeably downplayed. In contrast to publications from later years, where his name was avoided altogether, Stalin was still mentioned, but he takes his place alongside the Communist Party and the masses of peasants and workers of the USSR. In this 1955 pamphlet, Stishov asserted:

The soul and inspiration of the nation-wide struggle to smash the enemy was the glorious Communist Party – the leading and guiding force of Soviet society, the battle-hardened vanguard of the Soviet people. The war clearly showed the wisdom and far-sightedness of the politics that the Party had developed under the leadership of the great Lenin and subsequently continued under the leadership of the Central Committee under the leadership of I.V. Stalin. (p. 6)

In summarizing the ten basic topics to be covered in teaching about the Great Patriotic War, Stishov clearly made a point that reveals how much this version of official collective memory differed from previous versions in which Stalin had been the main character. There he wrote that:

Every theme is organized in such a way that it orients students to discover the role of the Communist Party as the inspiration and organizer of the nation-wide struggle against the Fascist aggressors and to discover the role of the masses of people as the decisive force in the rout of the enemy. (p. 8)

As a final point for comparing official Soviet accounts of World War II, consider a history textbook edited by M.P. Kima (1976) and published more than two decades after Stalin's death. As was the practice throughout most of the Soviet period, this was the only history textbook used by tenth-grade students in the USSR at the time. It had been cleared by various Soviet authorities and had a print run of almost 2.5 million copies. The eighty-three pages that make up Chapter 3 of this textbook were devoted to the "Great Patriotic War of the Soviet Union 1941–1945."

Like the previous two accounts of World War II I have outlined, this one involves a mix of Marxism-Leninism and Russian/Soviet nationalism and exceptionalism. For my purposes, what is most striking, however, is that this text was written in such a way that Stalin had largely disappeared altogether. He does not surface in any of the twenty-five photographs in the chapter, including one photograph of major commanders of the war effort. He also does not appear in any of the twenty sections of "Documentary Materials." These are standard sections in Soviet textbooks that included original source material. Not a single one of these items has Stalin's name associated with it despite the fact that many of them were written by him or at his behest. For example, a directive of July 29, 1941, from the Soviet People's Commissariat is included at the end of Section 6 of this chapter. This commissariat was headed by Stalin, and many would indeed say it was an instrument of his personal control over the war effort. Nonetheless, no mention is made of his name.

In contrast, the name L.I. Brezhnev, the Soviet leader in 1976 when this book was published, does appear as author of an item of documentary material. In fact, Brezhnev did participate in World War II, but he was neither a major figure in the event nor an authoritative analyst of it, to say the least. Furthermore, the material on Brezhnev that is included in this chapter comes from a volume of his speeches and articles published many years after the war, and has nothing to do with his personal experiences. This excerpt is a pronouncement by Brezhnev about the importance of the Battle of Stalingrad. It repeats a standard Soviet description of what occurred there and why it was important not only for the USSR but for the entire world.

Among other things, the excerpt quotes from a letter written by President Franklin Delano Roosevelt. Brezhnev apparently did this in order to support claims about the importance of this battle. What is not said, however, is that this letter was written by Roosevelt *to Stalin*. Any experienced Soviet reader would recognize the shadowy presence of Stalin behind this text, but those who produced it managed to avoid mentioning him.

The brief comparison I have made among these texts from 1949, 1955, and 1976 touches on several points. First, one can see at least the outlines of the mixture of Marxist-Leninist theory and Russian nationalism in all of them. In all three publications, the account of World War II was formulated in Marxist-Leninist terms involving a struggle between Fascist and capitalist forces, on the one hand, and the masses of people led by the Communist Party, on the other. At the same time, however, each recognized the exceptionalism of individuals and national groups, a tendency that runs counter to the general line of reasoning of Marxism-Leninism about how large-scale social and economic forces determine the course of history.

Second, each of these versions of the past presents itself as the one true history – that is, as a state-approved civic truth. Each is characterized by a tone of certainty, if not dogmatism, about the causes and agents of historical events, a tone that characterizes virtually all official Soviet histories from the 1920s on. In such accounts, there is no doubt or ambiguity about who was responsible for historical events and about why these events occurred in the way they did.

Third, this tone of certainty characterizes several historical accounts that in fact differ from, and in some cases contradict, one another. For example, in 1949 it was Stalin who played the major role in leading the war effort, in 1955 it was the Communist Party, and by 1976 one might think that Brezhnev had been a major figure. Changes of this sort in the one true account of the past were of course potentially embarrassing to the Soviet state. They confronted authorities with the task of constantly introducing new accounts of how and why major events occurred and of airbrushing old faces out of the picture. Keeping up with the version of official history that was true at any time was a complex matter for Soviet citizens. What made it even more complex was that in addition to keeping abreast of what the currently accepted account was, one had to pretend, at least in the public sphere, that previous versions had not existed, and avoid mentioning anything that would even suggest that one knew of them.

This constant process of knowing the one true history of the day and forgetting previous ones was a source of underground humor, but, keeping this confusing picture straight was often no laughing matter. The Soviet Union has been called a society "where remembering has been dangerous at least since the 1920s" (Khubova, Ivankiev, & Sharova, 1992, p. 89), as well as one that "had been forced into amnesia" (Passerini, 1992, p. 8). In this context, "false memories were forged, individuals were pushed to destroy their own letters and diaries, and an atmosphere of lies and falsehood was perpetuated" (Passerini, 1992, p. 8).

In sum, the production of official Soviet accounts of the past reflected several properties of collective memory. These accounts were characterized by a strong form of state-imposed univocality. This univocality took shape over the period of the Soviet Union's existence, with particularly important changes occurring during some of the darkest years of the 1930s. From that period on, the production of Soviet history was grounded squarely in the assumption that one immutable truth about the past existed. However, that truth changed from time to time, often for reasons that were not at all clear to Soviet citizens. With each new version of history produced by the Soviet state, old ones had to be altered, discarded, and in many cases actively suppressed. The guiding principle might be termed "dogmatic, but temporary, truth" about the past.

Soviet Schools and the Production of Univocal Collective Memory
No Soviet institution had greater responsibility for overseeing dogmatic, but temporary truths about the past than the educational system. This was part of a general effort to create the ideal Soviet citizen. During certain periods, the goal of this effort was formulated in terms of creating the "new Soviet man" or "Homo Sovieticus," supposedly a new level in the evolution of humankind, and in others its formulation was less ambitious. However, all periods were linked by a shared focus on the creation of committed Soviet citizens.

An early version of this orientation can be seen, for example, in the goals laid out by a 1918 congress of educational workers:

We must create out of the younger generation a generation of Communists. We must turn children, who can be shaped liked wax, into real, good Communists. . . . We must remove the children from the crude influence of their families. We must take them over and, to speak frankly, nationalize them. From the first days of their lives they will be under the healthy influence of Communist children's nurseries and schools. There they will grow up to be real Communists. (from Heller, 1988, p. 149)

The basic goals of the Soviet educational system were not always formulated in such frank terms, but the general orientation remained quite consistent throughout the USSR's existence. The means for reaching these goals, however, changed. As was the case for history writing, the decade or so following the 1917 Revolution was one of relatively open debate and experimentation in Soviet schools. Following this, however, the state imposed increasing control, and did so with a vengeance during the "cultural revolution" of the early 1930s (Fitzpatrick, 1984). In this revolution:

self-management was replaced by the exclusive authority of the director (the principal) and "firm discipline"; instead of the "collective" mode of teaching (the "brigade method") there were traditional classes, lessons, and timetables. In 1934, "stable" curricula and textbooks were introduced, so that throughout the Soviet Union all the schools would be teaching the same subject with the same textbooks at any given time. For each subject there was one textbook, approved by the Party Central Committee. (Heller, 1988, p. 149)

The Soviet leadership was quite clear about the importance it attached to ideological commitment in this regard. Writing after Stalin's death, but still very much during Soviet times, the British scholar Nigel Grant (1964) described this commitment in the following terms:

The aim of Soviet authorities has always been the building of a new kind of society, and they have used the educational system, deliberately and consciously, as a means of attaining this goal. It is, therefore, designed not merely as a machine for the production of scientists, engineers, and technicians, but as an instrument of mass education from which the younger generation gain not only their formal learning, but their social, moral, and political ideas as well. (p. 15)

And a decade after Grant had outlined the goals of education in the USSR, the Soviet author Smirnov (1973) described the ideological responsibilities of schools in the following terms:

...all educational institutions are confronted with the task of giving a clear and convincing account of the mass character of the revolutionary struggle and the need for socialist transformations. It is impossible to bring up true sons of the Motherland [i.e., the USSR], steadfast ideological fighters, without fostering respect for the history of their own people, their own culture. It is essential that every Soviet person should understand that the socialism built in his country according to Lenin's plan acts as the most powerful, effective and humane force which along with the other socialist countries today stands in opposition to imperialism. All Soviet people must fully understand that no mistakes committed in the process of building socialism, no problems of the present day can remove the historic significance of the building of socialism or diminish its achievements. (p. 274)

Even during the final stages of the Soviet Union's existence, one could find the Central Committee of the Communist Party arguing that "The Party aims to achieve a situation in which a person is educated here not simply to be a processor of a certain quantity of knowledge but primarily to be a citizen of a socialist society and an active builder of Communism" (Heller, 1988, p. 150).

An essential means for pursuing this ideological mission was the authority and highly centralized nature of the Soviet state. This meant, first, that planning was its responsibility. Once established in the 1930s, the centralized planning of education was a constant part of education in the Soviet Union.

All aspects of Soviet education are...planned in detail, from the finance of universities to the curriculum and teaching methods for the elementary classes, from building programmes to admission figures for the colleges.... It is a fair assumption, then, that anything we observe in the Soviet schools will rarely be unofficial or accidental, but will usually have been consciously planned for the purpose of running a system of mass education designed for the rearing of the 'new man' and the building of a communist society. (Grant, 1964, p. 31)

The centralization of control over education did not stop with planning, however. Soviet authorities also went to great lengths to monitor the implementation of their plans and ensure they were carried out as intended. The result was a level of uniformity that has seldom, if ever, been matched in a large-scale society. Again quoting Grant (1964):

One of the most prominent features of Soviet education, which highlights its differences from other large-scale systems of mass education, is the extent of tight control exercised by the central authorities, and the degree of uniformity enforced in principle and practice through the length and breadth of the Soviet Union. In such a vast and varied country there are naturally some local differences, and there are also plenty of instances of things happening at school level without the knowledge or approval of the higher authorities... In the formulation of basic policy, however, and to a considerable extent in the details of school practice, the authorities in Moscow keep a firm grip on what happens in schools and colleges from Riga to Vladivostok. (p. 32)

With regard to the information about history that students encountered in Soviet schools, this meant that central control existed at several levels. First, the written materials they used were closely controlled by the state. Second, the specific way these materials were to be used was planned in detail. And third, the state closely monitored whether these plans had been carried out. All of these levels were devoted to ensuring that students were exposed to the sole, but temporary, dogmatic truth about the past.

The effectiveness of the state in controlling the production and use of textual resources for history instruction can be seen in the responses to a set of interviews conducted by Elena Ivanova (1999) in the Russian-speaking eastern section of Ukraine. Ivanova interviewed ten adults, all of whom were around the age of fifty in 1999 and hence had been in secondary school during the 1960s – well before glasnost, perestroika, or other forms of decreased central control by the Soviet state. One of the questions she posed to each interviewee was, "Did your teacher ever indicate to you that certain information in the [history] textbook or the course had to be learned but that you should not believe it? If so, what was that information?"

Although this is a small interview study and we know little about the representativeness of the sample, the uniformity and vehemence of the responses to this question are quite striking. All ten interviewees stated unequivocally that their teachers never gave any indication that information in history textbooks should not be believed. Responses ranged from dismissive comments such as "Never" and "Certainly not. It was impossible" to more elaborate ones such as "I do not remember such things. I am sure it was absolutely impossible. It simply could not have been because it could never happen" and "Ha! I am sure she believed herself in each line of the textbook. . . . A strange question. Certainly she could not have said something like that."

Ivanova (1999) reports further that the nonverbal responses to this question were striking. When she asked the interviewees whether their high school history teacher had given any indication that something in the textbook was not to be believed, they invariably responded by looking at her in disbelief. They found it hard to conceive that this was a serious question since its answer was so obvious. In contrast to their responses to some of the other questions, responses that revealed some hesitation, "Their subjective awareness about their negative response in this case was 100%. They answered immediately and without any hesitation."

State Production of Textual Mediation for Official Collective Memory

In this chapter, I have outlined some of the motivations that states have for producing an official account of the past in general and how this process played out in the Soviet state in particular. Such representations of the past seldom fall neatly under the heading of analytic history or collective memory. On the one hand, states usually claim that the account they produce is based on objective historical scholarship, and to some degree this is the case. On the other hand, states have a strong interest in seeing their version of official history being accepted by citizens in such a way that they become a loyal imagined community. The intent is not simply for students to know the official history, but to believe it, to take ownership of it as a usable past, and this suggests that collective memory rather than historical memory is involved.

These observations apply to any state, but they were played out in a particular fashion in the USSR. After an initial period of relatively open debate, Soviet authorities exerted a very high level of control over the official account of the past available to its citizens. This does not mean that contestation and negotiation did not occur, but there was a powerful central figure or committee that resolved any disputes in a way that was not open to further challenge, at least for the time being. Furthermore, little of this went on in the public sphere, and any particular official history that came out of this did not reflect public discussion.

Instead of making available a range of perspectives and accounts of the past, the Soviet state controlled textual resources very closely, and ended up presenting its account as the sole, authoritative, unquestionable truth. The extent of control the Soviet state imposed on this process resulted in what might be called the totalitarian state's dream: a univocal account of the past that had no competitors, at least in the public sphere. This strict univocality did not mean that one account emerged and remained unchanged. Instead, there were constant changes, each of which resulted in a new univocal account, something that can be described as "dogmatic, but temporary, truth" about the past.

The processes I have outlined in this chapter present a striking picture of how official history was produced during the Soviet years. Although some of the more oppressive of these tendencies moderated in the last years of the Soviet Union's existence, the inertia of several decades continued to create a setting in which the univocal state sought to exercise complete control over collective memory. It was in this context that the massive changes associated with the break-up of the Soviet Union were destined to occur.

At the time, it was very difficult to predict what would happen, or even to characterize the setting in which it was occurring. Now, with almost two decades of hindsight, one thing is fairly clear when it comes to collective memory. An important force involved in the transition that had been unleashed stemmed from alternative voices that had been silenced for decades and now had a kind of pent-up energy. In his analysis of nationalism, Isaiah Berlin (1991) described this sort of phenomenon using the image of a bent twig that will snap back when its restraints are removed. As will become clear when I address textual production and consumption in the chapters that follow, nationalism may not always have been the relevant issue, but Berlin's image is a useful one more generally when trying to understand the forces that came into play in post-Soviet Russia.

5

Narrative Dialogicality and Narrative Templates in the Production of Official Collective Memory

In the last chapter, I outlined several general issues about the way modern states seek to control collective remembering. Starting with the observation that social groups presuppose memory, I examined some of the motivations and means that states have for producing an official account of the past. The specifics I outlined in connection with the Soviet Union provide an example of how such motivations and means may be taken to an extreme, but they reflect tendencies that exist in one form or another everywhere.

A general point of Chapter 4 was that all states are committed to promulgating an official account of the past. Such accounts typically look more like collective memory than analytical history, and efforts to control collective remembering through the production of textual resources are almost invariably coupled with the tendency to discount or suppress alternative accounts. Furthermore, it is not uncommon for the official accounts to be presented as immutable, even when they are not.

In this chapter, I shall explore some of these issues further by going into more detail about the production of textual resources for collective remembering in Russia. In particular, I shall be concerned with such production during the transition from the Soviet to the post-Soviet era. This setting is unique for several reasons, two of which I shall examine in what follows. The first is related to the "bent twig" phenomenon outlined by Berlin (1991) and concerns the rapidity and scale of change in Russia following the break-up of the USSR. This swift, massive transformation has only a few parallels, and makes Russia a unique natural laboratory for the study of collective memory dynamics. The second has to do with how these dynamics were influenced by deeply embedded cultural factors in Russia that have exerted their influence for centuries, both during times of transition and times of stability. And under this latter heading of Russian cultural factors, I shall be concerned with two issues in particular. The first of these is a pattern of radical oppositional thinking that analysts have viewed as characterizing Russian culture for the past several centuries. This tendency for drawing sharp boundaries between stark opposites – black and white, good and evil – has implications for how accounts of the past can be written and revised. Among other things, it suggests that producing new accounts of the past requires the outright rejection of previous ones and generating something completely different.

The second aspect of Russian culture that I shall consider serves as a conservative force acting in the opposite direction. Instead of encouraging radical change, it provides for a kind of continuity. What I have in mind here is a schematic narrative template (Chapter 3) for making sense of the past. As I have been arguing throughout, narrative form is taken to be a cultural tool for grasping together a set of events into a coherent whole. As such, it serves as the basic instrument in distributed memory. The particular way of grasping together actors, motivations, events, turning points, and so forth can be expected to take on particular forms in particular settings, and Russia is no exception in this regard. As will become evident, the tendency to use an underlying "triumph-over-alien-forces" narrative has insured continuity in collective memory even in the midst of what appears to be great change.

The Transition in Collective Remembering: Unleashing the Struggle over the Past in Post-Soviet Russia

From today's vantage point, it is difficult to recall the rapidity and volatility of change that occurred with the disintegration of the Soviet state. The late 1980s and early 1990s witnessed events that were hard to fathom at the time and would have been unimaginable even a few years earlier. The feeling was one of being on a roller coaster without knowing where it was headed.

An essential part of this turmoil was the transformation in official collective memory. Although constant revision of official history had been part of Soviet life for decades, it had tended to involve relatively minor changes rather than open questioning of the fundamental story line itself, and it certainly did not involve challenging the veracity and trustworthiness of official voices. From this perspective, individuals might have made mistakes or even been wreckers or enemies of the state, but the system itself and its basic story line remained intact, if not sacrosanct.

All of this changed with the break-up of the USSR. Criticisms and alternative accounts that would have been considered blasphemous and grounds for prosecution in earlier years were now openly discussed. This was part of the almost immediate response to the extremely tight control that Soviet authorities had exerted for decades over textual resources. For the first time, public discussion occurred about topics such as Stalin's repressions and the dubious nature of the 1917 Revolution, and the result was an outpouring of reanalysis, writing, and heated debate. As authors such as Shlapentokh (1996) have argued, there was something very sharp – indeed

Manichaean – about the reactions that arose in the wake of the disintegration of this totalitarian system. The bent twig had been unleashed.

In this context, national groups, historians, and the governments of newly emerging states were all anxious to enter the fray. However, the extreme centralization of the Soviet state meant that the relevant actors came to their new task with little experience, and hence they often generated a great deal of confusion as well as insight. Nonetheless, there continued to be a strong inclination to proceed as rapidly as possible, something that was inspired in part by fear that the centralized Soviet state might reemerge and stop efforts to write post-Soviet histories in their tracks. Now that it was finally possible "to tell the truth about history," people were insisting that it be done without delay.

The year 1988 witnessed a landmark event in this process. On June 10 of that year, the government newspaper *Izvestiya* announced that high school history examinations on the Soviet period for the higher grades were being cancelled. The reason given for this was that "even the best and most inquisitive teachers presented the history of our homeland in a monstrously distorted and unrecognizable form" (*Izvestiya*, June 10, 1988, p. 1). The Rector of the Moscow State Institute of Historian-Archivists, Yuri Afanas'ev, went even further: "I can give you my assurance that there is not a single page without falsification. It is immoral for young people to take exams based on such a textbook" (from Husband, 1991, p. 460). In essence, the state was openly admitting that much of what students had learned about history in school was not true and never should have been considered as such.

This public announcement actually was consistent with long-standing doubt, "hypocrisy and double-speak" (Boym, 1994, p. 224) by Soviet citizens about official information. In recalling attitudes toward the press, for example, Boym (1996) reports, "nobody believed it ... We didn't believe anything that was in the newspapers" (p. 32). Indeed, the media had become so suspect in the eyes of many segments of the Soviet population that they assumed truth could be divined by thinking precisely the opposite of what was reported. One result of this was that Westerners sometimes found themselves in the ironic position of trying to convince Russian friends that stories in newspapers such as *Pravda* ("Truth") really were true!

This attitude of doubt was nowhere more pronounced than in the case of the official history produced by the Soviet state (Tulviste & Wertsch, 1994). Although belief in official history had been waning for several years before 1988 in the USSR, these accounts had retained at least a patina of acceptance. It could still be dangerous – to one's career prospects if nothing else – to openly call official accounts into question, even during the final years of the Soviet Union's existence. This was a context in which much of the population accepted the need to operate within the official "frame" (Goffman,

1974) of Soviet ideology, at least in public, while simultaneously believing in private that it was time to admit that the emperor had no clothes. As can be imagined, in such a setting the official acknowledgment that what had been taught about the past was not true was a signal event.

When trying to understand efforts to rewrite history after the break-up of the Soviet Union, the first inclination of many observers has been to point to the availability of newly unearthed information. For example, the dust jacket of a 1996 best-selling biography of Stalin proclaims that the author was "granted privileged access to Russia's secret archives" and as a result was able to produce "the first full-scale life of Stalin to have what no previous biography has entirely gotten hold of: the facts" (Radzinsky, 1996). Such assertions suggest that newly uncovered information was the key to understanding how authors could write Soviet and Russian history in new ways. As will become clear, however, a kind of dialogue with previous narratives played a far more essential role in this process.

Forces of Change: Narrative Dialogicality

Revisions of official history typically involve responses to earlier accounts, but analysts such as Yuri Lotman and Boris Uspenskii (1985) have argued that the dynamics of this process take a special form in Russia. They see these dynamics as being governed by a sort of binary opposition that has operated in Russia for the past several centuries. Such a binary-model culture involves "a bipolar field ... divided by a sharp boundary without an axiologically neutral zone" (p. 31). The absence of this neutral zone in Russia provides a point of contrast with the West, where "a wide area of neutral behavior became possible, as did neutral societal institutions, which were neither 'holy' nor 'sinful,' neither 'pro-state' nor 'anti-state,' neither good nor bad" (p. 32).

Lotman and Uspenskii base their argument on an analysis of Russian culture up to the end of the eighteenth century, but as was often the case for Soviet authors, their line of reasoning also had clear implications for the very context in which they were writing. Hence their usefulness when trying to interpret the transition to the post-Soviet context. From Lotman and Uspenskii's perspective, the key to understanding the mechanisms for generating new forms of textual mediation in this context is that every new period in Russian culture "is oriented toward a decisive break with what preceded it" (p. 31).

Among the oppositions that structured Russian culture from the conversion to Christianity straight through to Peter's reforms, one of the most stable has been the opposition between "the old and the new." The activity and significance of this opposition is so great that from the subjective position of the "native speaker" of the culture, it has at various stages included or subsumed other singularly important contrasts such as "Russia versus the West," "Christianity versus paganism," "true faith versus false faith," "knowledge versus ignorance," "upper class versus lower classes," and so on. (p. 33)

As envisioned by Lotman and Uspenskii, this tendency toward radical opposition and negation is coupled with, and tempered by, the *"regeneration of archaic forms"* (p. 33, italics in the original). Even in the context of efforts to make a radical break with the past, one is likely to "encounter a good many repeated or very similar events, historical-psychological situations, or texts" (p. 31). The issue, then, is to identify what forces are involved in making a radical break with the past and what forces operate to insure an element of continuity.

These ideas provide important insights when trying to understand the "dialogue of narratives" that has been involved in writing history in post-Soviet Russia. When producing new accounts of the past in this context, the focus has been on rebutting and replacing previous narratives. Specifically, it has involved taking particular ideas in Soviet narratives such as class struggle, capitalist imperialism, and the leadership role of the Communist Party as points of critique and rebuttal.

This process was grounded in the dialogic function of narrative outlined in Chapter 3. This is not to say that new official histories are determined solely by the functions of narratives. Obviously, other political and cultural forces play a role as well. However, processes of narrative organization and dialogic engagement provide essential semiotic resources that mediate and constrain the production of new official histories, and it is these resources that will be of primary concern in what follows.

When examining these issues, the process that Bakhtin (1984) outlined under the heading of "hidden dialogicality" provides a useful starting point.

Imagine a dialogue of two persons in which the statements of the second speaker are omitted, but in such a way that the general sense is not at all violated. The second speaker is present invisibly, his words are not there, but deep traces left by these words have a determining influence on all the present and visible words of the first speaker. We sense that this is a conversation, although only one person is speaking, and it is a conversation of the most intense kind, for each present, uttered word responds and reacts with its every fiber to the invisible speaker, points to something outside itself, beyond its own limits, to the unspoken words of another person. (1984, p. 197)

In my analysis of Soviet and post-Soviet textbooks, I shall be concerned with how the voices producing the narrative texts function in the capacity of Bakhtin's "speakers." Specifically, I shall be concerned with how the voices of Soviet texts seem to be "present invisibly" and leave "deep traces" on post-Soviet Russian texts. As will become evident, this invisible presence has taken on a particular form in this case.

Important insight into this particular form can be found in the ideas of Andrei Kvakin (1998) about "Manichaean consciousness," ideas that draw on the line of reasoning developed by Lotman and Uspenskii. In Kvakin's view, this form of consciousness characterizes many aspects of post-Soviet Russian society. From such a perspective, "the world is divided strictly into the light and darkness, true and false, our own and alien" (p. 39). As Kvakin notes, authors such as Berdyaev (1992), Lotman and Uspenskii (1985), and Raeff (1966) have traced the roots of Manichaean tendencies in Russian culture to points well before the twentieth century, so it should not be viewed as a peculiarly Soviet phenomenon.

Kvakin sees the presence of Manichaean consciousness in many aspects of post-Soviet Russian society, but he is particularly interested in how it is manifested in political discourse. According to him, "Manichean methods have once again been applied: the mildest critiques of 'democratic' leaders or the absence of negative evaluations of the Communist regime automatically gives rise to attaching the 'red-brown' label to others. The 'uncompromising struggle,' the division between what is 'our own' and what is 'alien' arises anew" (p. 42).

In Kvakin's view, this political discourse has spilled over into efforts to write new accounts of the past. In criticizing what he views as an unfortunate continuation of old habits, he argues that it is "intolerable to label the positions of one or another side of a debate as simply 'correct' or 'incorrect'" (p. 42). To do so is to participate in the practice of using "invective as a tool of political argument" (p. 40).

The kinds of Manichaean practices criticized by Kvakin give rise to collective memory, and simple forms of it at that, as opposed to analytical history. Indeed, it is difficult to imagine conditions more conducive to creating accounts characterized by the properties of collective memory outlined in Chapter 3 – in particular, the tendency to employ a single committed perspective and the tendency to be impatient with ambiguity about the motives of the actors in a narrative. In this case, it is not so much a matter of the content of narrative texts that is remembered as it is a matter of the practices and habits one employs when responding to others. As such, the sort of Manichaean consciousness discussed by Kvakin can be viewed as a version of "habit memory" as discussed in Chapter 3.

Kvakin's account of Manichaeanism in contemporary Russian consciousness and public discourse has important implications for the nature of hidden dialogicality in the cases I shall be examining. One may be in the habit of reacting and responding to "the unspoken words of another person" (Bakhtin, 1984, p. 197) in several ways. For example, one may respond by extending, criticizing, or studiously ignoring the words of others. Or one may treat the words of others as "thinking devices" (Lotman, 1988) that are useful for productive elaboration and extension. Or one may follow the more Manichaean path of radical opposition and negation, light as opposed to darkness, truth as opposed to falsity. Kvakin's analysis suggests that it is important to be on the lookout for tendencies of the last sort of hidden dialogicality when examining the production of new texts about the past in post-Soviet Russia.

Forces of Continuity: The Triumph-Over-Alien-Forces Schematic Narrative Template

Whereas binary thinking and Manichaean consciousness suggest a tendency toward radical change in collective memory, there are also forces that have provided for continuity during the transition from the Soviet era to the post-Soviet era. These forces of continuity are grounded in what Lotman and Uspenskii (1985, p. 33) term the "regeneration of archaic forms," and they derive from the cultural tools that mediate collective remembering. In this connection, I shall be concerned with a schematic narrative template (see Chapter 3) that shapes collective remembering in Russia such that continuity is maintained in the midst of what appears to be radical change.

The line of reasoning I shall follow continues to draw on the ideas of figures such as Mink (1978), who viewed narratives as "cognitive instruments" that make possible the "configurational act" of grasping together information about setting, actors, events, motivations, and other elements in particular ways. In contrast to being concerned with specific narratives with their concrete settings, actors, and events, I shall be concerned in what follows with the more abstract level at which schematic narrative templates operate.

In the Russian case, the narrative template at issue is what I shall title "triumph-over-alien-forces." This is a narrative template that may be instantiated using a range of concrete characters, events, dates, and circumstances, but its basic plot remains relatively constant and contains the following items:

1. An "initial situation" (Propp, 1968, p. 26) in which the Russian people are living in a peaceful setting where they are no threat to others is disrupted by:

2. The initiation of trouble or aggression by an alien force, or agent, which leads to:

3. A time of crisis and great suffering, which is:

4. Overcome by the triumph over the alien force by the Russian people, acting heroically and alone.

To many it will appear that there is nothing peculiarly Russian about this narrative template since it may be found just about anywhere. For example, by replacing "Russian" with "American" it would seem to provide a foundation for American collective memory of the Japanese attack on Pearl Harbor in 1941. My point is not that this narrative template is available only to members of the Russian narrative tradition or that this is the only schematic narrative template in this tradition. Obviously, this is a cultural tool employed by many people around the world, and there are other items in the cultural tool kit of the Russian narrative tradition. However, there are some concerns that suggest this template plays a particularly important role and takes on a particular form in the Russian narrative tradition, and hence in collective remembering.

The first of these concerns its ubiquity. Whereas the United States and many other societies have accounts of past events that fit this narrative template, it seems to be employed more widely in the Russian tradition than elsewhere. It forms the basic plot line for several of the most important events in Russian history, including the Mongol invasion in the thirteenth century, the Swedish invasion in the eighteenth century, Napoleon's invasion in the nineteenth century, and Hitler's invasion in the twentieth century. Indeed, many would say this narrative template is *the* underlying story of Russian collective remembering, and hence contrasts with the items that people from other nations might employ. For example, it contrasts with American items such as the "mystique of Manifest Destiny" (Lowenthal, 1992, p. 53) or a "quest for freedom" narrative (Wertsch, 1994; Wertsch and O'Connor, 1994).

Of course, one obvious reason for the ubiquity of this narrative template in Russian collective remembering is that it reflects actual experience. Over its history, Russia clearly has been the victim of several invasions and other acts of aggression, and my intent is not to argue that this narrative is without foundation. Instead, it is to examine how this narrative template is organized and how it plays a role in shaping new accounts of the past. As will become apparent, the triumph-over-alien-forces narrative template plays an extremely important role in collective memory, even in instances where it would not seem relevant, at least to those who are not "native speakers" (Lotman & Uspenskii, 1985) of this tradition.

Part of the reason for the ubiquity of this narrative template is that it has great flexibility. In particular, the notion of "alien" extends beyond what would typically come to mind for most Western observers, and allows it to refer to characters other than non-Russian or non-Soviet actors. While foreign actors serve as the characters that initiate many narratives in collective remembering, Russian counterrevolutionaries and other actors who originally appear to be one of "us" from a Russian perspective, but turn out to be "alien" traitors or "wreckers," may play this role as well.

Given the ubiquity and flexibility of the triumph-over-alien-forces narrative template, consider some additional properties that give it a unique flavor in the Russian context. First, regardless of whether alien parties are foreign or domestic, their basic motivation in the narrative is aggression toward the genuine "us" of the Soviet Union or Russia. Such characters cannot exist in a neutral space when emplotting the past for collective remembering in this context. Instead, they are always on one or the other side of an uncompromising struggle.

In a sense, this is to be expected in any instantiation of this narrative template, but it takes on particular form in the Russian case in the extent to which the opposition between good and evil, light and darkness, us and them is emphasized. As Kvakin has outlined, this is part of the public debate among professional historians, but it also affects everyday processes of collective remembering and the production of its textual mediation. For example, Fran Markowitz (2000) has outlined the basic opposition between whether someone is ours or alien ("nash ili chuzhoi") as it played out in classroom discussions in the mid-1990s after the break-up of the Soviet Union. Describing a discussion led by the teacher "Vladimir Borisevich" in a Moscow school in 1994, she reports:

Vladimir Borisevich did not equivocate with terminology. At the beginning of the term he told students that he was just going to say *nashi* [ours] for the troops of the Soviet army "because that is what they are, right?" "Right," the students responded, agreeing with his declaration that the former Soviet Union and the present Russian Federation are both "us." (p. 80)

The interpretation of the alien is a further reflection of the binary thinking and Manichaean consciousness outlined earlier – namely, alien personages are starkly differentiated from "our own" (Kvakin, 1998, p. 42), and they are opponents in an uncompromising struggle. They are separated from us by "a bipolar field ... divided by a sharp boundary without an axiologically neutral zone" (Lotman & Uspenskii, 1985, p. 31). Hence there are no neutral parties in this narrative.

At least one additional aspect of the triumph-over-alien-forces narrative provides further insight into how it functions in the Russian context. The first two of the four items in the narrative template outlined earlier are usually combined to emphasize that the Russian or Soviet people were in a benign state of peace that had every reason to continue had alien aggression not occurred. From this perspective, there was no reason for any trouble to arise *except for* belligerence by a malicious alien force, and this lends an element of victimization to the account. Given that Russia was depicted as non-threatening in this narrative template, attack by an alien agent comprises a step in the plot that makes it hard not to interpret Russia as a victim of a devious, unprovoked aggression.

Again, to make this point is not to argue that Russia has not in fact been the victim of attacks. It clearly has, and these attacks have been traumatic events in its history. The issue is not so much one of the criterion of accuracy (Chapter 1) as one of how events can be emplotted in the service of creating a usable past. It is a matter of interpreting the characters' motives and the outcomes that follow. The choices involved affect the ability of a narrative to serve as what may be termed an "identity resource," and in the Russian and Soviet case the tendency has been to use narratives whose starting point is victimhood at the hands of an alien force.

Before leaving this point, it is worth noting that alternatives to the triumph-over-alien-forces schematic narrative template do in fact exist and have been used to grasp together major events and tendencies in Russia's past. Perhaps the most obvious alternative can be termed the "Russian empire" narrative template. Just as there is evidence to support the triumph-over-alien-forces narrative template, there is evidence to support this interpretation, the big difference being that it is usually employed by people other than Russians as a textual and identity resource. For example, it is not difficult to encounter people from Ukraine, Latvia, Estonia, and elsewhere who assume that the Russian empire narrative template provides the obvious interpretation of the motives and actions of Russia's leaders.

Furthermore, the Russian empire narrative template is not something one encounters only in national groups' collective memory. It also lies behind numerous accounts in analytical history. For example, in his book *Empire*, Dominic Lieven (2000) has outlined longstanding practices by Russian and Soviet governments that lend themselves to such an interpretation. Discussing earlier periods of history, he writes:

In 1462 the grand prince of Moscow ruled over 24,000 square kilometres. In 1914 Nicholas II ruled over 13.5 million. The tsarist state was one of the most effective mechanisms for territorial expansion ever known. To many European observers in the nineteenth and early twentieth centuries there appeared something inexorable, remorseless and unstoppable in its advance. (p. 262)

Lieven points out that despite its ideological hatred of imperialism, the Soviet government had, if anything, even more pronounced tendencies in this direction.

Subsequently, as supreme leader, Stalin was very strongly guided in his foreign policy by traditional tsarist perspectives on territorial expansion, geopolitics and power. His leading lieutenant and foreign minister, Molotov, commented later that 'like no one else, Stalin understood the great historical destiny and fateful mission of the Russian people – the destiny about which Dostoevsky wrote: the heart of Russia, more than that of any other nation, is predestined to be the universal, all-embracing humanitarian union of nations. He believed that once the world-wide communist system had triumphed . . . the world's main language, the language of international communication, would be the language of Pushkin and Lenin. Molotov added that 'my task as minister of foreign affairs was to expand the borders of our fatherland.' (p. 295)

In sum, several aspects of Russian culture can be expected to shape the way that collective memory reflects both radical transformation and underlying continuity in the transition from the Soviet to the post-Soviet

Russian era. The radical change in this setting reflects forces that might be expected to be at work in any context of rapid social transformation, but it also takes on special form in this case. Specifically, the tradition of Manichaean consciousness has given rise to a particular form of narrative dialogicality. Standing in contrast to this, the elements of continuity in this setting derive from the use of an underlying cultural tool – namely, the triumph-over-alien-forces schematic narrative template. An understanding of these two opposing tendencies provides the framework for examining the production of official collective remembering in the sections that follow.

Soviet and Post-Soviet History Textbooks and Instruction

Compared with what exists today in Russia, history instruction in the Soviet Union was both monolithic and monologic. Across all eleven time zones of that massive state, students in the same grade were literally on the same page of the same history textbook on any given day of the school year, and the official history taught allowed little room for competing voices. In the wake of the events in 1988, this changed dramatically. Many history teachers found themselves in the position of having to organize their instruction around whatever materials they could find. They used texts ranging from old Soviet textbooks to newspapers to family stories. The setting in which the changes I shall examine occurred, then, was one in which history instruction was moving from being part of a system of rigid, centralized control to being shaped by dispersed, local decision-making.

As a means for getting some sense of the transformations at work in this context, consider the following facts about some high school history textbooks published in Russia in 1976, 1989, 1992, and 1995 (see Appendix A at the end of this chapter). These four textbooks were selected from a wider set of materials as a way of documenting some of the changes in historical representation that occurred before, during, and after perestroika. Each of the first three volumes was published as the *sole* Soviet history textbook for a given grade level (the 1976 text for ninth graders, the 1989 and 1992 texts for tenth graders), whereas the 1995 version was one of several competing textbooks for a grade level (eleventh grade).

As shown in Appendix A, there are major differences in the print runs for the Soviet and post-Soviet texts, something that reflects differences in how these texts were produced and used. In contrast to the Soviet context, when there was only one basic history textbook for each grade level in the USSR, the Ministry of Education of the Russian Federation worked with several private publishing firms in the 1990s to produce multiple, competing accounts of history. Furthermore, some teachers in Russian schools used none of these materials for budgetary or other reasons.

The conscious effort to introduce an element of multivoicedness into history education in the 1990s was led by figures such as Aleksandr Asmolov (personal communication, 1998), who served as Deputy Minister of Education for the Russian Federation between 1992 and 1998. Under his leadership, the Ministry of Education insisted that at least two, and preferably more, history textbooks be produced at each grade level. As in the battles of "history wars" (Linenthal & Engelhardt, 1996) elsewhere, the suggestion that more than one voice should be recognized as producing a legitimate narrative about the past was hotly disputed in post-Soviet Russia. In pursuing their agenda, Asmolov and others found themselves in a political and cultural maelstrom. They were publicly attacked by organizations such as Pamyat' (Memory), an extreme Russian nationalist organization, and they often found themselves and their families as the targets of personal threats.

As Mendeloff (1996) suggests, the efforts by Asmolov and others to foster multivoicedness in the production of official history in post-Soviet Russia were not always successful. Despite their efforts, it is likely that a great deal of uniformity in history instruction continued to exist. This new homogeneity stemmed in part from the continuing influence of the triumph-over-alien-forces narrative template, but it also received institutional support from the fact that many schools and teachers used materials recommended by the Russian Ministry of Education. While Asmolov and others fought to encourage this Ministry to develop multiple textbooks for each grade level, it still served as a sort of centralized endorsement agency with conservative tendencies. For example, it produced a textbook list called the "Federal Set," and items on this list are much more likely to be used by teachers, especially in rural areas, than the myriad books and other materials produced by individual schools or other sources. In short, while the rigidly enforced centralization of the Soviet years no longer existed, new sources of homogeneity emerged in its place.

In order to examine some of the factors involved in struggles to come up with a new picture of the past in post-Soviet Russia, I shall concentrate on two historical events covered in Soviet and post-Soviet history textbooks: the Russian Civil War of 1918–1920 and World War II. In the case of the Civil War, I shall argue that a hidden dialogicality grounded in Manichaean consciousness has yielded a new form of emplotment for grasping together events and actors. Different results from such hidden dialogicality have emerged in the case of World War II: in this instance, the emplotment remains largely unchanged, but the dialogue of narratives has yielded other transformations, especially in the characters who occupy central roles. There is also an element of continuity provided by the underlying triumph-over-alien-forces narrative line, but it takes on different forms in the two cases.

Soviet Narratives of the Russian Civil War: Foreign and Domestic Enemies in the Triumph-Over-Alien-Forces Narrative Template
In Soviet era textbooks, the Civil War was emplotted as beginning with the kind of alien aggression that characterizes many aspects of collective remembering in Russia, and it goes on to reflect the triumph-over-alien-forces narrative template in other respects as well. Thus, it begins with intervention and aggression by foreign actors, events that then gave rise to belligerent acts by domestic counterrevolutionaries. In this account, the USSR was a victim of alien intervention that unexpectedly and artificially changed its otherwise peaceful course of action while recovering from the 1917 Revolution. This is reflected in the titles of the sections and chapters. For example, the fifty-page section in the text by Berkhin and Fedosov (1976) for the ninth grade is called "The Soviet land during the period of intervention by imperialist governments and the Civil War (1918–1920)." The first chapter in this section is titled "The beginning of military intervention by the imperialists and the Civil War." The corresponding section and first chapter in the 1989 text by Korablëv, Fedosov, and Borisov have identical titles.

"The beginning of military intervention by the imperialists and the Civil War" in the 1976 text begins as follows:

Causes of the intervention and the Civil War. A new period in the history of the young Soviet government began in the summer of 1918 – a period of liberation and of class warfare of the workers and peasants of Russia against the combined forces of international imperialism and internal counter-revolution – a period of civil war. This period extended from May-June 1918 to November 1920. This was thrust upon the Soviet people above all by international imperialism, which organized military intervention. Its goal was to destroy the world's first socialist government of workers and peasants, "to extinguish the fire of socialist revolution begun by us," wrote Lenin, "and threatening to call out to the entire world" (vol. 37, p. 39). It strove to liquidate the center and foundation of the worldwide proletarian revolution. (p. 211)

Some change in this pattern of presenting the beginning of the Civil War appeared, at least in the chapter headings, in the 1992 text by Zharova and Mishina. Instead of setting off the Civil War in a separate section whose title clearly marks that it began with – and because of – foreign intervention, it is covered in a more inclusive chapter, "At the cliff of a historical turning point. The development of psychological confrontation in society into open civil war and the establishment of a dictatorship of the proletariat in Russia (July 1917–1920)." This new version comes closer to the treatment of the Russian Civil War found in contemporary Western historical scholarship (e.g., Figes, 1997) in that the Civil War is viewed as an extension of the October Revolution. From this perspective, the appropriate narrative is one that grasps together the October Revolution and the Civil War as part of extended civil strife, counterrevolution, and the emergence of a dictatorship.

Even with these new chapter and section titles in the 1992 text, the old Soviet narrative in which foreign intervention played a crucial role in initiating the Civil War continues to be in evidence. For example, the authors introduce notions of imperialist intervention, and describe it in the following terms:

The mind behind the idea for open foreign intervention in Russia was Winston Churchill. He worked out the plan for reconstituting the German Army for the struggle with the Bolsheviks and then undertook the efforts to unite the counter-revolutionary forces with the goal of overthrowing the Soviet government and breaking up Russia into a multitude of weak political units. These plans were supported by the U.S. State Department. The U.S. delegation to the Paris peace conference brought with it a map of the "Proposed Borders of Russia." On this map Karelia, and the Kola Peninsula, the Baltics, Ukraine, a significant part of Belorussia, Transcaucasia, Siberia, Central Asia, and other areas were outside the borders of Russia . . . In the struggle against Soviet Russia Churchill even contemplated the use of chemical weapons. (pp. 213–214)

Hence in all of these Soviet-era history textbooks, the unprovoked intervention of alien forces was given a prominent role in the account of the Civil War, and up to the very end of the Soviet era it was viewed as marking the beginning of this conflict. This pattern is clearly reflected in the chapter titles of the 1976 and 1989 texts. The fact that it was more subtle in the 1992 text suggests that changes were underway during the transition from Soviet to post-Soviet Russia.

In all of these Soviet textbooks, the events of the Civil War were systematically presented such that foreign intervention was mentioned before the war was mentioned, something that reflects the assumption that the intervention *caused* the war. Furthermore, this emplotment of the Civil War served to separate the story of the Revolution neatly from the story of the Civil War. The former ended with a triumphant victory for the Communist Party and the people, and the latter began with the intervention of alien forces.

After the beginning of the Civil War, the subsequent emplotment in the Soviet textbooks follows the contours of the triumph-over-alien-forces narrative template. It moves through the low points of defeats and setbacks for the Reds and a period of great suffering for the people and then turns to a triumphant and final victory. The early defeats by external and internal enemies were so serious that "Terrible 1918" is used as a chapter heading in the 1976 text. However, this section of the narrative is followed by one that focuses on the Reds' decisive, heroic triumph (indeed, rout – "razgrom") over external and internal enemies. In this connection, for example, the 1976 text has chapters titled "The rout of the spring (1919) combined campaign of the Entente," "The decisive victory of the Red Army," and "The war with the Polish bourgeois-landowners. The rout of Wrangel's army."

In these narratives, such victories are presented as resulting from heroic efforts over seemingly impossible odds. In accordance with the triumph-over-alien-forces narrative template, the Russian people had to act alone and heroically. As noted in the 1989 textbook:

"A historical miracle." That is what V.I. Lenin called the victory over the White Guards and the international imperialists. It was a victory of our devastated country which was besieged from all sides in a duel with opponents who began with immeasurably greater strengths. The enemies had at their disposal a multitude of armies and a huge stock of arms, and they succeeded in surrounding the Soviet republic on all sides, cutting it off from regions that provided food and raw materials. But "we held our ground against everything" V.I. Lenin said with pride. (p. 238)

Hence the sense of an ending that shapes the Soviet narratives about the Civil War is provided by decisive victory over alien aggressors. After some initial low points, the rout of enemies produced the upward sweep of the plot, an upward sweep that is so powerful and triumphant that it is termed "a historical miracle."

Post-Soviet Russian Accounts of the Civil War:
A Counter-Narrative of Tragedy

Post-Soviet accounts of the Civil War found in Russian high school textbooks differ markedly from their earlier counterparts. Of particular importance for my purposes is the fact that they are emplotted in a fundamentally different way. Hidden dialogicality is clearly in evidence in that the Soviet narrative is "present invisibly" in the new text, and the new text "reacts with its every fiber to the invisible speaker, points to something outside itself" (Bakhtin, 1984, p. 197). Specifically, at many points the new text seems to be operating in accordance with the strictures of binary thinking, and hence is more concerned with asserting that things did *not* happen the way they were presented in Soviet texts than with saying what did happen.

In this new account, the Civil War did *not* start with foreign intervention, its sense of an ending is *not* provided by glorious victory of the Reds, and its actors are *not* the "collective individuals" identified by Ahonen (1992, 1997) as populating Marxist-Leninist accounts from the Soviet era. In all of these respects, the post-Soviet text can be viewed as rebuttals to their Soviet counterparts. My analysis of this post-Soviet emplotment focuses primarily on a 1995 high school textbook (Ostrovskii & Utkin, 1995), but similar patterns can be found in other recent textbooks such as the one by Danilov, Gorinov, Leonov, Lugovskaya, Senyavski, and Naumov (1996) for college students.

The account of the Civil War in the 1995 post-Soviet Russian textbook is provided in a relatively short section (twenty pages) titled "Revolution in Russia. March 1917–March 1921." This section treats the Civil War as part of a larger set of events, including the October Revolution of 1917. Rather than assuming that the Revolution had a clear-cut beginning and end that neatly separates it from the Civil War, the authors specifically note that "Revolution in Russia was not a single, punctual event, but a process that extended over several years" (Ostrovskii & Utkin, 1995, p. 188). Ostrovskii and Utkin further note that the protracted nature of events in Russia has strong parallels with many other revolutions. This again stands in marked contrast to accounts in earlier textbooks in which the Revolution was presented as an exceptional, even unique, event in human history.

The treatment of the Civil War as a natural extension of the Revolution means that the narrative resources used to grasp together events are quite different from those used in Soviet textbooks. Specifically, the war is re-emplotted in such a way that it is viewed as growing out of internal disputes in the Soviet Union. Consistent with this is the fact that foreign intervention is given a minor role at best. In striking contrast to the emphasis given to foreign intervention as a cause of the Civil War in Soviet texts, there was virtually no mention of it in this post-Soviet volume. The term "intervention" is absent from chapter and section titles, and "imperialism" is a term that never appears. One of the few references to intervention is the dismissive comment that "The assistance of European countries to Poland [during the Soviet-Polish war of 1920–21] was greater there than their help to the White movement in Russia" (Ostrovskii & Utkin, 1995, p. 162). Indeed, the only extended comment about the role of Britain, the United States, and others who had been cast in the role of alien forces in previous accounts is one that asserts that their efforts actually did more to help the Reds than the Whites.

The White Army did not participate jointly in the military actions [of a landing by allied troops in the North, South, and Far East]. But the very fact of the landing was used by Bolshevik propaganda to stir up distrust in the White movement. Assistance by the allies in the form of finances, arms, and uniforms was of a limited character, and could not exert an influence on the course of the White actions. (p. 157)

As outlined earlier, Soviet accounts of the Civil War emplotted its events as beginning with foreign intervention, which interrupted the course that history otherwise would have taken and led to a dark and dangerous period. This was then followed by triumph over all odds and the rout of alien forces. In contrast to this "historical miracle," which gives Soviet narratives their upward sweep, events are configured in a quite different way in the post-Soviet accounts. In the 1995 textbook, the events are emplotted in terms of a downward sweep that eventually led to disaster for virtually everyone involved. Events leading up to the end are presented as opportunities missed rather than steps toward an inevitable and glorious outcome. The tragic ending is presented as something that might have been avoided had various actors had the foresight, determination, and courage to avert it. The Whites are presented as clearly lacking in this regard.

Tragically for the White movement, a significant part of the country's intelligentsia, being apathetic and nonbelievers, refused to support it. This break led to a situation in which the Whites did not succeed in creating a normal civil government for the country. They were forced to concern themselves with military matters since they did not have serious experience with such work, and they committed irreparable mistakes. Forced requisitions without financial guarantees alienated the peasants, who initially approved of the Whites, and the same pattern occurred with people banished by the Bolsheviks. (p. 157)

In striking contrast to the Whites, the Reds are portrayed by Ostrovskii and Utkin as being decisive, and ruthless in their efforts to take power and organize their forces.

Communist power did not . . . vacillate. It was hard and cruel, executed with a certainty that the laws of history lay behind it. But its victory was not a matter of historical predestination. Instead, it is possible to identify two important conditions that underlay it. First, it was founded on organized violence never before seen in history. No one had ever recognized the possibilities of such violence before 1917. Second, the anti-bolshevik opposition in the armed forces and the anti-bolshevik opposition among the people were unable to unite into a unified whole. The reason for this was the long-standing rift between the people and the intelligentsia. . . . (p. 189)

In sum, Ostrovskii and Utkin emplot the events of the Revolution and Civil War in such a way that the narrative clearly has a downward sweep. Indeed, they could have used the title used by Figes (1997) in his account of these events: *A People's Tragedy*. From this perspective, events leading up to the end are viewed as opportunities tragically missed rather than as causes leading inexorably toward a grand triumph.

Further elements of silent dialogicality grounded in Manichaean consciousness appear in the treatment of the actors in the 1995 textbook. The first point to note here is that the major actors no longer are imperialist interventionists, White Guards, and others, on the one hand, who are pitted against the Reds led by the Communist Party with Lenin at its head, on the other. Furthermore, instead of generally treating actors as collective individuals motivated by class interests and revolutionary zeal or by counterrevolutionary false consciousness, the post-Soviet textbook points to common, and often base, motives of unique individuals and groups concerned with local issues. This is reflected, for example, in the following passages:

The peasants from the central regions of Russia did not actively come out against the Bolsheviks, being engaged in the spontaneous demobilization and the return to farming. But in the spring of 1918 the peasants' mood underwent a change. More and more they expressed their discontent with the new power. The situation began to change, and not to the Soviets' benefit. The main force operating in opposition to them became the so-called "democratic counter-revolution," which united the former Socialist Revolutionaries and other moderate socialist parties and groups. They came out under the banner of restoring democracy in Russia and a return to the ideas of a constituent assembly. In the summer of 1918 these groups created their own regional governments: in Arkhangelsk, Samara, Ufa, Omsk, and also in other cities . . . The suspicious and scornful approach that local soviet powers took toward [White elements such as] the Czechs led them to armed conflict . . . At this time Trotsky, combining the most brutal measures for laying down discipline and for attracting the old officer corps into the Red Army, succeeded in creating a regular, battle-worthy army. The officers were recruited by force (officers' family members were held as hostages), and some also volunteered. As a rule, the new army attracted those who thought that in the old army they had not realized their professional capacity. (Ostrovskii & Utkin, 1995, p. 146)

As presented in this narrative, then, the characters involved in the Civil War differed quite strikingly from those found in Soviet accounts. Instead of wishing to participate in the Revolution, peasants simply wanted to return to farming; rather than engaging in counterrevolution, the Czechs were simply responding to hostile treatment by local soviets; and rather than joining the Red Army out of a new form of universal, class-based patriotism, men joined out of fear or for ignoble personal gain. All of these motives and actions gain their significance from the new, tragic emplotment that grasps them together.

In sum, the relationship between the post-Soviet textbook account of the Civil War and its Soviet precursors can be understood in terms of a form of the hidden dialogicality that gave rise to a counter-narrative. Furthermore, this hidden dialogicality reflects several aspects of binary thinking and Manichaean consciousness in that it mentions many of the same events but reverses their interpretation from strongly positive to strongly negative, heroic to evil, and so forth.

This counter-narrative is characterized by a different beginning, by a different sense of ending and associated narrative contour (falling, as opposed to rising sweep of the plot), and by the actors and motives that make sense within such a plot structure. The result is a 1995 text that grasps together events and actors into a tragic narrative that argues in diametric opposition to the "invisible speaker" in earlier Soviet narratives organized around a triumphalist sense of an ending.

These points about the 1995 official history indicate a radical break with previous accounts. However, an element of continuity can also be seen to be at work, something that stems from the triumph-over-alien-forces schematic narrative template. This is reflected first in the continuing existence of alien enemies in the new version. Instead of focusing on foreign enemies such as Western imperialist forces and Churchill, however, the new version focuses on enemies within the Soviet Union such as Lenin, Trotsky, and the Communist Party. In the 1995 text, these actors are presented as disrupting what would otherwise have been a more democratic course of history. Indeed, Ostrovskii and Utkin make a special point of noting that their "victory was not a matter of historical predestination" (p. 189).

While these new enemies came from within the Soviet Union, they are portrayed as alien in that they were not truly part of Russian society. They stood apart and were often at odds with it, making it necessary to use unusual coercive force to get the population to act in their cause. These "hard and cruel" aliens are portrayed in the 1995 text as victorious largely because they relied on a level of "organized violence never before seen in history" (p. 189). The only way they could force others to join their effort was through coercion, including holding officers' families as hostages, and attracting misfits and others who "had not realized their professional capacity" (p. 146).

The points I have made up to now support the continuing influence of the triumph-over-alien-forces narrative template insofar as alien actors are concerned. However, they do not address how some sort of triumphal ending fits into the picture. Indeed, the tendency to rewrite the 1917 Revolution and the Civil War as one grand tragedy would seem to contradict any notion of triumph. It turns out that this aspect of the plot continues to exist, but in a somewhat different form and in a different time frame.

For many people in post-Soviet Russia, the seven decades beginning with the Revolution and ending with the dissolution of the USSR are taken to be an abnormal period. From this perspective, the Soviet era is viewed as a period of crisis and darkness that was only overcome with the re-emergence in the late 1980s of a relatively democratic government that reflects the will of the Russian people. In this account, actors such as Lenin, Trotsky, and the Communist Party appear as alien forces who disrupted an earlier, relatively peaceful and untroubled time. They are alien in the sense that they introduced ideas that were unnatural and alien to Russian society, a point made by Slavophiles and Russian nationalist writers such as Solzhenitsyn (1976). The time of darkness and suffering introduced by these alien forces was only overcome by the triumph of the Russian people over communism at the end of the century. Hence, even in this case, which at first glance suggests radical change in the cultural tools used to interpret the past, there is an underlying element of continuity provided by the triumph-over-alien-forces schematic narrative template.

Soviet Accounts of World War II: The Party as Hero in the Triumph-Over-Alien-Forces Narrative Template

The process of revising the World War II narrative in post-Soviet textbooks follows a path that is in some ways quite different from that used in the case of the Civil War. Instead of fundamentally re-emplotting the account around a new sense of ending, post-Soviet accounts of World War II look much the same as their Soviet precursors. There is little sense in which they involve new ways of grasping the events together. This continuity with earlier accounts has been noted by Mendeloff (1997), who argues that the new narratives continue to be organized around well-established themes of Russian exceptionalism, heroism, and victimization, themes that reflect the influence of the triumph-over-alien-forces schematic narrative template. Hence, forces of continuity play a greater role and forces of transformation a lesser role than in the case of the rewriting of official history about the Civil War. Given the role of the World War II narrative as a continuing "dominant myth" (Weiner, 1996) in Russian life, this is perhaps to be expected.

My comparison of Soviet and post-Soviet accounts of World War II will draw on a somewhat different set of textbooks than those used in the discussion of the Civil War. The reason is that in Soviet instructional practice, the year 1940 was a dividing point between what was covered at two grade levels, and hence the Civil War was covered in one textbook and World War II in another. I will examine Soviet textbooks published in 1964 and 1975, along with the same post-Soviet Russian textbook from 1995 that I used when examining the Civil War (see Appendix B at the end of this chapter).

Like recent Russian textbooks, Soviet accounts made a distinction between World War II, which began on September 1, 1939, and the Great Patriotic War, which began when the USSR was invaded on June 22, 1941. In both cases, the entry of the Soviet Union into the war was presented as the event that transformed relatively unimportant, smaller scale hostilities into the massive conflict whose major focus was the struggle between Germany and the USSR. Furthermore, Soviet and post-Soviet textbook accounts of World War II are emplotted in the same basic way. Both presuppose that the Soviet Union, which was not threatening anyone, was the victim of an unprovoked attack by Germany. Following heavy initial losses the Soviet Union, acting heroically and largely alone, managed to achieve victory over great odds.

An additional similarity between Soviet and post-Soviet accounts can be found in the central role given to the USSR in the plot. From this perspective, the USSR was *the* central character in the war, and the motives and possibilities for others' actions were determined or made possible by what it did. For example, in the 1975 text the author includes the following passage in a section titled "The Fundamental Turning Point in the Course of the Second World War: The International Significance of the Rout of German-Fascist Forces at Stalingrad."

The Battle of Stalingrad was the greatest military-political event of the Second World War. The victory at Stalingrad was the beginning of a fundamental turning point in the course of the Second World War in favor of the USSR and of the entire anti-fascist coalition. The Red Army began an offensive from the banks of the Volga that was completed in the unconditional capitulation of Hitlerite Germany. The defeat of the German Army, which was unprecedented in history, sobered the ruling circles of Japan and prevented it from entering into war with the USSR. It also brought to a halt the calculations by the leaders in Turkey, who formally were neutral, but in fact were helping Germany and were waiting for the fall of Stalingrad to declare an alliance with Germany. The rout of the Hitlerites who had thrown their most important forces into the Soviet-German front, created propitious conditions for an attack by Anglo-American forces in North Africa. (p. 27, italics in the original)

As indicated by passages such as this, the main character in this narrative is the USSR, a point that is further elaborated by statements about the exceptionalism of the suffering and the heroism that characterized Soviet, as opposed to other countries' efforts.

In terms of the events in the plot structure, Soviet accounts of World War II point to the German attack on the USSR as transforming it from a small-scale conflict into the major struggle known as the Great Patriotic War. The narrative then goes on to identify several events that led to the defeat of Germany. The first of these is the successful defense of Moscow in the winter of 1941–42. As noted in the textbook passage quoted, the Battle of Stalingrad is then put forth as *the* major turning point of the entire narrative (of World War II and the Great Patriotic War). From this perspective, Stalingrad was the high point of the German offensive and the beginning of the end for Germany. Indeed, events in the war from this point on, events such as the Battle of the Kursk salient and the advance to Berlin, are presented as part of a march to inevitable victory.

The similarities I have noted between Soviet and post-Soviet accounts of World War II have to do with the events included and the basic plot line of the narrative. While these similarities are striking, their existence should not be taken to suggest that the two versions of World War II are identical. In fact, they are strikingly different in certain respects, but the differences in this case concern the characters involved rather than the plot structure of the narrative. And as in the case of the rewriting of Civil War history, this difference reflects a process of silent dialogic rebuttal of official Soviet accounts.

The most important point to note in this respect is that in Soviet-era textbooks, a Marxist-Leninist theoretical framework was consistently used to define the characters and interpret their motives. Various characters' actions were invariably formulated in terms of class struggle, imperialist designs on socialist states, and so forth. For example, the chapter on World War II in Krivoguz, Pritsker, and Stetskevich (1964) opens with the following words:

Like the First World War, the Second World War grew out of the contradictions of imperialism. The victorious powers of World War I – England, France, and the U.S. – divided the world into spheres of interest and tried not to give up or divide what they had seized. However, in accordance with a law of imperialism, the unequal economic and political development of countries led to a change in the interrelationship of forces in the capitalist world . . . Hence, *the main cause of the Second World War was the aggravation of the contradictions of capitalism, which gave rise to attempts by both imperialist groups* [England, France, the U.S. and Germany, Japan, Italy] *to rule the world.* (p. 118, italics in the original)

In such passages, the actions of characters are viewed as being inevitable outcomes of forces such as "laws of imperialism" having to do with inequalities in economic and political power. The major actors are classes and "collective individuals" (Ahonen, 1992) who operate in accordance with the dictates of class consciousness and other Marxist-Leninist categories. Furthermore, those actors who recognized the nature of these categories and the inevitable outcome of the struggle they entail occupy a superior moral position compared with others. These points surface in passages such as the following from the 1964 textbook:

Throughout the entire war a struggle went on within the antifascist coalition between two lines: the line of the USSR, which persistently strove to attain the fastest defeat of fascist powers and to create conditions for a just and lasting peace, and the line of the U.S. and England, which tried to subordinate the conduct of the war to its own imperialistic interests. (p. 131)

All the Soviet era textbooks I am examining in this analysis came out well after Stalin's death, and hence the tendency I noted in Chapter 3 to literally airbrush him out of the picture was already in effect. Instead of Stalin, the leading character in the entire narrative was now the Communist Party. It was portrayed as the main force that led the efforts of the Red Army and the masses of workers and peasants in the USSR as well as worldwide, and it did all this in a selfless and heroic manner. For example, according to Krivoguz et al. (1964):

The Communist Party played a leading role in the struggle against Fascism during the war years. Not sparing themselves and their lives Communists everywhere were in the first ranks of the fighters for the freedom and independence of all peoples. Despite the fact that the Communist Party underwent terrible persecution, they were able to pursue and realize a program of struggle with the occupiers. Communist Parties in Germany, Italy, Japan, and other countries in the Hitlerite coalition carried forth the struggle under particularly onerous conditions, advancing the goal of defeating their governments. The courage and deeply patriotic behavior of Communists during the hard years of the war evoked the admiration of the working classes. These facts provided clear and convincing evidence that only the Communists were capable of leading the people on a path toward freedom and delivering them from infamy. The authority and influence of the Communist Party quickly grew. (p. 135)

More picturesque and emotionally laden versions of these claims can be found in other Soviet-era history textbooks, especially those for younger readers. For example, some of the same points were made by Golubeva and Gellershtein in their 1984 textbook for fourth graders in a chapter about the Great Patriotic War in the Soviet Union. In a section titled "Everyone to the front! Everyone for victory!" they wrote:

Following the appeal of the Communist Party, all the people rose up in the sacred struggle with the enemy. The Soviet people carried on the Patriotic War against the fascist murderers. The Central Committee of the Communist Party guided all the work for the defense of the country and routing the enemy. A Governmental Committee for Defense was formed with I.V. Stalin as its head.

Millions of Soviet citizens fought the fascists. More than half of all the members of the Communist Party and of the Komsomol went to the front. The members of the Party and the Komsomol served as examples for the soldiers to see in the face of death. The best of the military joined the Party. "I ask to be considered a Communist" said soldiers going on the most dangerous military assignments.

During the war almost 12,000 people received the order Hero of the Soviet Union for their deeds. Of these about 9,000 were members of the Communist Party and the Komsomol. In museums one can see Party and Komsomol cards with bullet holes in them and covered with the blood of heroes who gave their life in battles for the motherland. (p. 178)

A central claim in Soviet accounts of World War II is that the Soviet Union stood largely alone in its struggle with Germany from June of 1941 until mid-1944, when the United States, Great Britain, Canada, and other Allies landed in Normandy. This landing, which is usually called "D-Day" in the United States, Britain, and elsewhere in Western Europe, is discussed under the heading of "opening the second front" in Soviet textbooks. The first point made in these texts is that the USSR had to operate alone and in heroic manner in the absence of others' help between 1941 and 1944. Krivoguz et al. (1964) note:

This struggle [between sides within the antifascist coalition] appeared first of all in the question of a second front in Europe. The creation of a second front would have significantly sped up the defeat of Germany. It was not for nothing that Hitler's forces sought with every effort to avoid a war on two fronts. Only the great certainty that the western powers did not intend offensive action made it possible for the fascists to throw 152 divisions into the Soviet-German front at one time. (p. 131)

As is the case for other events in this narrative, the treatment of the second front in Soviet textbooks is interpreted in terms of Marxist-Leninist theory in which individuals and groups act in accordance with their role in a worldwide class struggle over the direction of imperialism. Hence, Krivoguz et al. write:

Only upon becoming convinced that the Soviet Union, relying on its own strengths and without a second front, would complete victory over Germany, and fearing that the liberation of all Europe by Soviet forces would give peoples the possibility to establish a truly democratic order, the governments of the USA and England decided to open a second front. (p. 138)

Post-Soviet Russian Accounts of World War II: Russian People as Hero in the Triumph-Over-Alien-Forces Narrative Template

As already noted, post-Soviet accounts in Russian history textbooks are organized around the same basic plot and set of events as their Soviet precursors. The unprovoked attack by Germany in 1941, the battles of Moscow, Stalingrad, and the Kursk salient as turning points, the belated opening of the second front, and the victorious march to Berlin are all still included. Furthermore, an upward, triumphal sweep still supplies the sense of an ending that grasps the narrative together, hence continuing to make it an instantiation of the triumph-over-alien-forces narrative template. In contrast to their Soviet precursors, however, post-Soviet accounts of the war provide a quite different picture of the characters and motives involved.

The process of revision and rebuttal in this case follows a different path than what occurred in the case of the Civil War, since the switch in characters and motives is not tied to a fundamental switch in plot. Instead, it is a case of new characters appearing in an existing narrative framework. Specifically, the various peoples of the Soviet Union, especially Russians, are presented as being motivated by sentiments of national patriotism and as rallying around their culture and nation, making it possible to sustain the battle against the German invaders. Instead of the Communist Party, it was the Russian people, the Orthodox Church, and other traditional national and cultural forces that were viewed as leading the effort.

Ostrovskii and Utkin (1995) set the stage for the heroic deeds of Russians, as well as other national groups, by outlining Hitler's "Plan East."

In May of 1940, before the attack on our country, the leadership of fascist Germany set about planning for the subjugation of the people of Eastern Europe. This plan was titled "East." In accordance with this monstrous plan there was to be a liquidation of our country as a unified whole, a general annihilation or expulsion of a significant part of the population. There was a plan to Germanize the Estonians and Latvians, deprive them of their native language and culture. The Lithuanians were to share the fate of Slavic peoples. It was assumed that Germans would populate the liberated lands and after colonization these lands would be included in the great Reich.

In the occupied territories the goal was to exterminate 30 million Russians and 5 to 6 million Jews before the beginning of the expulsion. (p. 286)

As was the case in earlier accounts of the Great Patriotic War, the authors of this 1995 text emphasize the exceptional heroism and suffering of Soviet, especially Russian, people as they acted alone in their struggle against the alien aggressor. For example, in describing the desperate struggle to move from early defeats to the strategic offensive, Ostrovskii and Utkin write about the dark period in the following terms:

The defeats were bitter, and our forces suffered large losses. But the resistance they showed forced the aggressors to recognize that the character of war on the territory of the USSR was different from what they had seen on the Western Front. A week after the beginning of military action the chief of the German general staff, F. Galder, wrote in his diary, " The unyielding resistance of the Russians has forced us to carry out combat using all the rules of our military regulations. In Poland and on the Western Front, we were able to allow ourselves some flexibility and to refrain from following strict military principles: this is no longer admissible." (p. 259)

In outlining these events, the authors of the 1995 textbook repeatedly emphasize that the Red Army and the people were fighting for the motherland – *not* the Communist Party – something that consistently reflects the role of the "invisible speaker" of Soviet narratives in giving rise to the post-Soviet texts. In this connection, Ostrovskii and Utkin go out of their way to note that Stalin himself was quite aware of where the people's loyalties lay.

Already at the beginning of the war, a consolidation of society had emerged, not on the foundation of Communist ideology but on the basis of traditional patriotic values. Having in mind the people and the Party, Stalin admitted to the U.S. ambassador A. Harriman: "Do you think they carry on war for us? No, they carry on war for their mother – Russia." Out of this came a shift in political propaganda to appealing to traditional values. In addition to patriotic values, one would have to appeal to values of home and family and personal faith. Thus began an external "humanization" of the regime that continued under the pressure of the people. (p. 319)

This presentation of the actors' motives goes beyond simply saying that they fought the war out of loyalty to national as opposed to Communist ideology. Ostrovskii and Utkin argue that the actions of Stalin and the Communist Party had in fact been *detrimental* to the war effort, and as a result the Soviet Union, especially the Russians, began their struggle from an unnecessarily enfeebled position.

The fact that an enemy reached the Volga (something that had never happened in Russian history), plus the fact that this enemy was stopped only at the price of enormous sacrifice and losses, point to the historical weaknesses and unsteadiness of the regime. It was only the colossal moral and intellectual potential of the Russian people, their long-suffering and self-sacrificing nature that made it possible to preserve governability. (p. 319)

Indeed, it was only because Stalin and the Communist Party were pushed aside and more stable and competent parties were allowed to take over that a successful war effort could be mounted, according to Ostrovskii and Utkin.

While nominally remaining the infallible leader, Stalin in fact had to turn over almost all the real leadership for the war to military professionals. He also turned over leadership of the economy to professional organizers – economists. What occurred was a spontaneous "professionalization" of the regime. Purely ideological problems were pushed to the background. At the price of massive human and territorial losses, the war succeeded in taking on a protracted character that doomed Germany to defeat. (p. 319)

An interesting point about the post-Soviet accounts of World War II is that they include several new events and characters that create challenges to writers wishing to use the same basic narrative template. These are events and characters that have been officially unearthed or recognized for the first time in the last decade. For example, in their 1995 textbook, Ostrovskii and Utkin mention the Molotov-Ribbentrop Pact, the Soviet execution of Polish officers in the Katyn forest in 1940, and the massive network of Soviet prison camps (the GULAG). Such events would seem to be difficult to incorporate into a narrative in which Russians are first depicted as victims of German aggression and then go on to take on the role of triumphalist heroes. These difficulties are handled in a variety of ways. In some cases, information about a newly documented event (e.g., the Katyn massacre and the Molotov-Ribbentrop Pact) is simply inserted into the text with little apparent relationship to the overall narrative. In other cases, as in comments about the GULAG, the information is used as part of the exceptionalism of Russian suffering and heroism.

In general, the inclusion of "new" information in post-Soviet textbooks raises a set of challenges to emplotment that have not yet been adequately resolved. Specifically, it raises problems for authors as they attempt to employ the same narrative template to grasp events together while at the same time including new events that have little place in it. As a result, it sometimes seems that new information has been dropped into a narrative with little consideration for how or whether it fits into the overall text. All of this suggests that one can expect to see a continuing struggle between the competing demands of (1) including new information from archives, and (2) continuing to use a narrative template organized around Russian exceptionalism and heroism.

Conclusion

The break-up of the Soviet Union provided a context in which one can observe textual resources for collective remembering undergoing massive transformation in very short order. Many readers will be surprised, if not shocked, to see how drastically the new official history differs from the old. Anyone familiar with Soviet-era culture will understand that from that perspective, the new accounts are not just different, they are heretical.

When trying to account for this striking transformation, commentators have often focused on the role of newly available archival information. This is certainly part of the story, but I have argued that another factor has been equally, if not more, important in the process of rewriting official Russian history. Specifically, I have argued that the post-Soviet versions of this history are fundamentally shaped by what Bakhtin (1984) termed "hidden dialogicality." In this first round of producing post-Soviet textual resources, "each present, uttered word responds and reacts with its every fiber to the invisible speaker, points to something outside itself, beyond its own limits, to the unspoken words of the other person" (p. 197). The result of engaging in hidden dialogicality in this case is that the new official history takes the form of a rebuttal to Soviet accounts. The role of narrative is important because it provides the parameters within which the hidden dialogues have occurred.

The dynamics of hidden dialogicality take on a specific form in this context. It is not simply that the new texts respond to the "unspoken words of the other person." They respond in a way consistent with claims about the Manichaean consciousness and binary thinking that has long shaped Russian political and cultural discourse. This pattern means that much in the new texts is aimed at rebutting and standing in opposition to the old ones.

At the same time that radical changes have occurred in the textual resources for collective remembering, an element of continuity has been in evidence. I have argued that this continuity derives from a schematic narrative template – one that I have given the title "triumph-over-alien-forces." Even in a context where the narrative accounts of the past seem to change radically, this underlying narrative template insures a degree of continuity. The characters, events, and even the plot may appear to change in important ways, but the influence of this narrative template is present at a deeper level. As a result, there are certain aspects of the new accounts that do not look all that different from their Soviet precursors.

In my account, I have focused on two major episodes in twentieth-century Russian history: the Civil War of 1918–1920 and World War II. In the case of the Civil War, an important re-emplotment was involved in producing the new texts. The war has now been incorporated into a tragic narrative that starts with the October Revolution. This contrasts sharply with earlier accounts in which the Civil War is set off as a separate narrative that begins with imperialist intervention, has a triumphalist sense of an ending, and follows on the heels of another triumphalist narrative about the Revolution. Even in the context of this major transformation, however, the triumph-over-alien-forces narrative template continued to exert its influence, the result being that the tragic period of the Revolution and Civil War now represent one phase of a larger narrative that ends with the triumph of the Russian people with the end of the Soviet Union.

In the case of World War II, the same basic plot was involved in Soviet and post-Soviet Russian official accounts, but one set of actors and motives has been substituted for another. In this case, the triumph-over-alien-forces narrative template provides a central element of continuity. The process of revision is still very much in progress, however, since there have been a few attempts to include new events such as the Molotov-Ribbentrop Pact in the post-Soviet narrative, but they have not been fully incorporated into the plot structure.

Having mapped out these two paths for producing new official history, we are left with the question of why the account of the Civil War was revised in one way and the history of World War II in another. To speculate on this matter involves going beyond the sorts of textual evidence I have supplied here, and into the realm of the cultural and institutional forces involved in the production of official history. Since I have not presented extensive evidence on these issues, my comments on them must be taken as speculative. It strikes me, however, that one interpretation immediately presents itself.

As Weiner (1996) has noted, the heroic World War II narrative continues to serve as a positive "dominant myth" in many areas of the former Soviet Union. In this respect, it is an episode that stands in contrast to others from Soviet history, especially those having to do with events surrounding the Revolution. Part of this difference is simply a function of the fact that World War II is still part of the autobiographical memory of many people, whereas the Civil War is not. Perhaps more important, however, is the fact that in the new anti-Communist "official culture" (Bodnar, 1992), there is strong resistance, if not outright rejection, of heroic narratives about the origins of the Soviet state. While a small segment of the Russian population might still embrace such narratives, this is a minority position, and certainly not one held by the government. This is not to say that the tendency to transform earlier triumphalist narratives into tragic ones is driven solely by forces of politically expedient presentism. As suggested earlier, new accounts also have the strength of having much more in common with accounts that have emerged in internationally recognized scholarly research.

In contrast, World War II provides one of the few remaining positive historical narratives for contemporary Russians to employ when trying to make sense of their past and present. As Robert Cotrell (2001) notes, Hitler's defeat was "the one event in Russian history which all Russians can agree to have been a great and glorious moment. In May 1945 Russia got it right" (p. 32). As a result, the importance of a World War II narrative has probably grown over the past few years even as narratives about other events such as the October Revolution and the Civil War have been rejected or rewritten as tragedies. The World War II narrative is about one of the defining events in twentieth-century history, an event in which Russia and the Soviet Union clearly played a central, if not *the* central role in stopping a brutal and dangerous enemy. It would be painful and difficult to give up such a narrative as a resource for constructing new national identities in Russia.

The kind of hidden dialogicality between narratives that I have mapped out above has now gone through one round. While the textual transformations of the future may not be so radical as they have been in the past, it will undoubtedly continue. Events occurring in Russia as this book is being written provide a reminder of the difficulty in predicting who the players will be in shaping future accounts of the past. However, it is reasonable to assume that the hidden dialogicality among narratives that has shaped the process up to now will continue to do so in the future.

Appendix A: Soviet and Post-Soviet Russian Secondary School History Textbooks Used in Analyses of the Russian Civil War

I.B. Berkhin & I.A. Fedosov. *Istoriya SSSR. Uchebnik dlya 9 klassa* [History of the USSR. Textbook for the ninth grade]. Edited by Corresponding Member of the USSR Academy of Sciences M.P. Kima. Approved by the Ministry of Education of the USSR. First edition. Moscow: "Prosveshchenie," 1976. Print run = 3,900,000.

Yu.I. Korablëv, I.A. Fedosov, & Yu.S. Borisov. *Istoriya SSSR. Uchebnik dlya desyatogo klassa srednei shkoly* [History of the USSR. Textbook for the tenth grade of middle school]. Edited by Yu.I. Korablëv. Approved by the State Committee of the USSR on People's Education. Moscow: "Prosveshchenie," 1989. Print run = 3,110,000.

L.N. Zharova & I.A. Mishina. *Istoriya otechestva. 1900–1940. Uchebnaya kniga dlya starshikh klassov srednykh uchebnykh savedenii* [History of the fatherland. 1900–1940. Educational book for senior students of middle educational institutions]. Approved by the Ministry of Education of the Russian Federation. Moscow: "Prosveshchenie," 1992. Print run = 1,246,000.

V.P. Ostrovskii & A.I. Utkin. *Istoriya Rossii. XX vek. Uchebnik dlya obshcheobrazovatel'nykh uchebnykh zavedenii* [History of Russia: Twentieth Century. Textbook for general education institutions]. Eleventh grade. Moscow: Izdatel'skii dom "Drofa," 1995. Print run = 300,000.

Appendix B: Soviet and Post-Soviet Russian Secondary School History Textbooks Used in Analyses of World War II

I.M. Krivoguz, D.P. Pritsker, S.M. Stetskevich (1964) *Latest history (1917–1945). Textbook for middle school. 2nd edition.* Moscow: Izdatel'stvo Prosveshchenie. Print run = 700,000.

V.K. Furaeva (1975). *Noveishaya istoria (1939–1974 gg.). Uchebnoe posobie dlya desyatogo klassa srednei shkoly* [Contemporary history (1939–1974). Textbook for tenth grade of middle school]. Under the editorship of V.K. Furaeva. Recommended by the Ministry of Education of the USSR. Sixth edition, corrected and expanded. Moscow: Prosveshchenie, 1975. Print run = 1,400,000.

V.P. Ostrovskii & A.I. Utkin. *Istoriya Rossii. XX vek. Uchebnik dlya obshcheobrazovatel'nykh uchebnykh zavedenii* [History of Russia: Twentieth Century. Textbook for general education institutions]. Eleventh grade. Moscow: Izdatel'skii dom "Drofa," 1995. Print run = 300,000.

A.A. Danilov & L.G. Kosulina (1995) *Istoriya Rossii. XX vek. Uchebnaya kniga dlya 9 klassa obshcheobrazovatel'nykh uchrezhdenii* [History of Russia. XX Century. Textbook for grade 9, general education institutions]. (Recommended by the chief commission for the development of general middle education, Ministry of Education, Russian Federation.) Moscow: Prosveshchenie. Print run = 275,000.

6

The Consumption of Historical Narratives

Up to this point, my focus has been on the production of texts about the past. I have emphasized that what is produced are cultural tools in the form of narrative texts, not collective memory itself. This bears repeating because of the tendency to assume that it is somehow possible to produce collective memory directly. Such an assumption is reflected in analyses that imply that if we know about the narrative texts produced by a collective, we know what people will think, believe, and say. In actuality, even the most exhaustive study of text production cannot tell us whether narratives will be used in the way intended by their producers. Hence, when analyzing textually mediated collective remembering, it is essential to complement studies of the textual production with studies of textual consumption.

This point takes on special importance when considering patterns of textual consumption in settings such as the former Soviet Union. At several points in earlier chapters, I have alluded to the fact that Soviet citizens often did not believe the information they obtained from history textbooks, the media, and other official sources of information about the past. Indeed, people often said they did not believe such information precisely *because* it was produced by the state. All this suggests that it may be quite misguided to assume that one can know what people will believe or say simply on the basis of knowing what textual resources have been made available to them.

I shall approach these issues by invoking notions such as text and narratives as cultural tools introduced in earlier chapters. This means focusing on the dynamics of how speakers employ textual means when speaking and thinking about the past. Such dynamics cannot be understood by focusing on either the agent or textual mediation in isolation. Instead, they involve an "irreducible tension" (Wertsch, 1998) between these two elements of mediated action.

The Bakhtinian notion of text I adopted in Chapter 2 is grounded in this irreducible tension. From this perspective, text involves a structured system of signs such as a sentence or narrative, on the one hand, and the use made of this system of signs by a concrete speaker on a specific occasion, on the other. The first "pole" of the text involves "elements (repeatable) in the system of the language (signs)" (Bakhtin, 1986, p. 105); the second is "unrepeatable," involves "special dialogue relations" with the speaker, and "is revealed only in a particular situation" (ibid.).

A basic question in this kind of textual analysis is, "Who is doing the speaking," and as I have outlined elsewhere (Wertsch, 1991), the Bakhtinian answer is: at least two voices – the speaker's and the textual means being employed. These two voices derive from the unrepeatable and repeatable poles of the text, respectively. From this perspective, Sasha's account of World War II outlined in Chapter 1 presupposes a distributed version of collective memory because he employed the textual means provided by others to create a multivoiced account of these events. The distribution of responsibility may vary from instances in which the speaker takes the primary role and combines linguistic elements to come up with something quite novel and creative to instances in which a speaker simply parrots a widely used text. In the end, however, *all* such cases of collective remembering involve some form of an irreducible tension between agent and cultural tools.

In addition to the level of responsibility attributed to the two poles of an utterance, it is essential to consider other aspects of the relationship between them. It is not only the quantity of contributions from the speaker and textual means that is important, but also the quality of this relationship. Speakers may take many different stances toward textual resources provided to them. They may accept the text wholeheartedly and try to reproduce it without change, they may reject it, they may parody it, and so forth.

Of particular importance for my purposes is whether or not speakers approach a text as authoritative, or even sacred. If so, the text is taken to be something that does not invite modification or commentary from the speaker, and is to be used as is. Conversely, it may be taken to have a "creative function" (Lotman, 1990, p. 13), to be a sort of "generator of new meanings" (Lotman, 1990, p. 13) that emerge when a speaker assumes that he has the liberty to play with it and use it as he wishes.

Bakhtin addressed such issues in connection with the distinction between "authoritative" and "internally persuasive" discourse (1981, pp. 342–348). There he argued that "the authoritative word (religious, political, moral; the word of a father, of adults, of teachers, etc.) . . . demands that we acknowledge it, that we make it our own; it binds us, quite independent of any power it might have to persuade us internally; we encounter it with its authority already fused in it" (1981, p. 342). In such cases, "one must either totally affirm [the authoritative word], or totally reject it" (p. 343). One is not invited to engage in the give and take of dialogue, to "divide it up – agree with one part, accept but not completely another part, reject utterly a third part" (p. 343).

In contrast, internally persuasive discourse does not rest on such hierarchical differentiation of authority. Instead of being put in a position of either totally accepting or rejecting the words of another, the speaker is encouraged to engage in a kind of dialogue with what others say because "the internally persuasive word is half-ours and half-someone else's" (p. 345). In contrast to authoritative discourse, which is characterized by the dogmatism attached to words, one is invited to take the internally persuasive word as a "thinking device" (Lotman, 1988), as a starting point for a response that may incorporate and change what was originally said.

When examining instances of authoritative and internally persuasive discourse, it is useful to take into consideration how they are shaped by stable characteristics of the speaker, on the one hand, and the characteristics of particular speech situations, on the other. The distinction I have in mind is by no means always easy to maintain when examining concrete empirical cases, but it is nonetheless useful as an analytic strategy. In what follows, I shall discuss speaker attributes under the headings of "mastery" and "appropriation," and I shall examine issues having to do with contextual forces under the heading of the "contextual control of narrative texts."

Mastery and Appropriation of Textual Means

In discussions of textual consumption, or reception, that focus on characteristics of the speaker, one frequently encounters the term "internalization." As I have argued elsewhere (Wertsch, 1993), this is a term that tends to raise as many conceptual problems as it resolves, and for this reason I prefer to avoid it. Among other things, it encourages us to gloss over the distinction between "mastery" and "appropriation" (Wertsch, 1998), a distinction that plays an important role in textually mediated collective memory.

The mastery of textual resources concerns knowing how to use them. In the case of historical narratives, for example, mastery is reflected in the ability to recall them at will and to employ them with facility when speaking. But it extends beyond that as well to include skills such as being able to use historical narratives as a foundation for reasoning about the actors and motives behind the events being discussed. The focus on "knowing how" to use a cultural tool at the foundation of mastery involves fewer, and less philosophically questionable, commitments to internal mental representations than accounts that focus on the process of "knowing that" (Ryle, 1949), and it has the added advantage of being compatible with recent trends in cognitive science (Bechtel & Abrahamsen, 1991; Clark, 1997; Wertsch, 1998).

For my purposes here, it is important to comment on a limitation of the notion of mastery as well – that it falls primarily under the heading of cognitive functioning defined in a fairly narrow way. As such, it has little to say about any emotional commitment to the texts involved. To go back to the example outlined in Chapter 3 of using Microsoft Word:mac 2001, I can say that this is a cultural tool I have mastered (at however primitive a level), but purely as an instrumental, cognitive means.

The appropriation of textual resources concerns a different sort of relationship between agent and cultural tool and a different sort of motivation for using a text when speaking. It is a notion that derives from the Russian term *prisvoenie* as used by Bakhtin (1981). Its root and the verb *prisvoit'* are related to the possessive adjective *svoi*, which means "one's own." *Prisvoit'* means bringing something into oneself or making it one's own, and the noun *prisvoenie* means something like the process of making something one's own. This process involves the text's having "personal sense" (Leont'ev, 1981) for its user, as opposed to abstract, distanced "meaning." As such, a text that is appropriated may serve as an identity resource – a means for anchoring or constructing one's sense of who one is.

The opposite of appropriating a cultural tool is resisting it (Wertsch, 1998). Just because someone is exposed to a cultural tool – and just because she has mastered it – does not guarantee that she has appropriated it as an identity resource. Indeed, there are cases in which someone has clearly mastered a cultural tool, yet resists it. For example, Tulviste and Wertsch (1994) have outlined ways in which resistance may arise in connection with official histories produced by modern states. In this case, official Soviet accounts of events in Estonia were actively resisted by many ethnic Estonians, partly through their knowledge of alternative, unofficial histories. What was especially striking is that many of the individuals had thoroughly mastered the official history – in some cases better than any unofficial history – yet they clearly had not appropriated it.

There are several areas of theoretical and empirical study capable of providing insight into what appropriation is and how it can be fostered. Psychological research on identity and motivation are particularly relevant, and in this connection I shall draw on "self-determination theory" as outlined by Edward Deci and his colleagues (Deci, Eghrari, Patrick, & Leone, 1994; Grolnick, Deci, & Ryan, 1997). In their review of studies of familial socialization, Wendy Grolnick et al. (1997) argue that it involves "inner adaptation to social requirements so that children not only comply with these requirements but also accept and endorse the advocated values and behaviors, experiencing them as their own" (p. 135).

The theme of accepting, endorsing, and experiencing values and behaviors as one's own runs throughout the writings on self-determination theory. A perspective grounded in textual mediation differs in what is taken to be accepted, endorsed, and experienced – namely, narrative texts, as opposed to "values" and "behaviors" – but important parallels between the two approaches nonetheless remain. For one, both sorts of analysis can be viewed as being concerned with consumption. Indeed, Grolnick et al. touch on how consumption stands in opposition to production when they note that the "potential contradiction between the forces of socialization that attempt to promote compliance with culturally transmitted behaviors and attitudes, and the children's need to actively assimilate new values and behaviors if they are to accept them as their own" (1997, p. 135).

Self-determination theory can provide some useful insights into the analysis of how textual resources are appropriated. Specifically, it suggests how one might develop a more nuanced account of this process, and hence of textual consumption more generally. Using the term "internalization" to cover what I am calling "appropriation," Grolnick et al. argue:

Internalization . . . concerns the processes by which individuals acquire beliefs, attitudes, or behavioral regulations from external sources and progressively transform those external regulations into personal attributes, values, or regulatory styles... [T]his definition highlights that full or optimal internalization involves not only taking in a value or regulation but also integrating it with one's sense of self – that is, making it one's own – so the resulting behavior will be fully chosen or *self*-regulated. (1997, p. 139)

What is particularly useful in the account provided by Grolnick et al. (1997) is their effort to outline specific types and degrees of internalization. In their view, "internalization is... not an all-or-nothing phenomenon. Rather, it concerns the degree to which an activity initially regulated by external sources is perceived as one's own and is experienced as self-determined" (p. 140). These authors sketch a developmental path beginning with "external regulation," followed by "introjected regulation" and then "regulation through identification," and they argue that the most mature form occurs "when the identification has been *integrated* . . . with other aspects of one's self" (p. 141). In general, then, levels of internalization have to do with:

whether a value or regulation that has been taken in by the person has been fully integrated and thus has what we . . . refer to as an internal (rather than an external) perceived locus of causality. If a behavior is experienced as fully chosen and autonomously undertaken, it would have an internal perceived locus of causality, whereas if it is experienced as pressured or coerced by an internal force, it would have an external perceived locus of causality. In the latter case, the regulatory process would be within the person but would not have been fully integrated. (p. 140)

The line of reasoning outlined by these authors has interesting implications for analyzing the appropriation of textual resources. First, it buttresses the observation that cognitive mastery does not guarantee appropriation or the use of a text as an identity resource. For example, ensuring that students have mastered officially produced history texts through gate-keeping procedures such as examinations does not ensure that they have appropriated these texts. Indeed, as the research of Grolnick et al. suggest, exerting too much pressure in the form of external rewards and threats may encourage individuals to resist fully internalizing – appropriating – a text. The second point to keep in mind in analyses of consumption is that when appropriation *does* occur, it may take different forms and exist at different levels.

From the perspective of a state seeking to "turn out worthy, loyal, and competent members of the total society" (Gellner, 1983, p. 64), the aspiration is to achieve what Grolnick et al. term "regulation through identification" rather than "regulation through introjection." In this view, citizens should experience behaviors such as reciting an official narrative as "fully chosen and autonomously undertaken [with] an internal perceived locus of causality" rather than "pressured or coerced by an internal force [associated with] an external perceived locus of causality" (p. 140).

These desiderata raise two questions. First, how does the state, and its educational system in particular, go about maximizing the chances that regulation through identification, as opposed to regulation through introjection (or even something less) will occur? That is, how can state authorities get citizens not only to employ the "right" cultural tools when speaking and thinking, but experience this behavior as acting in accordance with their own volition rather than in response to external force? Second, how does the state or anyone else really know if they have been successful in their efforts?

It turns out to be extremely difficult to know for certain that someone has fully appropriated a narrative text – that regulation through identification is involved. It is far from clear what constitutes solid evidence for evaluating this. Of course, a fairly crude measure is employed by virtually every modern state – namely, procedures such as examinations on official history. As already noted, however, such procedures may touch on mastery alone and not tell us very much about appropriation. As such, they have inherent limitations.

The Soviet Union, with its totalitarian system, demanded much more than simple mastery in any event. Authorities in that context were not satisfied with whether someone merely knew an official text. What was demanded was that a citizen really believe – appropriate – it. This begs the basic question, however, of what it means to "really believe" a text or how we would recognize a case of such belief if we saw it. Being able to specify whether someone really believes, or has fully appropriated, an official text is no easy task, as many social scientists, as well as state security agencies, know all too well.

Perhaps the first general lesson that has been derived from this experience is that one must be prepared to employ multiple indicators and methods when trying to address issues of appropriation, believing, and so forth. Instead of using a single neat measure that provides direct insight into whether autonomous volition and regulation through identification exist, it is almost always necessary to rely on several indicators to corroborate observations. The second lesson I shall make in this connection goes beyond what self-determination theory usually addresses. I shall argue that appropriation is often not a function of the psychology of the individual. Instead, it is typically also a function of the context in which individuals act. When trying to examine what a people "really believes," it is often the case that it seems to believe one thing in one context and something different, and often contradictory in another. This is an issue I shall take up in more detail next.

Contextual Control of Narrative Texts

Given these points as background, I shall address the issue of how states seek to control the contexts for using official texts under two headings: (1) the control of narrative information, and (2) the control of narrative performance. The distinction I have in mind is not a hard and fast one, but it does provide a way to organize the discussion of several interrelated phenomena.

Before turning to these two headings, it is important to note that the textual resources involved – namely, narratives – introduce an element of control in their own right. The inherent tendency of narratives to "grasp together" settings, events, and characters into a single whole means that they inevitably introduce a coherent perspective – *a particular* perspective – into an account of the past. Furthermore, this is not some kind of neutral cognitive perspective. Instead, it involves what Hayden White (1981) has termed a "moralizing impulse." White (1981b) argues that in contrast to other forms for representing the past such as annals, chronicles, and abstract, scientific description, narrativity inherently introduces "morality or a moralizing impulse" (p. 22). The very fact that events are cast in narrative form means that they must be interpreted in terms such as that of "a story of failure or of success, of plans miscarried or policies overtaken by events, of survivals and transformations" (Mink, 1978, p. 140). As noted by Mink (1981), the efficacy of narrative as a "cognitive instrument" is grounded in this impulse.

[T]he value of narrativity derives from the force of an impulse to moralize events by investing them with a "coherence, integrity, fullness, and closure" that is imaginary – a fiction, though a necessary one which inherits its necessity not from the determinateness of the world but from our inability (however one explains that inability) to contemplate events without redescribing them as connected within a moral order. (Mink, 1981, p. 234)

From this perspective, then, narrative form does not provide a way of grasping together a set of events into some kind of neutral, objective representation. In the very process of invoking an imaginary coherence, integrity, fullness, and closure, narrative also introduces a moral order into the picture.

Claims by figures such as White and Mink about how the moralizing impulse of narrative is an inherent part of historical representation have been criticized by some as overstated. Such critics note that those pursuing research in analytical history have a host of methods and procedures that rein in the bias introduced by narrative form. However, there is little doubt that this moralizing impulse is a major factor in official collective memories such as those produced by Soviet authorities. Indeed, the "moral horizon" (Taylor, 1989) from which such narratives were written was often explicitly touted by state authorities. The result was a form of collective memory that had a powerful tendency to simplify, to see events from a "single committed perspective," and to be "impatient with ambiguities" (Novick, 1999, pp. 3–4).

When addressing issues of the control of narrative information and control of narrative performance, then, part of the picture is that the textual resources employed – narrative texts – have some of the control built right into them. This tendency is enhanced by the fact that such control tends to be transparent in the sense outlined in Chapter 1, and hence difficult to recognize, let alone resist. As White (1981a) notes, "Story forms not only permit us to judge the moral significance of human projects, they also provide the means by which to judge them, even while we pretend to be merely describing them" (p. 253). The narratives used in collective memory, then, appear to be objective in that they efface the presence of the narrator, or in the words of the linguist Emile Benveniste, "The events are chronologically recorded as they appear on the horizon of the story. Here no one speaks. The events seem to tell themselves" (1971, p. 208).

The Control of Narrative Information

I have already addressed certain aspects of how narrative information was controlled in the USSR in my comments about the state production of official accounts of the past. One cannot but be impressed by the fact that during the Soviet period, every school child at a particular grade level in every school across the eleven time zones of the country was studying the same pages of the same textbook on the same day.

What I did not address in my previous comments was the experience of consuming this highly controlled narrative information. It turns out that "control" is once again the operative word, but it is control of a different sort. The control of textual consumption in the Soviet Union involved a constant vigilance and monitoring of one's beliefs and actions, something made all the more difficult by the fact that dogmatic truths about the past changed from time to time. The issues that fall under this heading are complex and wide-ranging, and I make no attempt to address all of them here. Instead, I shall outline a set of issues under the subheadings: (1) control of doubt about official narratives, and (2) control of knowledge from competing narratives.

The two issues arise, at least for some citizens, when living in any state. However, the form they took, and the consequences for engaging in them, were quite different in the Soviet Union than in most other settings, and as such they provided a backdrop against which all other aspects of consumption were organized.

Control of Doubt about Official Narratives

In informal conversation as well as in published memoirs, people who lived in the Soviet Union report a range of reactions to official accounts of the past. There are some who believed these accounts wholeheartedly, and continue to do so even today; there are others who believed them during the Soviet years, and were later deeply disturbed to find out that their belief had been misplaced; and there are still others who report always having doubts. Furthermore, there were important differences among contexts in the kind of doubt people had. For example, it varied depending on the year in Soviet history one considers and depending on one's cultural context (e.g., doubt was more widespread in urban centers than in rural areas). In general, it is clear that by the end of the Soviet period, this doubt had became much more pervasive than in earlier years, and some observers would go so far as to claim that at least in urban centers, *no one* believed anything from the press or other official sources (Boym, 1994).

While claiming that no one believed may be too strong, many people who lived in the Soviet Union clearly did begin to have reservations about the official accounts of the past at some point in their lives. This occurred even during the most ideologically laden periods of Soviet culture, a point that comes through quite clearly in many memoirs and informal reminiscences. Many people who lived through the Soviet years have stories of how distrust began to emerge during childhood or youth and what they did to control it. The control at issue involved using current official accounts of the past as authoritative texts, almost as sacred objects that were to be accepted and used without modification or any indication that one did not believe them. To treat an official account of the past as internally persuasive discourse was to invite sanction in this setting, sanction that could range from disapproval to imprisonment or worse.

One of the major sources of misgivings in this setting was precisely that the official account of the past could suddenly change, with little or no explanation being given for why this happened. As noted in earlier chapters, dogmatic commitment to one – and only one – account of the past is a hallmark of collective memory, as opposed to history. The fact that from time to time this dogmatic truth changed abruptly and without explanation was often profoundly disturbing to people of all ages in the

Soviet Union, but it seems to have had a particularly strong impact on younger people.

The kind of picture I have in mind is reflected in a 1995 interview I conducted with a sixty-four-year-old man ("P.Z.") who had lived all his life in the Soviet Union and had participated in the transition to post-Soviet Russia. Observations about how increasing qualms about official accounts of the past arose as a result of abrupt, unexplained changes in these accounts came up again and again. For example, P.Z. made the following comments about his early school years in a city in Ukraine, where he was a student in a Russian-speaking school. The period he describes was one of the darkest periods of Soviet repression, the years of the "Great Terror."

P.Z.: Of course, an official history existed for me since my childhood, and at the same time almost since childhood there existed a doubt in its veracity. I am speaking of the years even before I was 10 since that is the year [1941] that the war started. We really didn't study history in the first three classes . . . , but my doubts in history began to emerge even then, because when I entered school in 1938, they began a process of executing military officers, including a marshal. And in our textbooks even during the first years of school there were portraits of heroes of the [Russian] Civil War [1918–1920]. Among them there was Tukhachevsky [one of eight generals from the Civil War who were charged with treason, tried in secret, and executed]. They could not change this textbook overnight. Therefore, the teachers told us to strike out these portraits. The students stared in disbelief at the portraits of Tukhachevsky and others. Voroshilov stayed in. Chapaev stayed in. Hence I have this memory from childhood, you understand. To strike out one and not another was something I could not understand. What was going on? I can't say that I showed any surprise because I was too little to participate in that discussion. And then the war started and history began to happen before my very eyes.

J.W.: So who was it again who told you that these were enemies of the people?

P.Z.: It was *the teacher* who told us. Here you have a textbook, here you have portraits. And these people turned out to be enemies of the people. And these others, Voroshilov and others, these are good. (Interview with P.Z., December 17, 1995)

Later in the interview, P.Z. spoke about his experiences in school upon returning to his home city. This was after he had spent three years in Kazakhstan, having been evacuated as a child away from the battle front. The same pattern of sudden, unexplained changes in official narratives about the past emerged again and again, leading to doubt in their veracity.

P.Z.: In [our city] we were lucky to have a nice teacher, M.K. She was an historian and was very pleasant, had a good sense of humor . . . I think she was about 30 years old . . . She was wonderful, sometimes inviting us young students to her home, and so forth. But there was no openness about the idea that there were two histories. . . . In the last year of school, the tenth grade, it was simply necessary to memorize when such and such congresses and meetings of the Party occurred. Before that there had been courses on the middle ages and the modern age, and then there was "The History of the USSR," as it was called. Not "The History of Russia," but "The History of the USSR"... And again the same thing began to show up. The sign [i.e., plus or minus] began to change. The Chechen Shamil in the Chechen war of the last century ... first Shamil was good, then Shamil was bad. First Ivan the Terrible was good and then he became bad. That is, we were already used to the idea that one should not believe this, so to speak official history, but in general it really was not history that they were writing.... The evaluations in official Soviet history, so to speak, changed all the time. Various events were presented in a good light and then in a bad light. We used a single textbook, but they would tell us that the text was old. There was a difference between the textbooks and the lessons we had. The teacher was probably told from someone higher up to evaluate certain events differently.... Thank God, we ... never asked M.K. about our history, but misgivings arose in us about the veracity of the history of the Soviet Union. (Interview with P.Z., December 17, 1995)

The sort of changes this interviewee had experienced reflects the processes of binary thinking outlined in Chapter 5 ("first Shamil was good, then Shamil was bad") and gave rise to a distrust of official history. This distrust from the 1930s and 1940s clearly grew in the Soviet population in subsequent decades. Khrushchev's 1956 "secret speech" to the 20th Party Congress criticizing Stalin was a watershed event for many Soviet citizens. Even those who had earlier believed official accounts became suspicious.

By the end of the Soviet period, there was very widespread doubt about official accounts of the past, something that is apparent from a 1995 survey in which approximately 200 teachers from Russia and Ukraine participated (Wertsch et al., 1997). The most striking finding from this survey was the lack of importance teachers attached to textbooks as sources of information about the past. When asked to rank ten sources (e.g., textbooks, discussion with family, films, novels), the teachers judged textbooks to be *least* important. When asked where they think their students should obtain information about history, teachers again placed textbooks at the bottom of their list. In contrast, they generally placed discussions with adults outside the family and discussions with friends at the top of their list of sources of information about history used by students. These two sources were also ranked at the top of the list of where teachers thought their students should obtain information.

The general picture, then, is one in which the very people charged by the state with promulgating an official account of the past expressed widespread doubt about the official accounts presented in history textbooks. The fact that such a level of doubt prevailed among teachers is striking, and it clearly was likely to have had an impact on the students. This is not to say that such a picture was characteristic of the Soviet period. Indeed, this survey may coincide with the high point of doubt about history instruction, since schools in 1995 were often still using Soviet-era materials even though official accounts had changed quite dramatically.

To say that doubt about official history was widespread during the Soviet years does not mean that it could be openly expressed. State authorities did a great deal to control the expression of doubt, and hence individuals were required to monitor themselves closely in this regard. One of the ways that authorities routinely controlled at least the expression of doubt was to monitor students' performance in courses having to do with official history. Students encountered these courses at several points in elementary and secondary school and again at the university level. A critical report from an instructor or a poor grade in such courses could threaten a student's career, or more, depending on the period in the Soviet epoch.

In the interview with P.Z., he recounted just such a situation in which a poor grade in a course on official history could have serious consequences that could be overridden only with the help of intervention by individuals in whom the state had solid trust.

P.Z.: On the governmental examinations on history in the first and second years of college I received two "3's" [the rough equivalent of a "C" in U.S. colleges]: a 3 in a regular course examination and a 3 on an exam on the Party and government. And for this reason I was not accepted directly into graduate study. They accepted me only after R.L. [a senior professor and Communist Party member] persuaded them by arguing, "Yes, of course he is a bad person, he's a pig and this whole thing is not good. He doesn't know the history of the Party very well. But you know, he is nonetheless a talented young man, so why don't we accept him? Let him start out as a correspondence student and see what happens.

It is important to emphasize that the grade that nearly kept P.Z. from entering graduate study was in a course that had nothing to do with his area of professional specialization – psychology. Instead, the course on the Party and government was taught by custodians of official state ideology (often referred to as "red professors") to students majoring in *any* subject. Among the responsibilities that these custodians had was to ensure to the best of their ability that students not only knew, but believed (i.e., had appropriated), official narrative texts about the past. Their concern with the latter led them to monitor students as they went through their courses and maintain a steadfast ideological vigilance over students in other respects.

Sometimes this quest to ensure the absence of doubt in an individual's mind was pursued in ways that would have been humorous had not serious consequences been attached to them. In his interview, P.Z. commented on one procedure in this connection.

P.Z.: We had a question on an official form that had to be filled out about our past. It asked, "Did you ever vacillate toward the Party line?" It was horrible. You had to ask yourself whether doubt had entered your mind or not and then to sign the form on which you gave your response. Relying on our typical Russian humor, one possible variant was, "I have vacillated but only in accordance with the Party line." And that was the standard situation for very many who vacillated along with the Party line. The Party says one thing today and another thing tomorrow. The Party's delusion was that it never made a mistake. Various people, they may make mistakes – except for Stalin. . . . This was the humorous situation – actually, it wasn't humorous but became second nature.

In the Soviet context, then, the issues of doubt and the control of doubt were inherent aspects of the consumption of official accounts of the past. Of course, the state hoped that students would not only master narrative texts about the past but also appropriate them, even when the one dogmatic, but temporary, truth about the past changed. Misgivings about this truth, however, provided a kind of psychological backdrop against which the consumption of official texts occurred in general. Such misgivings hindered the Soviet state's attempt to create loyal citizens. Instead of experiencing the appropriation of official narratives "as fully chosen and autonomously undertaken, . . . [having] an internal perceived locus of causality" (Grolnick et al., 1997, p. 140), an experience of external coercion was pervasive. In many cases, this experience did not require the immediate presence of a teacher or other Soviet authority. Instead, this role had been taken over by the individual in a form of self-monitoring. In short, it was essential to monitor one's doubts and to ensure that they did not become apparent to others – or even to oneself in some cases. This constituted a form of control over narrative information that was a pervasive part of Soviet life.

Control of Knowledge from Competing Narratives

The second form of control of narrative information I shall examine concerns accounts of the past that might compete or conflict with the official version. This is closely tied to what I have termed the "control of doubt" about the official narrative because such doubt typically arose as a result of encountering these competing accounts. When considering such competing narratives, an important starting point is the socially distributed nature of their production. Despite the fact that doubt and the control of doubt were often very personal issues in the Soviet context, major support for such doubt often came from social groups that sought to discover and produce alternative versions of the past.

The social processes involved typically occurred in private settings outside the gaze of the state, settings such as discussions with family and friends. The importance of such discussions is reflected in the survey results from the teachers reported earlier. The Soviet apartment kitchen was the favored setting for such discourse, the result being that the expression "na kukhne" (in the kitchen) was a shorthand way of referring to the culture of unofficial discourse.

Soviet authorities viewed the possession of alternative, unofficial accounts of the past to be sufficiently dangerous that they went to great lengths to keep them out of the hands of everyone but individuals with special security clearances. For example, many publications were strictly controlled, and many, if not most, libraries had a "spetskhran" (a special collection). The items in this collection were not routinely available even to Party members. Instead, access required special, high-level clearance, and the result was that only a very small circle of readers ever saw them.

As with so many aspects of Soviet society, this feature of life gave rise to political humor. Consider, for example, a Soviet political joke, or "anekdot," that appeared on the streets when the last Soviet leader, Mikhail Gorbachev, came into office. It reports on an imaginary telephone conversation between Gorbachev and his deceased mentor Yuri Andropov after Gorbachev had finally gained access to top-secret documents in the Kremlin safe about the Soviet Union.

Gorbachev: Yuri Vladimirovich! How could you do this to me? I opened the secret safe in the Kremlin and found out what a mess we are in! Heavy industry is in a shambles. Agriculture is about to collapse. The Young Communists are about to rebel. And it turns out that the Party committed many historical crimes that we have always denied. How could you leave me in such a mess!

Andropov [in a suitably distant voice on a special phone line from Soviet heaven]: Misha . . . Misha . . . calm down. We picked you out long ago as intelligent and energetic. You were an outstanding leader in the Komsomol. You've been a great success in the Party – and at such an early age, too! You made such rapid strides in coming up through the system, never failing to take on important new challenges. The Party spotted you at an early age as one of the great stars of the future. You of all people should know that this is something we cannot discuss over the phone.

As was typical of Soviet political jokes, this one pointed to something that was a real, and not very humorous, fact about Soviet society. In this case, it was the importance of not revealing to others in public – and sometimes not even to oneself – that one knows alternative accounts of reality, past as well as present. Even in cases where one did not believe the alternative, merely knowing it could be very dangerous. It was not unusual for the KGB to plant or "find" false documents or publications in an individual's apartment as a pretext for arresting him. Hence the control of knowledge from competing narratives was a constant concern in the consumption of accounts of the past. One had to control very closely what one did know and what one did not know – or *no longer* knew or believed – in order to function effectively in Soviet society.

This did not stop many Soviet citizens from going to great lengths to obtain information about alternative accounts of the past. They routinely read items that were published in the underground press, or "samizdat" (self-published literature), and a whole underground industry was devoted, at least in major urban areas, to reproducing samizdat texts. During the

Soviet years, for example, I saw many texts, some of which were hundreds of pages long, that had been manually retyped in triplicate and distributed clandestinely from one reader to another.

When discussing the emergence of his youthful doubts about official history in his interview, P.Z. relayed the following incident.

P.Z.: [When we were in the last years of our schooling in the 1940s] we experienced a growing doubt that the Soviet Union – and this is very interesting – was following the path that had been laid out by Lenin. A small group emerged – about five, at most six – guys from our class. I can remember almost all their names.

We got together in a park or at my home or at the place of someone else who had a big apartment in Kharkiv. And we decided that we had to go back, as it were, to original sources, to Lenin's works. And we had to look at the Stalinist edition [of Lenin's collected writings]. I don't know how we got this idea into our heads ... In actuality, Lenin's works had also been edited. And we decided that we ourselves had to start studying the underlying history of the Soviet period and look into whether it really was the case that Stalin was leading our country in the direction laid out by Lenin.

One of my father's colleagues in western Ukraine had been given a well-preserved library. It was forbidden [to have it]. It was dangerous. But the library had the works of Bukharin [a leading Party theorist who fell out of favor and was executed in 1938] and many publications that were forbidden. This was in 1948. And I began to look at these materials. There was Bukharin's volume *Historical Materialism*, and we read all of his works in order. I did this with the other guys by meeting in secret.

We didn't know how lucky we were that we didn't get a knock on the door, that typical Russian practice of the NKVD or KGB, because a few years ago there was a story in a magazine about a participant in a similar story in Voronezh. He had become a writer and had been imprisoned for ten years. There was a similar group of curious young people who got together, and when word got out, all of them were imprisoned. They spent ten years in prison. They were the same age as I was when we had our club, sixteen or seventeen years of age.... I think this was typical for many towns. It probably happened all over the place. And then for some reason it occurred to us that we should stop our activities.

I kept up contact with the members of our group, but I left for Moscow in [the late 1940s] for good. We had written a set of statutes for the organization. The general issue was quite simple, namely: Can we once again move forward along a Leninist path? It's hard to understand, but it never entered our heads that maybe Lenin was mistaken. And so what took place was not really a responsible sort of action. And then I went to Moscow and arrived here, and it is very interesting that over the course of many years when we have met, not a single person on a single occasion has ever reminisced about this passion we had. It has been many years. After five years Stalin died and we met during the 1950s and during the 1960s. One member of the group became a professor of mathematics and worked in [another city] and visited me in Moscow. We all remembered, but no one ever broached this in a discussion. What had been was past. No one judged it. It all passed by. No one was arrested, thank God.

J.W.: And why did no one ever discuss this?

P.Z.: You know, I am a sociable person and I could have brought it up myself, but I thought that they were not bringing it up and I would not bring it up. Try to understand, in the world of real politics this organization was stupid. We already understood that it was ... simply impossible. It was a naïve idea that we understood and could somehow go explain this to someone, to the people. But thank God we never approached a single worker or peasant [to enlist them in their cause of showing that the Soviet government was not following the true Leninist line].... We understood that we were only a few people and we met only infrequently. It's interesting that our little society was strictly limited ... Ours was a boys' school and there was a girls' school, and we often met the girls, but not a word was ever said to them about it. (Interview with P.Z., December 17, 1995)

A point that comes through in this episode is the importance of social processes that occurred outside the gaze of Soviet authorities. It is true that during the Soviet period, some individuals operating in isolation also created alternative narratives about the past, but almost all the cases described to me over the past quarter century involved a group. One outcome of this group process, however, was that the individuals involved were equipped – or saddled – with information from competing narratives about the past, and this outcome required close monitoring and control on the part of the individual.

The Control of Narrative Performance

In my analysis of the control of narrative information, I have focused on the information itself and said relatively little about when and where it was used. Even in the account I provided, however, I touched on the issue of how this information could and could not be used when participating in various contexts. In what follows, I shall address these contextual forces in more detail, invoking notions of "performance" and "performance region" to do so. From this perspective, the Soviet state sought to control more than just narrative information about the past. It also sought to control the performance regions in which this information could appear.

I begin with an illustration taken from the Soviet era. In 1954, the second edition of a Soviet primer for first-grade students appeared. Like all primers produced by Soviet authorities at the time, this one reflected the perspective of the state – specifically, the State Text-Pedagogical Publishing House of the Ministry of Education for the Russian Federation. This ninety-six-page book was composed almost entirely of introductory penmanship exercises and short readings. At the beginning and end, however, the book contained heavy-handed political messages. On pages 94 and 95, for example, readers encountered portraits of Lenin and Stalin identical to the ones that were hanging in virtually all Soviet school classrooms at the time. The texts that went along with these portraits differed, both in form and content, from the relatively apolitical ones about cute animals, loving mothers, and so forth that had populated the earlier pages, but they nonetheless were written with young students in mind.

The text about Lenin read as follows:

Vladimir Il'ich Lenin – leader, teacher, and friend of all working people. Lenin created the Communist Party. Under the leadership of Lenin our people established Soviet power, the power of workers and peasants.

Lenin desired that all who work would live well. Lenin loved children. He wanted all children to study.

Lenin bequeathed to us the possibility to live peacefully, work honestly, and to guard Soviet power. Lenin died, but his work lives.

The Communist Party is firmly leading the people in accordance with the Leninist path.

In striking contrast to this hagiographical official depiction of Lenin, the following political joke was making the rounds in the Soviet Union during the very same years that children were using this primer:

Dzerzhinskii [the founder of the first Soviet secret police] calls Lenin and asks, "Vladimir Il'ich [Lenin], when should we carry out our executions – before or after dinner?"

Lenin replies, "Before dinner, absolutely! And then give their dinner to the children – the children of the workers are starving!"

The stark contrast between these two views of Lenin raises the question as to which one reflected the "real" collective memory. Did Soviet citizens remember Lenin as a kind teacher and leader who cared about children, or did they remember him as a brutal executioner driven by ideological fervor? As already suggested in the discussion of the control of narrative information, formulating the issue in terms of such either/or oppositions may not be useful when trying to understand textually mediated collective memory in the Soviet context. In fact, many Soviet citizens were familiar with *both* accounts of the past.

As already noted, however, this did not mean that citizens could display knowledge of both accounts in any context. One could endanger one's career prospects – if not more – by reciting an anecdote in the wrong context, and invoking a hagiographical version in private discussions "in the kitchen" could make one the object of unending derision. What this suggests is that we must go beyond understanding memory in terms of how an individual or group possesses information in some static, decontextualized way.

When explicitly confronted with the question of whether memory is a sort of possession, many of us would say no, denying at least a strong form of such a view. No one should doubt, however, the power of the metaphors of possession that lurk behind expressions such as "having a memory" or "losing a memory." Such metaphors shape the way we think and speak about this topic in fundamental ways. As a result, even if one recognizes the dynamism and contextual specificity of the relationship between agents and narrative texts, there is a natural tendency to slip back into assuming that collective memory remains relatively constant across contexts. Hence one finds discussions of the "Soviet memory of World War II," the "American memory of Vietnam," and so forth, discussions that proceed as if these were static possessions. What I shall emphasize in what follows is how memory may vary as a function of context.

The line of reasoning I am pursuing may be viewed as an extension of ideas outlined by Bartlett (1932). Bartlett sought to avoid the pitfalls of taking memory to be a static object or attribute by focusing on remember*ing* rather than memory and by emphasizing that the former is a process involving the effort after meaning. Contemporary psychological studies of individual memory have taken this dictum to heart in a variety of ways, and a basic thrust of this research is that the effort after meaning is often capable of shaping, and even "distorting" (Schacter, 1995) representations of the past.

I wish to extend this line of reasoning by arguing that the effort after meaning often varies in a systematic way with the specific context in which remembering occurs. The starting point for this is the recognition that remembering is usually part of a more complex set of ongoing activities. Laboratory research in psychology typically tries to limit this complexity by controlling the context. Specifically, it focuses on how individuals function in contexts defined by, and limited to, the task of remembering.

The notion of performance I shall be using approaches things from a somewhat different perspective. Instead of focusing on remembering for remembering's sake, I shall be examining it as part of a complex context involving multiple activities. This is a point that has been emphasized by analysts such as Middleton and Edwards (1990a) and one that informs the analysis to follow of collective remembering in the Soviet era.

I approach the issue of how remembering is shaped by context from the perspective of notions derived largely from the writings of Erving Goffman (1959, 1974) and Richard Bauman (1986). From this perspective, human activities such as remembering and speaking about the past are shaped as much, if not more, by the complexities of the performance of which they are a part as by the attributes of the individuals involved. The context in which remembering occurs is heavily shaped by the efforts of performers to engage in "impression management" and the "presentation of self" (Goffman, 1959). This means that a memory performance may reflect the desire to present oneself in, say, a desirable light as much as the need to arrive at an accurate account of the past. Hence, context or situation is not viewed as a stimulus that simply switches memory on or off. Instead, it is viewed as supplying a dynamic force of its own that fundamentally shapes representations of the past.

Goffman (1964) discussed these issues under the heading of "the neglected situation." According to him, "social situations ... constitute a reality *sui generis* ... and therefore need and warrant analysis in their own right, much like that accorded other basic forms of social organization" (p. 134). He specifically contrasted this approach with analyses that take as their focus macrosociological variables, on the one hand, or the individual, on the other. With regard to the former, he argued that "it is not the attributes of social structure that are here considered, such as age and sex, but rather the value placed on these attributes as they are acknowledged in the situation and at hand" (p. 134). With regard to the latter, he went to great pains throughout his writings to show how human action is fundamentally shaped by contextual forces as opposed to attributes of the individual.

The notion of "regions" that Goffman outlined is central to how social situations operate. Regions are performance spaces that are bounded by time, space, and perceptual access. Goffman divided the space in which a performance is carried out into a "front region" and a "back region." The former is "the place where the performance is given" (p. 107), where the performer tries to "give the appearance that his activity in the region maintains and embodies certain standards" (p. 107). In this setting, "some aspects of the activity are expressively accentuated and other aspects, which might discredit the fostered impression, are suppressed" (p. 111). In accordance with his dramaturgical analysis, Goffman viewed performances in the front region as akin to performances on stage.

In contrast, a back region, or "backstage," is "where the impression fostered by the performance is knowingly contradicted as a matter of course" (p. 112). It is in this region that "the performer can relax; he can drop his front, forgo speaking his lines, and step out of character" (p. 112). As an example of how these performance regions differ, Goffman recounted what may happen when a waiter at a fashionable restaurant goes from the dining room to the kitchen. Upon passing through the door, the performer's comments, speech style, and demeanor may change from that of the attentive, respectful waiter to the informal, disrespectful complainer (e.g., "Sir, is there anything else I can get for you now?" vs. "That jerk at table 3 is drivin' me crazy!").

Goffman provided the following general characterization of these differences:

The backstage language consists of reciprocal first-naming, co-operative decision-making, profanity, open sexual remarks, elaborate griping, smoking, rough informal dress, "sloppy" sitting and standing posture, use of dialect or sub-standard speech.... The frontstage behavior language can be taken as the absence (and in some sense the opposite) of this. In general, then, backstage conduct is one which allows minor acts which might easily be taken as symbolic of intimacy and disrespect for others present and for the region, while front region conduct is one which disallows such potentially offensive behavior. (p. 128)

The performances analyzed by Goffman are typically carried out not by isolated individuals, but in "teams." It is usually a group, or team, that is concerned with impression management, performance, and the use of backstage and frontstage language. Part of the dynamics of such teams is that "one over-all objective ... is to sustain the definition of the situation that its performance fosters" (p. 141); a team tries to avoid revealing any "destructive information" (p. 141) that would call its performance into question. The result is that "a basic problem for many performances is that of information control; the audience must not acquire destructive information about the situation that is being defined for them. In other words, a team must be able to keep its secrets and have its secrets kept" (p. 141).

Public and Private Spheres of Discourse in Soviet Life

Goffman's claims about presentation of self, impression management, regions, and secrets have implications for collective remembering in any setting, but their implications are particularly striking in the Soviet context, where the distinction between the public and private spheres of discourse and memory was particularly stark. In the analyses that follow, I focus on how the public sphere served as a front region of performance and the private sphere served as a back region. With its totalitarian aspirations the Soviet state actually strove to make all aspects of its citizens' life transpire in the glare of public scrutiny. While it may never have succeeded to the degree envisioned in the novel *Nineteen Eighty-Four*, George Orwell's account does come to mind when trying to describe everyday life in that context. What this means is that the distinction between the public and private spheres, and indeed the very existence of the latter, were loaded issues. In an important sense, loyal Soviet citizens were not expected to *have* a private life. Instead, every aspect of life was supposed to be carried out in the public sphere.

The aspiration of the Soviet state to see and control all aspects of life has been noted for decades. In an essay published in 1927, Walter Benjamin observed "Bolshevism has abolished private life" (1978). As Boym (1994) notes, Benjamin "believed the Soviet regime meant to eliminate private life along with private property. For the Bolsheviks 'private' was politically dangerous and deprived of social meaning" (p. 73). In tracing the historical roots of this negative view of private life in Russia, Boym points to origins well before the appearance of Bolshevism, among other things noting, "there is no Russian word for privacy" (p. 26). Hence the Soviet attitude toward private discourse and memory seems to have drawn on something already well in place.

Despite the Bolshevik effort to do away with the private sphere, it appears that Soviet society always managed to harbor forms of private resistance. This resistance gave rise to the creation of alternative performance regions, or backstages, for discourse and memory. During the darkest periods of Soviet life such as the late 1930s, these tendencies were minimized – either through revolutionary fervor or state terror. They were also minimized during World War II and certain periods of the Cold War era.

Writing of the "everyday Stalinism" characteristic of the 1930s in the USSR, Fitzpatrick observes that "For *Homo Sovieticus*, the state was a central and ubiquitous presence ... a tireless regulator of life" (1999, p. 3). Authorities in schools and the workplace sought to monitor citizens' activities, but the most obvious and threatening agents of the state in this connection were the police. They zealously tried to control private spheres of discourse and memory.

Suspecting that citizens were unlikely to say what they really thought in public, the authorities – in particular, the NKVD – sought to extend their surveillance to citizens' "off-the-record" discussions, those that were outside the range of state surveillance. That meant attempting to monitor not only conversations in private homes and private correspondence, but also anonymous and subversive public communications like jokes, songs, rumors, verbal outbursts against the regime, and abusive letters to the authorities. (p. 183)

The rise of the private sphere and the accompanying backstage performances were nowhere more evident than in the operation of collective memory. By the 1960s and 1970s, Soviet citizens went to great lengths to maintain an ideologically acceptable presentation of self in public performances of commemoration, but the divergence between this and the private sphere was growing. In the period following Khrushchev's fall in 1964, Soviet authorities recognized this and worked even harder at creating official collective memory, especially of World War II (more specifically, the Great Patriotic War). However, these increasingly heavy-handed efforts only seemed to yield poorer and poorer results. According to Tumarkin (1994), "The fortieth [anniversary of the end of World War II in 1985] had marked the climax of the Great Patriotic War cult; at the forty-fifth, the cult was manifestly finished as an institution" (p. 190).

Tumarkin also notes that the "desacralization" of the public collective memory was largely a response to the heavy-handedness of Soviet authorities in their attempts to create a collective memory that would serve their current purposes. Precisely as suggested by self-determination theory, overly coercive efforts at socialization can result in resistance, rather than the internalization or appropriation of official texts. By 1990, this process of desacralization had given rise to a context in which acts of resistance to the official culture were no longer restricted to backstage performances. Coercing children to participate in official sacred rituals about the Great Patriotic War seemed to result only in further acts of resistance. As a Soviet teacher asked, "What on earth do you think was going on in their souls during those times? Those endless, monofaceted 'patriotic' games for show, the contests for composition of patriotic songs, poems, posters...?" (Tumarkin, 1994, p. 25).

In short, teachers and other representatives of the state were no longer able to get young people to perform appropriately in the public sphere. Instead of succeeding in getting students to remember, or even re-experience the past through authentic engagement with ritual and narrative texts, they encountered increasing resistance when it came to commemorative activities. Among other things, this was manifested in the fact that what had formerly been restricted to the backstage was now making its appearance in the front region.

Public and Private Performance, Double Consciousness, and Internal Emigration

In my discussion of the contextual control of narrative texts – especially narrative performance and the public and private spheres of memory – I have emphasized how the notion of performance, rather than psychological make-up, provides an appropriate analytic framework. Instead of focusing on attributes of individuals that are assumed to exist across contexts, my emphasis has been on how speaking and remembering varies, sometimes radically, across performance regions. Instead of talking about what people "really" believe, as if this can be assessed regardless of context, the focus has been on what they say or think in specific settings. This is not to say, however, that psychological and contextual analyses are unrelated.

One of the ways that some very concrete links can be made between the two has to do with the impact on the individual of repeated participation in certain performance regions. The radical divide separating public from private discourse in the Soviet setting provides a natural laboratory for exploring this issue. Of course, some sort of division between public and private performance exists in any sociocultural context, but it took on a specific form and had specific consequences in the Soviet context. This division changed over the history of the USSR, but a stark, rigid version was always more or less in place, and the failure to respect it – especially the failure to appreciate the need not to reveal private thoughts and memories in public – could have dire consequences.

The importance of this division, and the impact it had on individuals who lived in the Soviet context, were so great that an extensive discussion has grown up around them. This can be traced back several decades, even to the 1920s. For example, it is reflected in the image Boris Paternak presents of one of his characters from that period in *Doctor Zhivago*. In that novel, Pasternak wrote about a psychological affliction that he saw emerging in the aftermath of the Russian Revolution and Civil War. This was an affliction that grew out of the constant effort by the state to exert control over people's private thoughts and words.

It was the disease, the revolutionary madness of the age, that at heart everyone was different from his outward appearance and his words. No one had a clear conscience. Everyone could justifiably feel that he was guilty, that he was a secret criminal, and undetected impostor. The slightest pretext was enough to launch the imagination on an orgy of self-torture. Carried away by their fantasy, people accused themselves falsely not only out of terror but out of a morbidly destructive impulse, of their own will, in a state of metaphysical trance, in a passion for self-condemnation which cannot be checked once you give it its head.

As an important military leader who had often presided at military courts, Strelnikov must have heard and read any number of confessions and depositions by condemned men. Now he was himself swayed by the impulse to unmask himself, to reappraise his whole life, to draw up a balance sheet, while monstrously distorting everything in his feverish excitement. (Pasternak, 1981, p. 459)

This depiction of an individual's struggle to maintain the division between public and private life is striking in at least two respects. First, this struggle was not viewed as normal. It was instead pathological, involving a "disease," a "revolutionary madness." Second, it was a source of self-doubt and shame ("No one had a clear conscience"). People generally knew that they had few opportunities – perhaps only one – to let any dangerous private thoughts or memories slip into public discourse, and the constant vigilance required to maintain their façade involved ethical, as well as cognitive, issues.

Pasternak's observations about psychological processes and pathologies must be understood in terms of a context in which Soviet authorities were constantly searching for hidden enemies within the state and within the individual. These activities can be taken as a reflection of the power of the triumph-over-alien-forces narrative template (Chapter 5) to shape understanding and action. In this connection, consider the scathing critique of the magazines *Star* and *Leningrad* written in 1946 by Andrei Zhdanov, one of Stalin's protégés. In this piece, Zhdanov spoke of people who were Soviet citizens, but were nonetheless "aliens" in Soviet society. He applied this term specifically to the poet Anna Akhmatova and the satirist Mikhail Zoshchenko, two figures who in his view had infiltrated into the heart of the body politic. According to Zhdanov, Akhmatova and Zoshchenko were dangerous enemies of the state, and as such should no longer be allowed to walk the streets freely. Observers such as Radzinsky (1996) have argued that in this particular case the decree was really a reflection of Stalin's petty jealousy over the popularity of Akhmatova and Zoshchenko, but the fact that textual resources involving alien forces were so readily at hand made it possible for Zhdanov to formulate issues in this way and to obtain widespread acceptance of his interpretation. In this context, the implications of Zhdanov's pronouncement were quite ominous.

It is in trying to explain such episodes in Soviet life that "native speakers" of that culture are likely to invoke the notion of "internal emigration." This term seems to have been in circulation before Zhdanov's 1946 decree, but it probably took on a somewhat different and more forbidding tone afterwards. It referred to a process whereby individuals created an inner existence that stood apart from their public life. Internal immigrants were distinguished from dissidents in that they did not vent their opinions in the public sphere, but in many cases their feelings of alienation, outrage, and shame were as pronounced as those of people who made them known openly.

During the last two or three decades of the Soviet Union's existence, "internal emigration" was a term whose meaning was well known among certain segments of the population. In particular, the intelligentsia used it and could provide definitions and illustrations of it on demand. This does not mean that the phenomenon, or even the term, could be openly discussed. Far from it. One indication of its private nature is that it was part of the oral, rather than written, tradition of the USSR. When asked, for example, whether the term is "internal immigration" or "internal emigration" (terms whose pronunciations are identical in Russian), former Soviet citizens often express uncertainty over the matter.

Precisely because internal emigration was a cultural notion that could not be written about or discussed openly in Soviet society – and certainly could not be the object of an official research program – there is little concrete information about how widespread its understanding and use were among the population. Many observers believe that the notion was not widely used among working people in cities or peasants in rural areas. Furthermore, the term seems to have taken on different meanings depending on what one was emigrating *from*. For example, Estonians and other non-Russian ethnic groups who had been forcibly incorporated into the Soviet Union as a result of the Molotov-Ribbentrop Pact often spoke of internal emigration as a way to escape a Russian public sphere, whereas Russians spoke of it as a way to avoid the public sphere of the Soviet state.

In the post-Soviet era, it became possible to discuss and investigate internal emigration in a way that would earlier have been inconceivable. While people may no longer experience this phenomenon, they certainly can remember and talk about it. With this in mind, I collaborated on a study with Olena Ivanova of the Department of Psychology at Kharkiv National University in Ukraine to analyze internal emigration. Specifically, we collected and analyzed a set of interviews to identify the basic dimensions of the meaning of this term and how it was manifested during the Soviet era.

Ivanova carried out open-ended interviews on the subject of internal emigration in the summer of 1998 with ten individuals from Kharkiv, a large city in the Russian-speaking region of Ukraine. The interviewees ranged from 22 to 80 years of age, and all were, or had been, employed in intellectual professions. Ivanova, who personally knew all the interviewees, invited them to participate in the study. We chose this means for selecting participants since internal emigration is still a sensitive and highly personal topic, and interviewees are unlikely to be willing to discuss it with someone they do not know or trust. The interviews were conducted in Russian, the native language of all the participants, but all of them knew Ukrainian as well.

All the interviewees were familiar with the term "internal emigration" and were quite prepared to comment on it. Indeed, over half of them spontaneously provided some sort of definition. For example, Interviewee A explained, "Internal emigration is a separation of oneself from the social environment and feeling like an alien [in that environment]," and B said, "Internal emigrants are people who could not leave [the country] for some reason and who did not agree with the regime. And they did not manifest their disagreement openly." Other interviewees made additional comments that provide further insight into the meaning of internal emigration in this context. For example, Interviewee C stated, "It is estrangement from all the ideology of society," D said "I had my own world which felt the external world as something hostile," and E stated, "I never felt myself a part of society."

At first glance, it might appear that self-reports such as these could be found wherever alienation exists in the modern world – that is, just about everywhere. From this perspective, there is nothing unique about what was called internal emigration in the Soviet Union. There are several reasons for questioning this facile conclusion, however, and I shall explore these in terms of a few basic themes. The first of these is that internal emigration in the Soviet case was not a response to just any cultural or societal force. Instead, it was a form of resistance to a totalitarian state. The Soviet state sought to politicize all aspects of life, thus leaving individuals with little or no space for private, and possibly oppositional, opinion. Even in cases where ethnic issues were raised (e.g., anti-Semitism), they were viewed as operating through the actions of a state that sought to demand total loyalty and have total control over every aspect of people's lives.

The second theme I shall touch on has to do with the fear associated with internal emigration, a point noted by Pasternak when he wrote of the terror associated with the "revolutionary madness" of the 1920s. Most of the interviewees in our study recognized or spoke about this fear as being deep and long-lasting. It was described as being so powerful and constant that many people seemed never to lose it entirely, and some even mentioned that it is re-experienced as flashbacks in the post-Soviet era.

Re-experiencing of the sort associated with trauma (see Chapter 3), as opposed to simple remembering, seemed to be common.

And third, internal emigration was associated with a particular set of behaviors in the public and private spheres. Acting both individually and in groups, people in this context struggled to create means for resisting the Soviet state's totalitarianism. I turn to each of these three themes next.

Internal Emigration from a Totalitarian State

The role of the Soviet state in fostering internal emigration was clearly reflected in the interviewees' responses to a question about when they began to experience it. In answering this question, all the interviewees mentioned political events in the public sphere of the state or something closely associated with such events. The representation of these events and the impact they had on the interviewees fell into two general categories.

Some interviewees spoke about the onset of their internal emigration by associating it directly with incidents in Soviet public life. For example, Interviewee A mentioned the murder of Kirov (the Communist Party boss of Leningrad) in 1934 and C mentioned the struggle against "cosmopolitanism" (often taken as a code word for Jews) in the late 1940s. Other political events identified as giving rise to internal emigration were the 1956 Communist Party Congress in which Khrushchev denounced the "cult of personality" surrounding Stalin, the Daniel' and Sin'yavsky trial of 1965, and the Soviet invasion of Czechoslovakia in 1968.

A second way that interviewees talked about the onset of internal emigration involved a more personal perspective. In these cases, internal emigration was still tied to political events in the Soviet public sphere, but it was presented in terms of events that had a direct impact on one's private life. In particular, interviewees talked about events that had ominous implications for themselves and their families. Interviewee D said, "I remember two black suitcases with clothes and canned food sitting at home. My parents were waiting to be arrested . . . When I asked about the suitcases, Dad answered, 'We can be arrested,'" and Interviewee E stated, "During all of 1952 my parents were trembling with fear waiting for Jews to be evicted. My mother is a Jew and my father is Russian. Father was preparing to go with Mother."

In other cases, internal emigration was reported as stemming from a rare but very powerful comment made about political affairs by a trusted other. For example, Interviewee F said, "In 1949 my father and I watched the movie 'The Fall of Berlin.' There is a sequence in which Stalin says to Zhukov, 'It's time to finish the war.' And father said very quietly, 'Oh, at last!' And I heard sarcasm (toward Stalin) in his tone of voice. I was astonished and asked him about this, but he did not answer."

In general, all the interviewees traced the onset of their internal emigration, either directly or indirectly, to events in the political life of the Soviet state. The background for all these events is that they occurred in a state that aspired to have a total – and total*izing* – presence in people's lives, one that would leave no room for a private sphere.

The private sphere involved in internal emigration was not restricted to individual mental processes. It often emerged in the social context of small groups of trusted friends as well. On both the individual and social planes, however, operating in the private sphere was often difficult and sometimes dangerous, and it always involved resisting pressures from the state seeking to encroach upon it.

The Fear Associated with Internal Emigration

A second theme that ran throughout the interviewees' responses was fear. In general, memoirs and other reports of life in the Soviet Union mention the ubiquitous terror in that setting, so it was no surprise to see it emerge as a theme in reflections on internal emigration. One of the ways this fear was manifested was in the decision not to become a dissident, a decision that was often accompanied by the onset of internal emigration. Not becoming a dissident was dissatisfying to many, but it allowed individuals to engage in some form of opposition to the state without encountering unacceptably high levels of risk to their personal safety, or more poignantly, the safety of their children or other family members. A related reason for pursuing this less dangerous path was the widespread opinion that overt dissent would not in fact influence the Soviet state.

Nor surprisingly, reports of the role of fear in internal emigration were particularly prevalent among interviewees who had lived through the events of the 1930s such as the forced collectivization of agriculture, the mass starvation in Ukraine, and the major purges of intellectuals that hit its full stride a few years later. During these events, it was common practice for the NKVD (a forerunner of the KGB) to force people to denounce their relatives and friends as enemies of the state when those relatives or friends were arrested. For example, a 79-year-old interviewee reported, "My friend's cousin was imprisoned, and my friend had to denounce him at a large gathering at the University (we studied at the University at that time)...I heard the whole process. It was disgusting and terrible."

In addition to using, or threatening to use, force to coerce people to denounce others after they had been arrested, it was not uncommon to make arrests on the basis of denunciations provided by people who were willing, or had been forced, to provide them. In many cases, these were concerned with a failure to control narrative information or narrative performance, and hence with official collective memory. Many people lived in constant fear of being accused of saying, or even thinking, something outside the confines of official history or of participating in other crimes against the state. The kind of psychological pressure and fear associated with being the victim of such denunciations can be sensed from the following account provided by Interviewee G:

It was in 1937 or 1938. I had a friend who was arrested on the basis of a denunciation. It was a closed trial, but was overtly conducted in accordance with formal procedure. I was a witness for the defense. After being questioned, I stayed in the courtroom and heard the questioning of the three people who had written the denunciations.

The first denouncer lied by saying that while he was on a tram together with my friend, the latter saw a portrait of Comrade Stalin and shook his fist at it.

The second person making a denunciation stated, "Everyone was sent to a collective farm to work. I was ill and could not go. When I asked him (the accused) how the work had been going there, he smiled in such a way that it was clear that he did not approve of collective farms."

The third witness providing a denunciation said, "He behaved as if he were smarter than others, so it became obvious that he was an enemy."

These comments provide a striking reminder of the absence of private performance regions in the Soviet context.

The same interviewee reported another event that gave rise to the fear he associates with internal emigration: "December 1, 1934, was the day of Kirov's murder. A meeting took place at the University. Someone was shouting, 'There are enemies among you!' I became terrified. I wanted to go somewhere far away from all this." When speaking about the impressions caused by the arrest of various people, especially the old Communists, an interviewee of about the same age stated, "All this stirred up fear first of all. The fear that these events can somehow touch you and your family."

As already noted, some interviewees reported that this fear did not disappear once the objective conditions for it no longer existed. In this connection, Interviewee H reported:

The fear remains with me, it has not gone away, even now. This state [i.e., Ukraine] is so unpredictable that nobody knows what will come into the heads of its leaders. There is no law, no assurance that it cannot happen again. There is no stability. Anything could happen anywhere. When there was a coup in 1991, I thought that everything would turn back. Everything changes, but the KGB never changes.

Reflections on the origins and nature of fear differ, depending on the interviewee's generation. For example, interviewees who had been born just before or after World War II describe their feelings and the origins of these feelings in ways that differ from older ones – namely, it seems to be fear that is sensed or transmitted through others such as parents who had initially discerned a threat. In this connection, J reported:

I remember an atmosphere of fear very well. When a friend of our family was imprisoned at the beginning of the 1950s, my mother cut out the page he had inscribed in a magnificent book about Peter the First that he had given to us.

My mother's first husband suffered in 1937. Mother survived and escaped from Kiev to Kharkiv. But fear remained with her all her life.

In her study of death and memory in twentieth century Russia, Catherine Merridale (2000) has made similar points about the fear associated with memory, a fear that has lasted for many well past the end of the Soviet era.

Living memory is partial, and that is why it is so eloquent. In Russia, often, it has a quality of nightmare, the voice, occasionally, of solitary confinement, and hence that affinity with fate. Public silences about the famine [of the early 1930s] were a kind of violence, another Stalinist atrocity, enforced by twisted calculations and pervasive fear. Activists who work with survivors . . . know that the task of overcoming their legacy is far from over yet. They warn us of oblivion's costs. "While humankind survives," one of them wrote in the 1980s, "it must preserve the memory of its forebearers [*sic*] to remain human and to avoid becoming . . . people without memory, whom it is easier to make slaves." (p. 183)

A woman who was born a few years after World War II reported:

In general, there was always a feeling of fear. I was not afraid that I might be held accountable for jokes and talk. And I was not afraid of reading samizdat'. But I always had a feeling of fear. Perhaps it was genetic. I think this might have resulted from the absence of freedom. Our consciousness was paralyzed with fear, and it was difficult to go beyond the restrictions I had imposed, but which existed in reality as well. I was always fearful of losing my job, my apartment. The feeling was one of an entire absence of rights. You had submitted entirely to a fixed order and were unable to disobey it.

Anti-Semitism also influenced these feelings. My parents introduced the idea that I could lose a job at any moment. And I was always afraid of this. I was afraid of being fired for a trifle.

My mother was afraid of contacts with foreigners and foreign countries. Father had relatives abroad, and this was a grenade that could explode at any moment.

The feeling of fear remained in many people and was unconscious. But under conditions of political tension and change it was revived. It was terrible to listen in 1991 . . . Older people said that anything was possible.

By way of contrast, a few interviewees responded that they had *not* experienced a constant atmosphere of fear. Their responses fell into two categories. First, some of the younger interviewees said that they had been shielded from potentially dangerous political discussions at home. For example, Interviewee C said, "Was there an atmosphere of fear in my family? I don't know. I didn't feel it. My father did a great deal to protect me from politics, and there were no political conversations at home." Second, some of the older interviewees who said they had not experienced fear had been more active in their resistance to the regime. This sort of active resistance seems to have insulated them from experiencing such fear.

Fear was a pervasive part of life for many Soviet citizens, and hence it is no surprise that it shaped internal emigration. The state's attempt to create a totalizing public sphere meant that when individuals and small groups attempted to create private space, they were engaging in an activity that could be dangerous to themselves and to their family and friends. Nonetheless, such attempts seem to have been widespread for at least certain segments of the population. For them, it may have served as a sort of defense mechanism to resist total encroachment by the state.

Resistance Activities Associated with Internal Emigration

A third general theme that ran throughout the interviews concerns forms of resistance associated with it. Given that internal immigrants were not dissidents, this resistance did not take the form of overt public protest – behavior that could often lead to arrest and imprisonment. Instead, it took forms such as actively disbelieving official statements and believing the opposite of official information.

The first point to note in this regard is that some interviewees identified turning points in their lives when they were transformed from relatively uncritical consumers of official state information to active resisters. For example, Interviewee C reported, "Whereas in the eighth or ninth grade I was able to believe in official propaganda (for example that bad things happen in America), by the first year of my university studies I never believed any official information." Interviewee D reported the following incident:

Lenin was sacred during the 1960s, but I did not have a deep understanding of what the system really was at that time. When I read [during perestroika] how Lenin ordered local officials to kill 10 priests, 10 scholars, 10 people from some other category, etc. as a warning to others, it had an extremely powerful impact on me . . . In due course I began to understand more and more that the struggle had been meaningless.

And Interviewee F produced the following account:

My attitudes toward Communist ideology were formed as far back as during my childhood. In any case, I was quite suspicious of this ideology. Even so, it was a revelation to me to know about how many people perished. Twenty million during the war and twenty million during the years of the repressions. My attitude toward the Great Patriotic War had almost been an official one. But when I learned how many people were killed in vain, how many people were killed in our camps, my attitude changed. When I first heard this, I could not believe it completely. To kill one's own people during the war! And then at that very moment I understood that both the ideology and the people who inculcated it in us were criminal.

Such transformations are often reported as if they took the form of a sudden insight, but when probed more closely, many agree that they grew out of years of reading, reflection, and discussions in a narrow circle of friends "in the kitchen." Hence, social processes in the private sphere provided a foundation for forming the individual phenomenon of internal emigration.

The groups involved in such private performance regions were typically tightly knit and closed, often keeping other acquaintances and even family members at a distance. Many of the activities of these closed groups revolved around underground literature. The mere possession of such literature could bring very severe penalties, and attempts to discuss or reproduce it could be even more dangerous, so the group had to be composed of very trusted people. Nonetheless, many individuals managed to read such literature in private and discuss it in their private circle. In this connection, D stated, "I knew rather early that the things spoken about in officially published books did not correspond to reality . . . I began to read [underground literature] very early," F reported, "I read a great deal, thought it over, compared . . . ," and G said, "I had friends. We read philosophy, poetry, samizdat. I realized pretty well that the Soviet period was a dark period in our culture."

In sum, these interviews suggest a few basic issues worthy of further consideration when trying to understand internal emigration. First, internal emigration clearly was a familiar notion in the Soviet era, at least among the intelligentsia. Second, it amounted to something more than the alienation that one might find in any modern society, having emerged largely in response to the efforts of a state seeking to have a total and totalizing presence in its citizens' lives.

The totalitarian system of the state is tied to another theme that runs throughout these interviews: the deep and abiding fear associated with life in the Soviet Union. This fear took on different forms for different generations, and in some cases was so powerful that people reported flashbacks in their post-Soviet life. Internal emigration gave rise to a variety of private and public behaviors. While having to maintain a constant vigilance against revealing their private views in the public space, the interviewees often refused to believe information provided through official state channels. Support for this form of resistance typically came from reading underground literature and discussing it "in the kitchen" among a small, closed group of trusted friends.

Conclusion

In this chapter, I have considered various aspects of textual consumption. Starting with the observation that even the most complete account of text production does not directly inform us of what someone knows or believes, I outlined the notions of mastery and appropriation. In particular, I focused on cases in which someone may have mastered, but not appropriated a textual resource.

It became clear, however, that this line of reasoning about the psychological dimensions of consumption needs to be complemented with an analysis of the contexts in which people use textual resources. This is so because belief or appropriation is often not an all-or-nothing affair that can be used to characterize individuals across contexts. Instead, people often say and think one thing in one context and quite another in another context.

The most obvious way in which these points played out in the Soviet Union concerns the distinction between the public and private spheres of performance. The stark distinction that existed between these two spheres in Soviet life was unique in several respects. First, it was a distinction that was created and monitored by the state. Second, failure to recognize this distinction could have very powerful negative consequences. These forces gave rise to phenomena I have examined under the headings of the control of narrative information and the control of narrative performance.

The stark public-private distinction characteristic of the Soviet era was associated with social and psychological processes discussed under the heading of "internal emigration." Again, this was internal emigration away from a public sphere of discourse controlled by the state, and at least some people's encounters with state-sponsored violence in this connection had given rise to a deep-seated fear that continued to exist well after the Soviet Union had collapsed. At the same time, however, internal emigration often provided some of the motivation and resources for resisting state efforts at social and psychological control.

All of these points serve to complicate the picture of collective remembering. Instead of being some sort of steady-state attribute of individuals or groups, collective remembering turns out to involve an array of complex relationships between active agents and the narrative tools they employ. These relationships vary not only along cognitive and affective dimensions, but also as a reflection of performance contexts in which memory practices actually occur in everyday life.

7

Generational Differences in Collective Remembering

When Soviet authorities cancelled nationwide history examinations in 1988 (see Chapter 5), few could envisage the road that lay ahead. The Soviet population had little experience with public debate, so it was unclear how they could take on the complex process of negotiating new forms of collective remembering. Some sort of open discussion was needed, but the level of cynicism made it difficult to see how this could happen. From the perspective of Soviet authorities, the only thing that was clear at the time was that the old system for promulgating collective memory was broken, and their action amounted to little more than a public admission that this was so.

The attempt to renegotiate collective memory in these circumstances was based on the standard assumption that what was needed was to produce a new official account of the past that would replace the old one. And as I outlined in Chapter 5, this gave rise to major efforts by the state to create new textual resources, efforts grounded largely in the dialogic, as opposed to referential, function of narrative. It remains unclear, however, whether this effort has been very effective. In part, this is due to production problems such as the unavailability of textbooks or the funds to purchase them.

What is even less clear a dozen years after the end of the Soviet era is how the textual resources that are available have been used. How do people in Russia employ the new textual means provided by the government and other sources? What do they know today about major events of the past such as World War II? What do they believe? These questions take on a particularly interesting dimension in the post-Soviet context because it seems to involve something other than simply substituting one set of textual resources for another. Specifically, it appears to be a context whose most relevant characteristic is the decline of state legitimacy and authority. In this scenario, the state may no longer have the authority to control the consumption of textual resources for collective memory in the usual manner – and certainly not in the manner characteristic of the Soviet era. The decline of state legitimacy in post-Soviet Russia has been widely discussed, and in the most draconian analyses has resulted in talk about a "failed state."

I do not subscribe to such a radical view, but I would note that the current setting in Russia provides an extraordinary setting for studying questions about the role of the state in shaping collective remembering. In order to understand how various aspects of this complex picture fit together, it is useful to turn once again to the notion of memory as a distributed phenomenon. The focus on narrative as the cultural tool in this case inherently introduces the notion of voice. Both the specific narratives and the schematic narrative templates we employ when speaking about the past have a history, and this history is reflected in the perspective, or voice, they now inherently introduce when using them. It is impossible to employ them without introducing others' voices along with one's own. In some instances, we may be aware of the resulting multivoicedness and critically examine how our perspective comes into contact with others; in others we may not, in which case the narrative tools and voices remain transparent as they did to Sasha as outlined in Chapter 1.

In what follows, I shall pursue these issues by examining the consumption of narrative texts and associated dynamics of collective memory. My discussion will be organized around an empirical study of how these processes differ across generations. Specifically, I examine the processes of mastery, appropriation, and performance as they apply to official textual resources, and how these processes have changed in light of the fact that people in today's younger generation in Russia have experienced the disintegration of the Soviet Union during a formative period of their lives. The research of Schuman, Belli, and Bischoping (1997) and Conway (1997) suggests that this experience is likely to have a lasting impact on this generation's collective memory and political outlook.

The object of collective memory in my discussion will be World War II, and I shall be particularly interested in the impact of schooling in this regard. This is not to say that factors other than formal instruction do not affect collective memory for elements of this "dominant myth" (Weiner, 1996) in Russia. The press and popular media come immediately to mind. Nevertheless, several indicators suggest that encounters with history texts and discussions at school exert a major, if not overriding, influence in creating generational differences in this collective memory.

For example, this is supported by the sharp difference between people who completed their schooling during the Soviet era and those who came after. The contrast between these two groups is pronounced, and it is hard to attribute it to age or other influences. For example, an adult pattern of mastering official World War II narratives surfaces even for the youngest members of a group who finished secondary school during the

Soviet period. In the empirical study I shall discuss, these people performed much more like older adults, including adults many years their senior, than subjects who were closer in age but who were educated in the post-Soviet era. A twenty-seven-year-old and a fifty-five-year-old, both of whom had gone through Soviet schooling, were much more similar in this regard than, say, the twenty-seven-year-old and a twenty-one-year-old who had gone through education in the post-Soviet years.

The data for this study were collected as part of a larger study carried out in collaboration with Dr. Tatyana Y. Kosyaeva, a researcher at the Institute of Economics of the Siberian Branch of the Russian Academy of Sciences. Kosyaeva collected questionnaire and essay data from high school students and adults in the Siberian city of Novosibirsk in late1999 and similar data from high school students in Moscow in early 2000. Several items were included in this questionnaire, but I shall focus primarily on two. The first of these asked the subjects to "Name the five most important events of the Second World War," and the second asked them to "Please write a short essay on the theme: 'What was the course of the Second World War from its beginning to its conclusion?'"

The first of two groups in this study included thirty-eight adults between the ages of twenty-seven and seventy-two who had been educated during the Soviet period. The data for all these adults were collected in Novosibirsk, but many of them had not lived in that city for their entire lives. These subjects were recruited through the "snowball" method, meaning that Kosyaeva recruited acquaintances, who in turn recruited other acquaintances, and so forth. This procedure yielded a sample that included subjects whose mean age was thirty-eight years and whose occupations ranged from factory worker to retail store worker to graduate student. I shall call this the "Soviet-educated" group.

Individuals in the second, "post-Soviet" group of 139 subjects had attended school after the Soviet era. They were post-Soviet in the sense that they had completed all or almost all of their formal education after 1991, the year the Soviet Union officially dissolved. Twenty-three of these, ranging from seventeen to twenty-five years of age, had already left high school at the time the data were collected. They participated in the data collection session in Novosibirsk that also yielded the Soviet-educated group. The other 116 post-Soviet subjects ranged in age from fourteen to seventeen, but almost all were either fifteen or sixteen. Forty-two of these subjects came from three Novosibirsk high schools: either a non-elite school attended by students of a factory neighborhood, a special mathematical high school linked to Novosibirsk State University, or a private business high school. The other 74 post-Soviet subjects participated in a data collection session at a non-elite Moscow high school named after a hero of the Great Patriotic War. Among other things, this high school housed a museum of the war.

There were some minor differences among these subgroups of post-Soviet subjects. For example, a few of the details they mentioned about World War II reflected the textbooks they were using or comments by their teacher. However, none of these differences was sufficiently consistent or significant to make systematic distinctions among the subgroups, and for this reason their data will be combined under the heading of post-Soviet subjects in the analyses that follow.

As was the case for Sasha as outlined in Chapter 2, both the Soviet-educated and post-Soviet subjects in this study provided accounts of World War II that reflect a perspective quite distinct from what one would normally encounter among people from other nations. For example, whereas Americans could be expected to respond to a question about major events in World War II by listing items such as Pearl Harbor, D-Day, the Battle of the Bulge, the liberation of concentration camps by American troops, Guadalcanal, and Hiroshima and Nagasaki, the prototypical Soviet account included the German attack on Russia, the Battle of Moscow, the Battle of Stalingrad, the Battle of the Kursk salient, the Leningrad siege, and the Battle of Berlin. None of the 177 subjects in this study mentioned Guadalcanal, D-Day (although the "second front" appeared occasionally), or American troops' liberation of concentration camps, and only a few included Pearl Harbor or Hiroshima and Nagasaki as one of the five most important events of the war.

In other words, the narrative texts and voices employed by Russians and Americans continue to be quite distinct, even as the former group encounters a more open and heterogeneous set of textual resources for collective remembering. This is not to say, however, that the Russian group was homogeneous. Indeed, the point of what follows is that the two generations generated accounts of World War II that are strikingly different along several dimensions. I shall explore these differences under the heading of the mastery and the appropriation of textual means used in collective remembering.

Mastery of the Textual Means for Collective Remembering

As outlined in earlier chapters, the mastery of a cultural tool has to do with knowing how to use it. Questions of mastery are questions about the cognitive skills required to use a cultural tool with facility, regardless of one's beliefs or emotional commitment to it. Issues of belief fall under the heading of appropriation in the terminology used here, and may be quite distinct from mastery, especially in cases of politically loaded cultural tools such as the narrative texts that mediate collective remembering.

The first and most obvious way in which the two generations in this study differ is reflected in a simple measure of mastery – namely, the amount of information from specific narratives about World War II that they were able to provide. In general, the younger Russians in this study appeared to know much less from official accounts (or any other accounts for that matter) than did the older generation. For example, 84 percent of the Soviet-educated subjects listed five items in response to the questionnaire item asking for the five most important events of the war, whereas only 48 percent of the post-Soviet respondents did so. Conversely, more than one quarter (26 percent) of the younger group listed *no* events in response to this question, whereas this was the case for only 5 percent of the Soviet-educated subjects.

In some instances, the failure to list even a single event may have reflected an unwillingness rather than an inability to respond, and for the two Soviet-educated subjects who did not list any events, this seems to have been the case. In contrast, many of the post-Soviet subjects who failed to respond made additional comments such as "I don't know," suggesting that they were unable, as opposed to unwilling, to provide a list of items.

A similar pattern of differences between the two generations emerged in their essays about World War II. Although 18 percent of the Soviet-educated subjects produced no essay, all but one of these listed five items in response to the question about the most important events of the war. Furthermore, only one explicitly refused to write an essay (a seventy-two-year-old with unsteady handwriting), and his response ("I don't want to write. It's too complicated and long.") suggests that he actually had a great deal to say. Of the 82 percent of the older subjects who did write essays, the vast majority (74 percent) produced texts that were ten or more lines in length. This combination of findings suggests that when Soviet-educated subjects failed to produce an essay, it was because they were unwilling, as opposed to unable, to do the task.

The post-Soviet group presents a quite different picture. Twenty-eight percent of the group failed to produce any essay at all, and of these more than half also failed to list even a single item when asked about the five most important events of World War II. Furthermore, of those who did not produce an essay, a sizable minority (26 percent) made comments such as "I don't know" or "I can't remember." And finally, of the 100 subjects who wrote essays, fewer than half produced ten lines or more. Indeed, many of their responses hardly qualify as essays at all. The average length of their texts was only eight lines, whereas the corresponding figure for the Soviet-educated group was twenty-three.

The findings I have reported thus far paint a uniformly negative picture of the mastery of textual means by the post-Soviet generation. To leave matters at this, however, only tells us what the younger subjects were *not* doing, and this can be taken to imply that both groups were trying to do the same thing, but the younger subjects were simply not as good at it. This does not seem to be the case, however, for several reasons. For example, some post-Soviet subjects included information in their lists and essays that was never included by Soviet-educated adults. And more generally, they seemed to be following a different strategy involving a different set of cultural tools to generate their responses than was the case for the older generation. Specifically, many of them used a strategy built around the use of a schematic narrative template rather than a specific narrative about the events of World War II.

As outlined in Chapter 5, a prototypical Soviet version of a specific narrative about World War II (actually, for the Great Patriotic War beginning with the 1941 German invasion) includes the invasion, the Battle of Moscow, the Battle of Stalingrad as the turning point in the war, the Battle of the Kursk salient, and the Battle of Berlin. This is consistent with the triumph-over-alien-forces schematic narrative template, but it goes well beyond it in terms of specific information. The Soviet-educated subjects typically identified specific events in their essays, including details about circumstances such as dates and locations. Of those who wrote essays, for example, 38 percent mentioned the Battle of Moscow, 32 percent included the Battle of Stalingrad – usually as the turning point in the war – and 26 percent mentioned the Battle of the Kursk salient. This contrasts with 14 percent, 9 percent, and 8 percent, respectively, for the post-Soviet subjects.

A typical version of the older subjects' accounts of World War II can be seen in the following essay by a thirty-three-year-old woman (Subject SE5) from Novosibirsk.

In 1939, Germany attacked Poland. In June of 1941, German forces, treacherously and without declaring war, invaded the territory of the USSR. The Great Patriotic War began. The Germans advanced almost all the way to Moscow, seizing a great deal of our country's territory. The turning point in the war was the Battle of Stalingrad. There the Germans received a well-deserved rebuff. After that, Soviet forces attacked and gradually drove the German forces from our territory. Then began the liberation of other countries: Czechoslovakia, Poland, Bulgaria, Hungary, Yugoslavia. The Soviet forces reached Berlin and routed Fascist Germany, bringing fascism in Europe to a halt. The allies of the USSR were England and the USA. They opened a second front. The main role in the victory over Fascist Germany was shouldered by the simple Soviet people, the simple *Russian* soldier. For the Russian people, the Great Patriotic War was emancipatory.

This essay has many of the hallmarks of the kind of text written by most Soviet-educated subjects. To be sure, it includes some "post-Sovietisms" such as singling out "the simple *Russian* [as opposed to Soviet] soldier," but it follows a basic Soviet pattern in most respects. For example, it describes the German attack as being undertaken "treacherously and without declaring war," a stock phrase that was memorized by generations of Soviet students. Other expressions such as "well-deserved rebuff" and "routed Fascist Germany" are also stock phrases found in many official Soviet accounts. And finally, this subject's text is organized around the major battles at Moscow, Stalingrad, and Berlin, events that provide the basic anchors for the official specific narrative presented for decades in textbooks and Soviet media.

An important characteristic of this essay is that it reflects a reliance on a specific narrative, as opposed to a more abstract schematic narrative template. In this connection, it is useful to consider the *level of description* involved. As Mink (1978) and other narrative theorists have observed, events may have the appearance of being defined independently of any narrative in which they are embedded, but in actuality the narrative often does a great deal to shape their boundaries and interpretation. Depending on one's purposes, events can vary along several dimensions. Of special importance for my purposes is the fact that they can range from narrowly defined, concrete events involving particular, identifiable individuals acting in a limited, local setting to vaguely defined happenings involving unspecified actors and settings.

I shall term events of the former sort "concrete" and those of the latter sort "abstract." For example, Hitler's committing suicide qualifies as a concrete event in that it involved a specific, identifiable individual acting in a relatively limited, concrete setting. In contrast, the suffering inflicted in World War II concentration camps – at least when described in these vague terms – counts as an abstract event since it does not specify the agents involved or the setting in which they acted.

If concrete and abstract events can be taken as anchoring the ends of a continuum, it is also possible to identify a plane of "mid-level" events. Under this heading, I have in mind items such as the Battle of Moscow. Such mid-level events typically involve large groups – as opposed to single individuals – operating in an extended setting, so they do not qualify as concrete; but their setting is clearly limited, so they also do not qualify as abstract. In the essay of the Soviet-educated subject provided earlier, the level of description is consistently at the middle level, something that characterizes essays by the older subjects in general.

Turning to the younger subjects' essays and lists of important events in World War II, one finds a quite different pattern. To begin with, it was not uncommon for these younger subjects to focus on a few very concrete events in their responses. For example, eight of the post-Soviet subjects included Hitler's death or Hitler's suicide in their list of the most important events of the war, whereas this item never appeared for the Soviet-educated adults. Furthermore, five members of the younger group included raising the Soviet flag over the Reichstag in Berlin (an event concretely depicted in a famous photograph) as one of the five most important events, whereas this never appeared in the older subjects' lists.

Like the sort of "human-interest stories" mentioned by Dower (1996) in his critique of popular accounts of the NASM exhibit (Chapter 3), the post-Soviet subjects' inclusion of events such as Hitler's suicide seems to reflect an orientation toward concrete individuals and events, and to take these to be the core of "a simple, unilinear story line" (p. 80). This level of description does not deal with complex, mid-level events that involve larger groups acting for reasons that make sense only against the background of specific historical circumstances.

It is worth noting that the absence of such concrete events in the older subjects' essays clearly was *not* due to a lack of knowledge on their part; they all unquestionably knew at least as much about these episodes as did the younger group. Instead, mention of such events by younger subjects reflects what appears to be a different pattern for identifying information and grasping it together into a narrative, a pattern that has arisen along with – and perhaps because of – their limited mastery of official state history. In contrast to the older subjects, who relied on mid-level events and specific narratives built around these events to provide an account of World War II, the post-Soviet subjects used a combination of concrete events that seem to reflect isolated bits of knowledge, on the one hand, and a schematic narrative template as reflected in the mention of abstract events, on the other. Indeed, the inclusion of the concrete events often seemed to serve the role of pointing in a vague manner to the narrative template.

As outlined in Chapter 6, the schematic narrative template in this case applies to many events in Russian history, including the Great Patriotic War. Specifically, the triumph-over-alien-forces narrative template includes:

1. An "initial situation" in which the Russian people are living in a peaceful setting where they are no threat to others is disrupted by:

2. The initiation of trouble or aggression by an alien force, or agent, which leads to:

3. A time of crisis and great suffering, which is:

4. Overcome by the
   triumph over the alien force by the Russian people, acting heroically and alone

Several of the subjects in the post-Soviet group seemed to be relying primarily on this narrative template when writing their essays, a pattern that was sometimes indexed by their reference to abstract events. For example, in their list of important events in World War II, ten of the post-Soviet subjects – but no Soviet-educated subject – included an abstract event that falls under the heading of item 3 in this narrative template. This could be in the form of vague references to the large number of Russians who were killed or had suffered in German concentration camps. Such references were never specific as to time and the parties involved and hence do not qualify as mid-level event descriptions.

This pattern of using the triumph-over-alien-forces narrative template was sometimes combined with the mention of one or two concrete events by the younger subjects in order to come up with an essay. The result is a patched-together text that does not include the sort of mid-level events and specific narratives found in the Soviet-educated subjects' accounts. For example, several post-Soviet subjects focused on Hitler and his concrete acts, as reflected in the following essay by Subject PS42, a fifteen-year-old student from Moscow:

The beginning [of the war] was very unexpected for the whole world except for Hitler. Also unexpected was the massive amount of bloodshed, the human losses, the Fascist concentration camps. The emergence of a second Napoleon, Adolf Hitler, was also unexpected and strange. The course of the war was hard for the countries of the defenders. Terrible, hard, bloody.

This very short essay includes only an indirect reference to one of the mid-level events usually mentioned by Soviet-educated subjects (the beginning of the war). Instead of building the account around other such events such as the battles of Moscow and Stalingrad, this subject used information about Hitler as an individual, hence relying on information that places the agency for events in a concrete individual rather than in mid-level entities such as "German forces" or "Hitlerites," expressions often used by Soviet-educated subjects.

An extreme example of this tendency to reduce World War II to specific events involving Hitler can be found in the "essay" of Subject PS56, another post-Soviet subject. Instead of even alluding to any mid-level events – or any abstract events, for that matter – he simply wrote: "1940. Hitler was alive. – 1945. Hitler died." The entire Great Patriotic War was thus viewed through the lens of personalized concrete events.

In the case of Subject PS42, the mention of concrete events is coupled with the triumph-over-alien-forces narrative template as reflected in the comments about bloodshed and human loss, comments tied to item 3 in this narrative template. Other elements of this template are reflected in this text as well. For example, the emphasis on the unexpected nature of the attack suggests that Russia was peaceful and non-threatening as specified in the initial situation, or first element of the narrative template.

Perhaps most striking in this regard, however, is this subject's comment about Hitler as a "second Napoleon." This comment suggests that he viewed the two figures as being essentially similar, and that in his view the story of Hitler and World War II is basically the same as the story of Napoleon and the invasion of Russia in the early nineteenth century. These two stories appear to be stamped out of the triumph-over-alien-forces narrative template, and for all practical purposes can be reduced to it. Such an approach echoes Eliade's comment (Chapter 3) that "popular memory finds difficulty in retaining individual events and real figures" (1954, p. 43), instead preferring the "transfiguration of history into myth" (p. 37).

To some it may appear that this student's use of the parallel between Napoleon and Hitler grew out of some original (though simplifying) thought of his own. However, texts involving this parallel are part of a cultural tool kit generally available in Russia, something that is reflected in the fact that it was also used by another post-Soviet subject (PS107) in this study. In this case, the essay reads as follows:

> In reality this was a victory of the Russian spirit. The Hitlerite forces were stronger. In his time Napoleon's forces were also stronger, but everyone knows how all that ended. There they all talked about strategy, but it was totally crazy. Russian spirit! It's interesting that with our spirit it turns out that we somehow cannot defeat Chechnya. As for the course of the war, I won't discuss it. It is boring and in essence unimportant. What is important is the result.

> P.S. In reality I am for peace for the whole world. Only don't think that I am a hippie. That's not the case. In reality peace for the whole world is impossible while there are different religions, different nationalities, politics, etc.

One would be hard-pressed in this case to find any of the mid-level events that are typically used by Soviet-educated subjects to organize their essays. Indeed, the subject wanders over a range of topics and opinions in this essay, and to the extent he refers to events at all, they are at the abstract level. What he does use, however, again suggests a reliance on the triumph-over-alien-forces narrative template. This is clearly reflected in the Hitler-Napoleon parallel, and it also is alluded to in the comments about the exceptionalism of the Russian spirit.

People who were educated in the Soviet context find this sort of essay to be either pathetic or simply humorous. In their view it is uninformed, lacking in detail, and full of unsolicited and inappropriately provided personal opinion. Again, however, interpreting it in purely negative terms provides little insight into what the subject was doing, and misses the point that it is more than simply an incomplete version of what Soviet-educated subjects would produce. This is apparent here from the references to Napoleon, something that never appeared in the older subjects' essays. This young subject's attempt to assimilate the complex story of the Great Patriotic War into the simplifying schema of the triumph-over-alien-forces narrative template distinguishes it from older subjects' responses, and it is the assumptions that go along with the strategy he employed that make the details "boring and in essence unimportant."

In sum, the Soviet-educated and post-Soviet subjects in this study demonstrated quite different levels of mastery of official accounts of World War II. In comparison with the post-Soviet group, the responses of the Soviet-educated subjects contain more information from specific narratives built around events described at a middle level of specificity. These and other characteristics reflect a mastery of official, state-produced texts that is relatively uniform across the subjects, despite the fact that they range in age from twenty-seven to seventy-two years of age.

In striking contrast, the post-Soviet group of subjects generally provided much less information about World War II. In many cases, their essays are so devoid of information that they are considered to be pathetic or humorous by anyone who went through the Soviet educational system. It is difficult for Soviet-educated people to believe how little the post-Soviet subjects seem to know about World War II. Even older people who had been severely critical of Soviet official history find it surprising, if not offensive, that young people know so little about the event that is still a source of great pride in Russia and is still considered the defining event of the twentieth century.

Again, however, the paucity of information provided by the post-Soviet subjects does not simply reflect a failure to master the same set of textual resources employed by the older generation, although this clearly was part of the story. Instead, several pieces of evidence suggest that the younger subjects seemed to be following a different strategy to come up with their accounts of World War II. Without knowing about specific narratives and mid-level events, at least some of the subjects seemed to be trying to construct accounts by drawing directly on the triumph-over-foreign-forces schematic narrative template. In some cases, this was the only foundation for their texts, and to the extent they introduced events, these were abstract. In others, they pointed to this narrative template with a few concrete events, and by this means arrived at a sort of skeletal account.

The differences I have outlined between the Soviet-educated and post-Soviet groups have some important implications when trying to understand the general dynamics of collective remembering. First, they suggest that the collective memory promulgated by a state can dissipate very quickly when official efforts at producing it are no longer forceful and effective. In the course of a single decade and generational change in this case, official texts that routinely had been mastered and appropriated by nearly everyone in the Soviet Union seem to have been forgotten to a degree that many find unimaginable. Put another way, this indicates just how much constant effort and vigilance are required by a state to keep a pattern of official collective remembering intact. Instead of viewing this case as a relatively standard substitution of one official collective memory for another, then, it seems more appropriate to describe it in terms of a general disintegration of official, state-sponsored collective memory for World War II in the younger generation. And this, in turn, appears to be part of the disintegration, or at least diminution, of state authority and legitimacy.

In this connection, it is worth noting an interesting ambiguity in the term "natural laboratory" as I have been using it. Up to this point, I have taken it to refer to a naturally occurring instance of the rapid transition of a sociocultural setting. But the data on textual mastery that I have reviewed in this chapter suggest that another sense of "natural" may also be involved. Specifically, the post-Soviet context may be one in which ongoing efforts by a state to promulgate an official account of the past have faltered, and people are demonstrating patterns of collective remembering that are less artificially constrained by state control – and in that sense, more natural. Among other things, the "unnatural act" (Wineburg, 2001) of disciplined historical thinking may be less likely to occur in such settings. Of course, this is a matter of degree, given that the new Russian state has been quite active in trying to promulgate new textual resources for collective memory.

The evidence I have presented, then, suggests that collective memory does not simply disappear when state authority and legitimacy decline. Instead, a pattern emerges that relies on a combination of narrative templates and a smattering of information about concrete events. These may very well come from the popular media, private discussions at home, and other informal sources that lie outside of state control. The narrative template in this case is one that certainly was consistent with official history. Apparently its availability does not depend on official efforts by the state, but is part of a more general cultural heritage.

At this point, it remains unclear whether the tendencies I have outlined for narrative templates to replace officially sanctioned specific narratives are general ones. It is possible that the kind of patterns demonstrated by the post-Soviet subjects would surface in any case where state authority and legitimacy dissipate. Alternatively, it is possible that the special circumstances of the setting I have been examining underlie the results. For example, it is conceivable that the new patterns of textual mastery found among the younger subjects in this study are part of a specific kind of reaction to Soviet totalitarianism. This could be a particular version of the "bent twig" phenomenon discussed by Berlin (1991).

Regardless of whether or not this point is unique to post-Soviet Russia, more general claims about collective remembering as mediated action apply. Even though it may be more difficult to identify the textual resources underlying collective memory in a context of diminished state legitimacy, there is little doubt that these resources – and the voices they involve – are still at work. This might mean that in place of stock phrases and specific narratives built around mid-level events, people must rely on more-or-less readily available items from their cultural tool kit, items such as narrative templates and a mix of abstract and concrete events. But the process is still one of active agents employing cultural tools.

A major point that distinguishes the two generations in this study is how the voices of others emerged in their accounts of the past. The use of expressions like "treacherously and without declaring war," "well-deserved rebuff," and "routed Fascist Germany" by a Soviet-educated subject (SE5) are so striking that one is readily tempted to ask, "Who is doing the speaking?" A decade and a half after the demise of the USSR, the use of such expressions suggests that it is possible to hear a Soviet voice in older generations' collective memory. By contrast, words from such a voice would be quite out of place in the world of the post-Soviet subjects.

Finally, while such differences might make it seem that the two generations in this study have nothing in common when it comes to collective memory, it is important to remember that the triumph-over-alien-forces narrative template continues to provide an underlying cultural tool and force of continuity for all of them. Exactly how, and how much, they rely on it varies greatly, but the perspective of this narrative template surfaces across the board in comparison with what people from other societies such as Germany, Japan, or the United States might say about the past. Unique forms of textual mediation and the voices embedded in them continue to bind all the Russian subjects together and set them off from what one would expect to hear from others.

Appropriation of the Textual Means of Collective Remembering

While the generational differences I have identified in connection with the mastery of textual resources are striking, equally interesting issues emerge in the case of appropriation. I shall explore these by examining various aspects of the relationship between the voice of concrete speakers and that of the textual resources they employ. In this connection, several questions emerge, questions such as: Does the speaker's voice appear in some overt way, or does it remain invisible? Does the speaker take a critical stance toward the textual resources he uses? Does he comment on what others have said in a way that indexes acceptance or rejection?

When approaching essays from the perspective of appropriation, it is useful to employ the basic opposition between treating textual resources as "authoritative" (Bakhtin, 1981), on the one hand, and as "thinking devices" (Lotman, 1988; Wertsch, 1998), on the other. As noted in Chapter 6, an authoritative text is associated with a voice of power and authority, and hence one is not invited to engage in the give and take of dialogue, to "divide it up – agree with one part, accept but not completely another part, reject utterly a third part" (p. 343). In contrast, approaching a text as a thinking device involves a more dynamic and interactive stance on the part of the individual employing it. In this case, the textual resource is viewed as the starting point for an active dialogue rather than something to be simply accepted or rejected.

The distinction between approaching narratives as authoritative texts and approaching them as thinking devices can be used to provide several insights into differences between how Soviet-educated and post-Soviet subjects consumed official accounts of World War II. As will become evident, the Soviet-educated subjects in this study displayed a tendency to accept and use the official textual material "with its authority already fused in it" (Bakhtin, 1981, p. 342), whereas the post-Soviet subjects tended to take the texts as thinking devices.

Based on the essays they produced, the Soviet-educated subjects generally seemed unable or unwilling to take official texts as thinking devices. They seldom entered into dialogic contact with the historical narrative produced by the state (the Soviet Union, in their case), and they were reluctant to let their own voice emerge to question or comment on the events recounted. In the most striking version of this tendency, adults wrote essays that sound as though they came straight out of Soviet textbooks. These took the form of objective-sounding narratives that seemed to tell themselves with little or no input from the individual conveying them. Instead of active engagement with the textual resources, subjects seemed to be passive "conduits" (Reddy, 1979; Wertsch, 1998) for official history. In many cases, subjects reproduced exact phrasings from the official history taught in Soviet schools.

This tendency was undoubtedly reinforced by the fact that the textual resources involved had many of the classic marks of collective memory, as opposed to analytic history. They tended to simplify, reflect a single committed perspective, and have no patience for ambiguity. Such narratives tend to grasp together the setting, events, and characters into tight plot structures with all the loose ends neatly wrapped up. When one begins to use them, it is difficult to imagine, let alone overtly introduce, other information or competing perspectives. In this sense, part of the control of consumption is built directly into the textual resources being employed.

An example of this sort of account is the text of Subject SE5 outlined earlier in the discussion of mastery. This subject used the sort of mid-level events, specific narrative structure, and set phrases that could be found in Soviet textbooks. As another example, consider the following essay written by a 55-year-old man from Novosibirsk (Subject SE24).

The Second World War began September 1, 1939 with the seizure of Poland by Fascist Germany. The goal of this invasion was to bring their forces to the border of the Soviet Union for a future attack on it. For this the general headquarters of Hitler worked out the so-called plan Barbarossa, which indicated the direction of the main strike by Germany and the further conduct of the war on the territory of the USSR. According to the intention of Hitler and his brothers-in-arms, this war had to be flash-like (a "Blitzkrieg") and unexpected. This was realized on June 22, 1941. German forces crossed our western borders and began attacks along the entire front from the Barents Sea to the Black Sea. But the main attack was toward Moscow, which they approached in the fall of 1941.

Lacking success there, the Germans changed tactics and decided to force their way through to the Volga in the area of Stalingrad and make their way to Moscow from there. But they also experienced failure there. The war took on a long, drawn-out character. The basic turning point occurred after the Battle of the Kursk salient, where the back of the Fascist beast was broken. The Red Army went over to the attack and began to liberate the Soviet land, a task that was finished in 1944. Then began the liberation from the Fascist yoke of the countries of Eastern Europe, where our army was welcomed as liberators. In May of 1945 Germany's capitulation was accepted, and May 9 was declared the day of victory. In 1946 the Nuremberg Trials were begun, where the Fascist ringleaders were judged.

This essay takes the form of a specific narrative built around the German attack in 1941, the battles of Moscow, Stalingrad, and the Kursk salient, and so forth. It remains consistent with the triumph-over-alien-forces narrative template, but it goes well beyond that in that it is constructed around the sort of mid-level events used in official narratives rather than staying at a more abstract level. Hitler was mentioned, but he was not used as a concrete, personalized substitute, or index for Germany or German forces in general as he was for some of the post-Soviet subjects outlined earlier. And as was the case for the other Soviet-educated subject I mentioned, this subject used expressions that appear to come directly from official texts about Soviet history, expressions such as "the Fascist beast," "the Fascist yoke," and "Fascist ringleaders."

The fact that stock phrases of this sort were used by several of the Soviet-educated subjects suggests that they did not take them to be particularly marked or overly ideological. In fact, their ready use indicates that the words and the perspectives they reflect are relatively transparent to many of the Soviet-educated subjects in the sense outlined in Chapter 1. Such transparency is an important part of authoritative texts in such settings. Instead of viewing expressions such as "the Fascist beast" as loaded with the value-orientation of a particular speaking consciousness, they were used in a straightforward way to talk about what "really happened." And because they were transparent, they were not reflected upon or challenged – processes antithetical to the authoritative word.

In comparison with the patterns exhibited by the Soviet-educated subjects, the post-Soviet subjects' accounts of World War II were more variable in length and content. Even more important for my purposes, they involved several patterns of appropriating official texts not used by the other group. The variability in the essays of the younger group makes it impossible to categorize them in any neat way. It is possible, however, to outline a range of variation extending from patterns similar to those of the Soviet-educated subjects to patterns indicating that textual resources were taken as thinking devices. I shall begin with cases in which a post-Soviet subject appropriated official textual means in ways quite similar to the older subjects. Under this heading, consider the following essay written by a fifteen-year-old subject from Moscow (PS25):

World War II for the world began as such in 1939. The beginning of the war did not presage great danger for the world and for Europe. Those opposing Germany could not, however, forestall the fact that the Fascist empire would visit misfortune on them, and before long, having concluded a mutual non-aggression treaty with the USSR, Germany attacked Europe. The inaction of the USSR was a major reason for why the war was so protracted and terrible. The course of the Second World War was very tragic. The USSR lost 20 million people. On June 22 Germany attacked the frontier posts of the USSR. And in a very short period it advanced up to 400 kilometers deep in the country. Then for two years, already now encountering great difficulty, the Germans made deep advances into the country, almost reaching Moscow, but they were unable to secure it and Soviet forces beat them back from there. The Battle of Stalingrad was a complete turning point struggle with the German forces. After that the Soviet forces no longer suffered defeat and pursued their victory march to the capital of Germany, and two valiant soldiers raised the flag over the Reichstag, completely smashing the Fascist aggressors!!!

In several respects, this essay mirrors those produced by Soviet-educated subjects. Indeed, it is the most Soviet-like of all the essays by the younger subjects. It uses a standard set of mid-level events (the German invasion, the battles of Moscow and Stalingrad, the march to Berlin) to construct a specific narrative about the war, and it even uses some stock phrases (e.g., "Fascist aggressors"). Nonetheless, even this most Soviet-sounding essay from the post-Soviet group is distinguished from those of Soviet-educated subjects by a few significant points. First, the writer makes specific mention of the non-aggression treaty, a complication in the official narrative that is seldom noted by Soviet-educated subjects. In addition to mentioning this pact, the subject explicitly comments that it made the war more protracted and difficult than it otherwise might have been. This critical note is presented as an objective observation, but it clearly indexes the speaker's voice emerging alongside the narrative. It is also something that never appeared in the essays of the Soviet-educated subjects. And finally, this young subject includes the soldiers' raising of the flag over the Reichstag, a point – along with the exclamation marks at the end of the essay – that never appeared in Soviet-educated subjects' essays.

Even with these emerging indications of the speaker's voice in this essay, its similarity with those written by many Soviet-educated subjects is striking, and sets it off from the other post-Soviet essays. These other essays were distinctive in how they allowed the speaker's voice to emerge in the text. Rather than serving as a passive conduit for official texts, young subjects often revealed a more active stance by treating at least some aspects of the textual means as a thinking device. In this connection, consider the short essay by the post-Soviet Subject PS10:

Until the USSR entered the war, it had taken on the character of a "Blitzkrieg." It was very fast and quick. After all, in 3 years Germany had conquered all of Europe. But on meeting the powerful opposition of the USSR, Germany changed its strategy, and the effect of surprise did not hold. And if one believes the documents, the war came to a finish in effect with: the suicide of Hitler, Eva Braun, Borman, etc.

This has several of the characteristics of post-Soviet subjects' essays already discussed. It fails to mention most of the major events included in official accounts, and the events that it does mention are abstract or concrete, rather than presented at a middle level of description. What is most interesting for my purposes, however, is this subject's comment, "And if one believes the documents . . . ." This is a clear marker of the speaker's voice, and it is a comment that was inconceivable during the Soviet period. This does not mean that Soviet citizens never doubted official information, but the idea of saying so in a public communication such as an essay about history was unheard of. Instead of serving as an unquestioning conduit for others' words and assessments, then, this comment reflects the fact that the subject was speaking for himself as well, thereby using textual resources as thinking devices.

The final essay by a post-Soviet subject that I shall present as an illustration of how texts can be treated as thinking devices reads as follows:

The Second World War, as all wars, brought a great deal of grief to every city, every home, every family. This was base treachery on the part of Germany, who used the defenselessness, a peace treaty => (and consequently) the unpreparedness of the Soviet Union. The course of the world war was connected with many tragic events. World War II was the result of the greediness of governments, when everyone wants to chop off a piece of something and devour it. The end of the war was welcomed by everyone since their losses had reached such huge proportions.

The possibilities for a speaker to treat a text as a thinking device and for the voice of the speaker to surface overtly are extended much further here than in the previous cases I have outlined. In fact, this essay contains very little *but* the speaker's voice. Instead of reflecting others' voices and textual resources, the essay is composed primarily of this subject's commentary on the actors and actions of World War II. No essay by a Soviet-educated subject included any such commentary, which is not to say that no adult shared this young person's opinion. However, it is to say that the older subjects apparently did not view it as appropriate to make such statements in the relatively public performance region involved in producing a written account of World War II. Indeed, when people who are products of Soviet-era education read this essay, they usually find the student's comments shocking or humorous. From their perspective, it is baffling that anyone could believe that he had been invited to provide an extended account of his opinion in this context.

In sum, the analysis I have outlined in this section reveals some striking differences between the two generations in terms of their appropriation of official history texts. As reflected in their tendency to reproduce official accounts in their essays, the Soviet-educated adults approached them as authoritative, and their personal voice seldom surfaced to question or comment on them. The post-Soviet subjects, in contrast, were much more likely to take the official narrative as a thinking device, as a starting point for a dialogue.

Recognizing these generational differences in patterns of textual consumption raises the question as to what it is that they actually reflect. Both the Soviet-educated and post-Soviet subjects had been exposed to the new information about history that has emerged in the past fifteen to twenty years, something that would suggest that the two groups are equally good candidates for approaching official texts as thinking devices. The fact that they did not do so suggests the need to look to other reasons for the difference.

One explanation that suggests itself is grounded in the performance regions found in Soviet and post-Soviet instructional settings. All the Soviet-educated subjects had finished high school by the time the USSR officially disbanded, and many had finished school well before that. In contrast, the post-Soviet subjects in this study had participated in new discussions of official history while they were still in school. In this context, the discourse of history instruction differed quite strikingly from its Soviet precursor, not only in content but also in terms of issues of narrative performance. Specifically, official texts are today often treated by teachers and students in a way that would be quite alien, if not blasphemous, in the Soviet era.

Given this, it is useful to return to a distinction outlined in Chapter 6 between two candidate explanations for the difference between the Soviet-educated and post-Soviet subjects. First, this difference could be attributed to divergent belief systems of individuals: Soviet-educated subjects believe one thing about World War II and post-Soviet subjects believe another. Such claims are grounded in psychological notions such as appropriation, introjection, and integration into a self-system, and they focus on the individual and assume relative stability across contexts. In Chapter 6, however, I raised questions about the viability of this approach in my discussion of narrative performance. The alternative interpretation would focus on how members of the two generations distinguish between public and private spheres of discourse (front and back regions), presentation of self, and impression management. While it may be difficult to unravel some of the issues involved in this case, there are reasons to explore this latter line of reasoning in more detail.

The first of these is that it was not uncommon during the Soviet era for adults to make strikingly different comments about matters such as World War II in the privacy of their own homes and in the public sphere. Many people who were quite capable of providing official-sounding accounts in the public sphere had different things to say in discussions and anecdotes appropriate for "the kitchen." This again suggests problems with assuming that one can speak about what individuals believe in any unified, stable way. Instead, the stark and rigidly enforced distinction between public and private verbal performance in Soviet life gave rise to such phenomena as internal emigration.

In contrast to the Soviet era, one of the properties of today's life in Russia appears to be a decrease in these tendencies and a completely different approach to what Goffman (1959) termed "impression management." Members of the younger generation in Russia have little experience with internal emigration, and often are not even sure what the term means. This is one reflection – a healthy one it would seem – of the demise of the state as a totalizing presence in people's lives, and is part of a general loosening of the ironclad distinction between public and private spheres of discourse. The kind of questioning, open-ended commentary, and even irreverent approach that post-Soviet subjects took toward official accounts of World War II might have been found in private discourse in the Soviet era, but such comments definitely could not appear in the public sphere. This was so even when everyone present in a public setting might have shared, and known that he had shared, a similar critical view.

All of this suggests that the differences between the essays of the Soviet-educated and post-Soviet subjects may be more indicative of differences in interpretations of discourse in the public sphere than of differences in stable beliefs about what really happened in the past. Whereas the Soviet-educated subjects in this study seemed to maintain a reverent stance toward the official texts, many of the younger subjects did not. Instead, their essays reflected a willingness to treat official narratives as thinking devices, and take them as starting points for an active dialogue in which their voice might have as much weight as an authoritative text.

In contrast to the adults, then, who seemed to operate with two sharply divergent forms of narrative performance (one for the public sphere and one for the private sphere), the students seemed to ignore, or simply be oblivious to, this distinction, at least in its extreme Soviet version. In short, the difference between adults and students may have less to do with differences in what individuals "really believe" than with differences in whether or not they observe a sharp distinction between public and private discourse and follow a practice of revealing personal opinion only in the private sphere.

Conclusion

Throughout this chapter, I have illustrated my claims using data from an empirical study conducted in Novosibirsk and Moscow, two major metropolitan centers in Russia. To the extent that these data serve only to illustrate theoretical claims, issues of how adequately they represent post-Soviet society in general are not particularly important. However, in the course of my argument, I have made broader claims about the situation in post-Soviet Russia today as well, and this means the question of the representativeness of the data I have used deserves comment.

The first point to make in this regard is that the study drew on subjects at sites other than Moscow. A common criticism of contemporary social science research in Russia is that it often relies exclusively on data from Moscow, but that this metropolis is quite unlike the rest of Russia. This is what motivated the effort to include subjects from another region – namely, Novosibirsk in Siberia. Furthermore, efforts were made to obtain subjects from a range of class and educational backgrounds. Hence the post-Soviet subjects were drawn from various high schools, and the Soviet-educated subjects in Novosibirsk came from various professional and class backgrounds.

For some readers, questions will undoubtedly remain as to how well the tendencies I have discussed on the basis of these data are representative of the broader picture in contemporary Russia. There is no simple way to respond to such concerns, but three points are worth making. First, I have examined several theoretically motivated claims, and in all cases the differences between the two generational groups have been in the expected direction. Second, in many cases these differences have involved no overlap between the two groups. Third, and perhaps most important, the results of this study replicate those from another study conducted at another site in the late 1990s.

This study was carried out in the autumn of 1998 by O.F. Ivanova of the Department of Psychology at Kharkiv University in Ukraine. Although the subjects were in Kharkiv, Ukraine, they were in many respects very similar to those examined in this chapter in cultural orientation since they came from the eastern, Russian-speaking region of that country. Sixty-four high school students ranging in age from fourteen to seventeen years and twenty adults ranging from twenty-two to seventy-four years of age participated in the Kharkiv study. They all responded to questions and requests for essays that were identical to those given to the subjects in Novosibirsk and Moscow.

While there are some differences between the Kharkiv group, on the one hand, and the Moscow and Novosibirsk groups, on the other, what is most striking about the results are the close parallels they present. As revealed in the analysis by Wertsch and Ivanova (1999), the generational differences discussed earlier in this chapter are closely mirrored by those found in the Kharkiv groups. This applies to the patterns of mastery as well as to those of appropriation, and it provides additional grounds for assuming that the findings I have discussed here are representative of some general trends at least in urban, Russian areas of the former USSR.

With these points about the nature of the data I have examined in mind, let me turn to some of the major conclusions to be drawn about the mastery and appropriation of official accounts of World War II in post-Soviet Russia. Perhaps the most important point to be made in this connection is that the state control of collective remembering seems to have diminished precipitously. In the span of a single decade and a generational change, there have been very significant changes in areas such as the mastery, appropriation, and performance aspects of official textual resources. In place of specific narratives grounded in a standard set of mid-level events, many subjects in the younger generation had much less to say when asked about World War II. Perhaps as a result of their diminished mastery, they fell back on the triumph-over-alien-forces schematic narrative template, often combined with a few concrete events to provide an account of these events. And from the perspective of appropriation, the subjects demonstrated tendencies to approach official textual resources as thinking devices rather than authoritative texts. The tendency to treat such texts as authoritative was strongly encouraged in the Soviet context, and as a result Soviet-educated adults are often shocked by the lack of respect reflected in the accounts of the post-Soviet subjects.

The upshot is that collective remembering has not simply declined in post-Soviet Russia. Such an interpretation suggests that knowledge about the past has simply disappeared, and leaves one with only a negative interpretation of performance by the post-Soviet generation. Instead of speaking of the disappearance of memory in the younger generation, it seems more appropriate to speak of how it is employing different strategies for coming up with its accounts of the past. On the one hand, these involve a heavy reliance on a narrative template, and this results in a kind of new rigidity in collective memory. Because so few facts from a specific narrative are involved, there is reason to expect that subjects' views are less open to question and criticism. In this way, their texts are characterized even more than official Soviet accounts by hallmarks of collective memory outlined in earlier chapters, hallmarks such as being committed to a single perspective, impatience with ambiguity, and unself-consciousness.

On the other hand, evidence concerning appropriation suggests that the post-Soviet subjects were *more* self-conscious about the textual resources they were using. Their tendency to take official narratives as thinking devices rather than authoritative texts meant that they were willing to engage with these texts in a critical way and provide their own comments and opinions in a way that Soviet-educated subjects were not. In short, the post-Soviet subjects were willing to engage with official textual material in a more critical way, but their knowledge about textual material in the first place was so much less developed than was the case for the older subjects that they often had little to comment on.

One could make many other points about the claims and data discussed in this chapter, but I shall conclude with these. Perhaps the most important point to be made from all of this is that even a drastic decline in the authority and legitimacy of those charged with controlling collective remembering does not mean that a collective's memory simply disappears. Instead, there seem to be quite active, compensating forces in textual consumption that are likely to give rise to alternative ways of representing the past.

Conclusion

This book is organized around three basic tasks. First, I have provided an outline of the meaning – or meanings – of "collective remembering." As discussed in Chapters 2 and 3, this term is widely used, but is still in search of coherent interpretation. Until we obtain some clarity on this front, we are likely to continue having trouble engaging in productive debate, especially debate that extends across disciplines and intellectual traditions. For this reason, I devote considerable space to reviewing existing thought on collective memory and how it can provide the foundation for moving ahead.

My review does not amount to a call for a single definition of collective remembering. We are a long way from reaching such closure – if indeed such closure is desirable at all. Instead, my goal was to reflect on the conceptual space within which discussions of collective memory have occurred. In Chapter 3, I laid out a framework for taking up such reflection, a framework organized around terms and conceptual oppositions such as individual vs. collective remembering, collective remembering vs. history, and remembering vs. re-experiencing.

While such an exercise in exploring this conceptual space is useful, it also raises the problem of how to narrow things down to more manageable proportions – for narrow things down one must. By listing so many dimensions and terms populating the conceptual landscape of thought about collective memory, it would appear that I have only managed to open a Pandora's box. How does one make the decision about which issues *not* to address? The most obvious response to such questions is to start talking about one's limited time and expertise (both true), but in fact my reasons for limiting the focus of this work have more to do with theoretical orientation. Specifically, by taking collective remembering to be a distributed phenomenon involving active agents using textual resources, and by considering the voices associated with these textual resources, I was inevitably led to focus on certain forms of memory and empirical phenomena.

The upshot of all of this is that the list of things that I have *not* examined is much longer than what I have. For example, I have only touched on the issue of re-experiencing, a topic that has been the focus of much of the study of commemoration (Gillis, 1994a). My focus has also given short shrift to the impact of informal learning at home and elsewhere out of school, something that Wineburg (2001) argues may have, if anything, more of an impact than that of formal instruction. And my focus on how textual resources are often transparent, or invisible to their users, has led me away from cases such as those explored by James Young (2000), in which texts are the object of explicit reflection. The list goes on and on, and about the only certain conclusion one can take away from it all is that there is no shortage of issues to take up in the future.

Listing all of these alternatives does not mean, however, that my choice of empirical phenomena is unmotivated. Instead, my concern with how modern states produce the textual resources for collective memory, and how these resources are consumed, reflects a decision to study what is probably the most important experiment in collective remembering in the modern world. It is hard to think of a more extended and massive effort to create and control collective memory than that mounted by modern states, especially through their education systems.

Things often seem to come in triads, and in this connection I would note that three basic themes run throughout my efforts to pursue the three tasks of this book. The first theme is that collective remembering is active. Hence the term *remembering* in the title of the book. I have argued that rather than being a thing, or possession, remembering is best understood as a form of action. Specifically, it is a form of mediated action, meaning that it is fundamentally distributed between active agents, on the one hand, and the cultural tools – especially narrative texts – that they employ, on the other.

The second theme is that collective remembering is essentially social. To say this is of course redundant, but it bears repetition and clarification. What I have in mind has to do with the way I have extended Halbwachs's claim that it is "individuals as group members who remember" (1980, p. 48) – namely, I have pursued this claim by drawing on the ideas of Bakhtin and others about semiotic mediation. Specifically, I have argued that the textual resources we employ in collective remembering always belong to, and hence reflect, a social context and history. This is what lies behind the term *voices* in the title of the volume. It means that instead of being neutral, or asocial, the textual resources employed in collective remembering bring with them a social position and perspective. Given this, it becomes obvious that even when a solitary individual engages in remembering, the exercise is likely to involve an inherently social dimension. In the sort of memory I have examined, it is no more possible to remember without invoking cultural tools that reflect a social heritage than it is possible to speak without employing language.

The third theme that runs throughout this book is that collective remembering is dynamic. As I outlined in Chapter 3, collective memory often makes claims of stability and constancy, but in fact it appears that one of the few genuinely durable attributes of collective memory is that it undergoes change. When examining the production of official history, for example, I proposed that both the dialogic and referential functions of narrative texts can provide impetus for change, and that they exist in a system of functional dualism that itself varies from one context to another. And under the heading of textual consumption, I outlined cases in which the control of narrative information and the control of narrative performance undergo rapid and drastic transformation.

As I have argued at several points, the transition from Soviet to post-Soviet Russia provides an ideal natural laboratory for examining these issues. To be sure, it is unrepresentative in some important respects. Instead of the more typical ongoing, incremental process, it was part of the massive turmoil surrounding the break-up of the USSR. The transformation involved was particularly wrenching because it began with a context of tight state control over collective remembering and moved to one that sometimes seems to be characterized primarily by chaos. The story of post-Soviet Russia is at least in part a particular story of how people respond to strict state control of collective memory once this control is relaxed, and in that respect it may not be representative of what occurs in cases where public negotiation of memory goes on in calmer circumstances. But in many important respects, the way this "bent twig" (Berlin, 1991) snapped back offers insight into underlying forces of state control of memory anywhere.

In pursuing these issues, I noted that there is a tendency to view new official histories as emerging primarily in response to the referential function of narratives, something that leads to claims about how access to newly opened archives has given rise to novel truths about the past in the post-Soviet context. In Chapter 5, however, I showed that the dialogic function can play an essential, if not overriding, role in this setting. This is the force that resulted in novel versions of official history in Russia sometimes looking more like lists of counter-claims and rebuttals than narratives grounded in new evidence.

Although a dialogic orientation of narratives may have taken on extreme form in this context, it is an important force in producing official history anywhere. For example, the "culture wars" that surrounded recent efforts to adopt a new set of history standards in the United States (Nash, Crabtree, & Dunn, 1997) would appear to have more to do with how one ideological voice responds to another than with new archives or other forms of information. In all cases, the issue is one of the relative weight given to the dialogic and referential functions of narratives, but the cases of textual production I examined are characterized by a prominent emphasis on the former.

I argued that the particular dynamics of the dialogic function of narrative texts in the Russian setting reflect the tradition of Manichaean thinking outlined by authors such as Lotman and Uspenskii (1985) and Kvakin (1998). This tradition seems to be very much alive, at least in the first generation of post-Soviet textbooks. At the same time, there is a countervailing element of continuity that continues to influence the production of new official textual resources. In my view, this continuity can be understood in terms of the triumph-over-alien-forces schematic narrative template. Thus, in addition to the radical disjuncture and transformation that seem to characterize processes at a surface level, a force of continuity, or *"regeneration of archaic forms"* (Lotman & Uspenskii, 1985, p. 33) also appears to be at work.

If the Russian case provides insight into several aspects of the production of collective memory, it is, if anything, even more revealing when it comes to how official narrative resources are consumed, or used. The differences between the Soviet-educated and post-Soviet generations' accounts of World War II delineated in Chapter 7 are striking. Indeed, many people who went through the Soviet educational system are astounded, if not offended, by them. As outlined there, the post-Soviet generation demonstrates little mastery, and even less appropriation, of the specific narratives built around mid-level events that were the hallmark of official collective memory in the Soviet years.

As I suggested in Chapter 7, however, this does not mean that collective remembering in the younger generation can be adequately characterized simply in terms of what they do *not* know or believe. Something else is emerging in place of the mastery of the specific narratives that formed the core of the essays by the Soviet-educated subjects. Specifically, subjects from the younger generation seem to rely on a combination of the triumph-over-alien-forces schematic narrative template and information about abstract and highly concrete events and personages to come up with their accounts of World War II. This new strategy may not yield satisfactory versions of this event in the eyes of many, but it should not be mistaken for nothing more than a poor version of the older generation's version of collective memory.

The evidence I reviewed in Chapter 6 suggests just how much constant effort and vigilance a state may be willing to devote to controlling the collective memory of its citizens. The Soviet state aspired not only to control narrative information, but also narrative performance. And the findings I outlined in Chapter 7 indicate what can happen in fairly short order if such effort and vigilance lapse. In the space of one decade, it appears that collective remembering, at least as manifested in the public sphere, has undergone drastic change in Russia. It can indeed be very dynamic.

Underlying my analysis of all these changes is the claim that collective remembering, at least of the sort dealt with in this book, is an inherently distributed phenomenon. It is defined by an irreducible tension between active agents and the textual resources they employ, especially narrative texts. From this perspective, it would be misguided to search for collective memory in libraries and other depositories of texts, on the one hand, or in individuals or groups considered in isolation from textual resources, on the other. If one starts from this perspective, one is naturally led to pose questions about how textual resources are produced by those who have the power and authority to do so and how they are consumed (mastered, appropriated, used in public and private performance regions, and so forth) by members of a collective.

My main focus has been on the modern state as the producer of official, obligatory narratives, and on how it also seeks to control the consumption of these textual resources. In the broader scheme of things, however, it is worth keeping in mind that such memory existed well before the emergence of states as we know them today. Observations such as those by Nora (Chapter 2) remind us that history and collective remembering have not always been understood in today's terms, and have not always been under the control of states.

Hence my analysis of collective memory is only one chapter in a bigger story. Over the past few centuries, the differentiation of analytical history from collective memory and an ensuing redefinition of the latter have been important developments in the Western tradition (Chapter 2). And if Anthony Aveni (1989) is right, even more pronounced differences often exist when one considers non-Western traditions. According to his account, cultures can be marked off from one another by their sense of time, and this may differ radically from what the modern state provides in the way of narrative resources.

It is also to be expected that the future will witness the emergence of new forms of collective remembering. In particular, it is likely that groups operating at levels other than the state will play new and more important roles. At the sub-state level, Bodnar has shown how this had already begun to take place in the United States as ethnic groups, local communities, and other collectives took on increasingly important roles in the negotiation of public memory during the twentieth century. We can also expect supranational efforts to emerge. Indeed, if authors such as Arjun Appadurai (1996) are right, these efforts are already well underway.

The more general point is that no matter how collective memory is formed and who controls it, the same basic structural tools – narrative texts – must be employed. This claim has parallels in the writings of figures such as Roman Jakobson and Petr Bogatyrev (1971) on the relationship between folklore and literature. In their article, they focus primarily on differences, but an underlying assumption is that the two forms are inherently linked by a basic set of narrative tools. Other authors, such as Jack Goody (1991), reinforce the notion that there are important differences between spoken and written textual practices and cultures, but in the end it is still narrative in some form that organizes human ways of knowing the past.

An essential question raised by the data I have examined concerns the various levels at which narrative organization influences collective remembering. The two levels I have outlined are specific narratives organized around mid-level events and schematic narrative templates that operate at a more abstract level. The findings I report suggest that the latter continue to operate even when the former seem to have largely disappeared in collective remembering.

In the case of production, attempts by post-Soviet Russian authorities to introduce new textual resources seem at first glance to have yielded radically new narratives, ones that could only be judged as blasphemous from a Soviet perspective. Despite the appearance of radical transformation motivated by binary thinking and Manichaean thinking, however, an important element of continuity comes through in new history textbooks and other state-sponsored accounts of the past, a kind of continuity that reflects the influence of a schematic narrative template. An analogous point can be made about consumption. There is no doubt about the existence of striking generational differences in the collective memory for World War II in Russia. These differences come into view in connection with the mastery of official narratives, their appropriation, and the control of narrative information and performance. At the same time, however, the triumph-over-alien-forces narrative template continues to make its influence felt in the post-Soviet generation.

These findings raise as many questions as they answer, especially questions about the nature of schematic narrative templates and their effect on collective remembering. Scholars of folklore (Propp, 1968), cognitive psychology, anthropology (Boyer, 2001), and other fields have long suggested that there may be some sort of basic universal vocabulary of concepts, or semantic primitives that shape all human understanding of the world. There is evidence to suggest that this is the case even in realms such as folklore and religion, where we usually assume cultural differences are very pronounced. It may be that schematic narrative templates are built out of these conceptual, or semantic, primitives, and this will be an important issue to pursue.

But this should not be taken to suggest that similarities among the schematic narrative templates of various groups are so great that differences among them are trivial or nonexistent. As noted in Chapter 3, schematic narrative templates are not some sort of universal archetypes. Instead, they reflect particular narrative traditions. We still know very little about how these traditions are to be understood or how they are transmitted from one generation to another. With regard to the issue of transmission, the data I have reported suggest that public socialization efforts found in formal schooling may be successful in promulgating specific narratives built around mid-level events, but other sites of socialization may play a role in the case of schematic narrative templates. These templates apparently can re-emerge in a generation even when formal instruction seems not to play a role. These sites of socialization may be private discourse settings, the media, and so forth.

The forms of collective remembering that emerge out of various schematic narrative templates may differ, sometimes radically, from one another. What often remains most interesting – and potentially dangerous – is how these differences give rise to distinct collective identities. In Chapter 5, for instance, I noted that in addition to using the triumph-over-alien-forces schematic narrative template to grasp together facts about Russia's past, it is possible to employ a narrative template about the expansion of a Russian empire. This narrative resource has been rejected out of hand by many Russians for centuries, but it is at the core of many others' interpretation of Russia's past. Both of these schematic narrative templates may be constructed out of a relatively small set of conceptual primitives, but they obviously differ radically, and it is this difference that on more than one occasion has led to massive misunderstanding and conflict.

Despite the fact that important questions about the nature of schematic narrative templates remain unanswered at this point, a couple of points can be made. First, schematic narrative templates seem to be deeply rooted in particular narrative traditions, so much so that they may survive the appearance and disappearance of massive efforts by states to inculcate specific narratives organized around mid-level events. Second, narrative templates are probably especially transparent in the sense outlined in Chapter 1. From my comments there about what Sasha told me about World War II, it appears that he was looking right through the narrative resources he was using. In his case, the resources were specific narratives and mid-level events. If anything, schematic narrative templates are likely to be even more transparent – and hence less accessible to our consciousness – than were the resources used by Sasha.

This is probably an important part of their effectiveness and staying power. Of course, it is also something that makes them even more impervious to rational argumentation and negotiation. As one considers the responses from the post-Soviet generation of respondents as reported in Chapter 7, it seems likely that they may be, if anything, less aware of the narrative resources they were employing than Sasha was. In their view, they were simply telling what happened. It might be extremely difficult to argue with them about specifics, if for no other reason than that virtually no specific, mid-level events were to be found in their texts.

In the end, my emphasis is not so much on particular forms of collective memory or particular settings in which it has emerged. Instead, I have been primarily concerned with how we can go about understanding what these forms are and how they might operate in any setting. Key to this enterprise are the claims that collective remembering is (1) an active process, (2) inherently social and mediated by textual resources and their affiliated voices, and (3) inherently dynamic. However we go about building on these claims, the voices of collective remembering promise to shape memory and identity for as long as we can peer into the future.

References

Ahonen, S. (1992). *Clio sans uniform: A study of the post-Marxist transformation of the history curricula in East Germany and Estonia, 1986–1991*. Annales Academiae Scientiarum Fennicae B:264. Jyväskylä: Gummerus.

Ahonen, S. (1997). The transformation of history: The official representation of history in East Germany and Estonia, 1986–1991. *Culture and psychology*, 3(1), pp. 41–62.

Aitmatov, Ch. (1988). *The day lasts more than a hundred years*. Bloomington: Indiana University Press (translated by John French; foreword by Katerina Clark).

Anderson, B. (1991). *Imagined communities: Reflections on the origin and spread of nationalism*. London: Verso.

Appadurai, A. (1996). *Modernity at large: Cultural dimensions of globalization*. Minneapolis: University of Minnesota Press.

Appleby, J., Hunt, L., & Jacob, M. (1994). *Telling the truth about history*. New York: Norton.

Asmolov, A. (1998). *Vygotsky today: On the verge of non-classical psychology*. Commack, NY: Nova Science Publishers, Inc.

Aveni, A.F. (1989). *Empires of time: Calendars, clocks, and cultures*. New York: Basic Books.

Bakhtin, M.M. (1981). *The dialogic imagination: Four essays by M.M. Bakhtin*. Austin: University of Texas Press (edited by M. Holquist; translated by C. Emerson and M. Holquist).

Bakhtin, M.M. (1984). *Problems of Dostoevsky's poetics*. Minneapolis: University of Minnesota Press (edited and translated by C. Emerson).

Bakhtin, M.M. (1986a). The problem of speech genres. In Bakhtin, M.M. (1986). *Speech genres & other late essays*. Austin: University of Texas Press, pp. 60–102 (translated by Vern W. McGee; edited by Caryl Emerson and Michael Holquist).

Bakhtin, M.M. (1986b). The problem of the text in linguistics, philology, and the human sciences: An experiment in philosophical analysis. In Bakhtin, M.M. (1986). *Speech genres & other late essays*. Austin: University of Texas Press, pp. 103–131 (translated by Vern W. McGee; edited by Caryl Emerson and Michael Holquist).

Bartlett, F.C. (1995). *Remembering: A study in experimental and social psychology.* Cambridge: Cambridge University Press (first published in 1932).

Bauman, R. (1986). *Story, performance, and event: Contextual studies of oral narrative.* New York: Cambridge University Press.

Bechtel, W. & Abrahamsen, A. (1991). *Connectionism and the mind: An introduction to parallel processing in networks.* Oxford: Blackwell.

Benjamin, W. (1978). Moscow. In *Reflections: Essays, aphorisms, autobiographical writings.* New York: Harcourt Brace Jovanovich (translated by Edmund Jephcott; edited with an introduction by Peter Demetz).

Benveniste, E. (1971). *Problems in general linguistics.* Coral Gables, FL: University of Miami Press (translated by Mary Elizabeth Meek).

Berdyaev, N. (1992). *The Russian idea.* Hudson, NY: Lindisfarne Press (translated by R.M. French).

Berkhin, I.B. & Fedosov, I.A. (1976). *Istoriya SSSR. Uchebnik dlya 9 klassa* [History of the USSR. Textbook for the ninth grade]. Moscow: Prosveshchenie.

Berlin, I. (1991). The bent twig: On the rise of nationalism. In I. Berlin. *The crooked timber of humanity: Chapters in the history of ideas.* New York: Alfred A. Knopf, pp. 238–261 (edited by H. Hardy).

Billig, M. (1990). Collective memory, ideology and the British royal family. In D. Middleton & D. Edwards, eds., *Collective remembering.* London: Sage Publications, pp. 60–80.

Billig, M. (1995). *Banal nationalism.* Thousand Oaks, CA: Sage.

Billington, J.H. (1966). *The icon and the axe: An interpretive history of Russian culture.* New York: Knopf.

Bodnar, J. (1992). *Remaking America: Public memory, commemoration, and patriotism in the twentieth century.* Princeton: Princeton University Press.

Bovingdon, G. (2001). The history of the history of Xinjiang. *Twentieth-Century China,* vol. 26, no. 2, pp. 95–139.

Boyer, P. (1993). Cognitive aspects of religious symbolism. In P. Boyer, ed., *Cognitive aspects of religious symbolism.* Cambridge: Cambridge University Press, pp. 4–47.

Boyer, P. (1994). *The naturalness of religious ideas: A cognitive theory of religion.* Berkeley and Los Angeles: University of California Press.

Boyer, P. (1999). Human cognition and cultural evolution. In H.L. Moore, ed., *Anthropological theory today.* Cambridge: Polity Press, pp. 206–233.

Boyer, P. (2001). *Religion explained: The evolutionary origins of religious thought.* New York: Basic Books.

Boym, S. (1994). *Common places: Mythologies of everyday life in Russia.* Cambridge, MA: Harvard University Press.

Boym, S. (1996). Mythologies of everyday life in Russia: A conversation with Svetlana Boym. *Ideas from the National Humanities Center,* vol. 4, no. 1, pp. 30–38.

Bruner, J. (1986). *Actual minds, possible worlds.* Cambridge, MA: Harvard University Press.

Bruner, J. (1990). *Acts of meaning.* Cambridge, MA: Harvard University Press.

Bruner, J.S. (1996). *The culture of education.* Cambridge, MA: Harvard University Press.

Burke, K. (1957). Literature as equipment for living. In K. Burke. *The philosophy of literary forms: Studies in symbolic action* (2nd ed). New York: Vintage Books, pp. 253–262 (originally published in 1937).

Calhoun, C. (1994). Social theory and the politics of identity. In C. Calhoun, ed., *Social theory and the politics of identity*. Oxford and Cambridge, MA: Basil Blackwell, pp. 9–36.

Calhoun, C. (1997). *Nationalism*. Minneapolis: University of Minnesota Press.

Campbell, D.T. (1988). *Methodology and epistemology for social sciences: Selected papers of Donald T. Campbell*. Chicago: University of Chicago Press (edited by E. Samuel Overman).

Caruth, C. (1995a). Introduction to "Trauma and experience." In C. Caruth, ed., *Trauma: Explorations in memory*. Baltimore: The Johns Hopkins University Press, pp. 3–12.

Caruth, C. (1995b). Introduction to "Recapturing the past." In C. Caruth, ed., *Trauma: Explorations in memory*. Baltimore: The Johns Hopkins University Press, pp. 151–157.

Cassirer, E. (1944). *An essay on man: An introduction to a philosophy of human culture*. New Haven, CT: Yale University Press.

Cassirer, E. (1946). *Language and myth*. New York: Dover Publications, Inc. (translated by Suzanne Langer).

Cassirer, E. (1955). *The philosophy of symbolic forms: Volume 1: Language*. New Haven, CT: Yale University Press (translated by Ralph Manheim).

Chang, I. (1997). *The rape of Nanking: The forgotten holocaust of World War II*. New York: Penguin.

Clark, A. (1997). *Being there: Putting brain, body, and world together again*. Cambridge, MA: The MIT Press.

Cole, J. (1998). The work of memory in Madagascar. *American Ethnologist*, Vol. 25, no. 4, pp. 610–633.

Cole, J. (2001). *Forget colonialism? Sacrifice and the art of memory in Madagascar*. Berkeley: University of California Press.

Cole, M. (1996). *Cultural psychology: A once and future discipline*. Cambridge, MA: Harvard University Press.

Cole, M. & Scribner, S. (1974). *Culture and thought: A psychological introduction*. New York: Wiley.

Confino, A. (1997). Collective memory and cultural history: Problems of method. *American Historical Review*, pp. 1386–1403.

Connerton, P. (1989). *How societies remember*. Cambridge: Cambridge University Press.

Conway, M.A. (1997). The inventory of experience: Memory and identity. In J.W. Pennebaker, D. Paez, & B. Rimé, eds., *Collective memory of political events: Social psychological perspectives*. pp. 21–45.

Conway, M.A. (2001). Personal communication.

Conway, M.A. & Playdell-Pearce, C.W. (2000). The construction of autobiographical memories in the self-memory system. *Psychological Review*, vol. 107, no. 2, pp. 261–288.

Conway, M.A. & Rubin, D.C. (1993). The structure of autobiographical memory. In A.E. Collins, S.E. Gathercole, M.A. Conway, & P.E.M. Morris, eds., *Theories of memory*. Hillsdale, NJ: Lawrence Erlbaum Associates, pp. 103–137.

Cottrell, R. (2001). Russia: Was there a better way? *The New York Review of Books*, vol. XLVIII, no. 15, pp. 32–34.

Crane, S.A. (1997). Writing the individual back into collective memory. *American Historical Review*, December, 1997, pp. 1372–1385.

Cronon, W. (1992). A place for stories: Nature, history, and narrative. *The Journal of American History*. vol. 78, no. 4, pp. 1347–1376.

Danilov, A.A., Gorinov, M.M., Leonov, S.V., Lugovskaya, E.P., Senyavski, A.S., & Naumov, A.P. (1996). *The history of Russia: The twentieth century*. New York: Heron Press (translated by Galina Ustinova; translated and edited by Vincent E. Hammond).

de Certeau, M. (1984). *The practice of everyday life*, translated by Steven F. Rendall. Berkeley: University of California Press.

Deci, E.L., Eghrari, H., Patrick, B.C. & Leone, D.R. (1994). Facilitating internalization: The self-determination theory perspective. *Journal of Personality*, 62, pp. 119–142.

Donald, M. (1991). *Origins of the modern mind*. Cambridge, MA: Harvard University Press.

Douglas, M. (1980). Introduction: Maurice Halbwachs (1877–1945). In Halbwachs, M. (1980). *The collective memory*. New York: Harper & Row (translated by Francis J. Didder, Jr. and Vida Yazdi Ditter).

Dower, J.W. (1996). Three narratives of our humanity. In Linenthal, E.T. & Engelhardt, T., eds. (1996). *History wars: The Enola Gay and other battles for America's past*. New York: Metropolitan Books, pp. 63–96.

Dumont, L. (1970). Religion, politics, and society in the individualistic universe. *Proceedings of the Royal Anthropological Institute*. pp. 31–45.

Ehlers, A., & Steil, R. (1995). Maintenance of intrusive memories in Posttraumatic Stress Disorder: A cognitive approach. *Behavioural and Cognitive Psychotherapy*, 1995, 23, pp. 217–249.

Eich, E. (1989). Theoretical issues in state dependent memory. In H.L. Roediger, III, & F.I.M. Craik, eds., *Varieties of memory and consciousness: Essays in honor of Endel Tulving*. Hillsdale, NJ: Lawrence Erlbaum Associates, pp. 331–354.

Eliade, M. (1954). *The myth of the eternal return: Or, cosmos and history*. Princeton: Princeton University Press (translated by Willard R. Trask).

Ellenburger, H.F. (1970). *The discovery of the unconscious: The history and evolution of dynamic psychiatry*. New York: Basic Books.

Enteen, G.M. (1984). Marxist historians during the Cultural Revolution: A case study of professional infighting, In S. Fitzpatrick, ed., *Cultural revolution in Russia, 1928–1931*. Bloomington, IN: Indiana University Press.

Erikson, K. (1995). Notes on trauma and community. In C. Caruth, ed., *Trauma: Explorations in memory*. Baltimore: The Johns Hopkins University Press, pp. 183–199.

Figes, O. (1997). *A people's tragedy: A history of the Russian revolution*. New York: Viking.

Fitzpatrick, S. (1984), ed. *Cultural revolution in Russia, 1928–1931*. Bloomington: Indiana University Press.

Fitzpatrick, S. (1999). *Everyday Stalinism: Ordinary life in extraordinary times: Soviet Russia in the 1930s*. New York: Oxford University Press.

Franklin, H.C. & Holding, D.H. (1977). Personal memories at different ages. *Quarterly Journal of Experimental Psychology*, 29, pp. 527–532.

Freud, S. (1955). *The standard edition of the complete psychological works of Sigmund Freud*, vol. 18. Translated under the editorship of James Strachey in collaboration with Anna Freud, assisted by Alix Strachey and Alan Tyson. 24 vols. (1953–74). London: Hogarth.

Fussell, P. (1975). *The Great War and modern memory.* Oxford: Oxford University Press.

Gardiner, J.M. (2001). Episodic memory and autonoetic consciousness: A first-person approach. *Philosophical Transactions of the Royal Society of London.* Vol. 356, pp. 1351–1361.

Gardiner, J.M., & Richardson-Klavehn, A. (2000). Remembering and knowing. In E. Tulving and F.I.M. Craik, eds., *The Oxford handbook of memory.* Oxford: Oxford University Press, pp. 229–244.

Gellner, E. (1983). *Nations and nationalism.* Ithaca, NY: Cornell University Press.

Gillis, J.R., ed. (1994a). *Commemorations: The politics of national identity.* Princeton: Princeton University Press.

Gillis, J.R. (1994b). Memory and identity: The history of a relationship. In J.R. Gillis, ed., *Commemorations: The politics of national identity.* Princeton: Princeton University Press, pp. 3–24.

Goffman, E. (1959). *The presentation of self in everyday life.* Garden City, NY: Doubleday.

Goffman, E. (1974) *Frame analysis.* New York: Harper and Row.

Golubeva, T.S. & Gellershtein, L.S. (1984). *Rasskazy po istorii SSSR dlya 4 klassa. Uchebnik dlya 4 klassa* [Stories about the history of the USSR for the fourth grade. Textbook for the fourth grade]. Moscow: Prosveshchenie.

Goody, J. (1991). The time of telling and the telling of time in written and oral cultures. In J. Bender and D.E. Wellbery, eds., *The construction of time.* Stanford: Stanford University Press, pp. 77–96.

Goody, J., & Watt, I. (1963). The consequences of literacy. *Comparative studies in society and history.* vol. 5, 1962–63, pp. 304–345.

Grant, N. (1964). *Soviet education.* Baltimore: Penguin Books.

Grolnick, W.S., Deci, E.L., & Ryan, R.M. (1997). Internalization within the family: The self-determination theory perspective. In J.E. Grusec & L. Kuczynski, eds., *Parenting and children's internalization of values.* New York: Wiley, pp. 135–161.

Halbwachs, M. (1980). *The collective memory.* New York: Harper & Row (translated by Francis J. Didder, Jr. and Vida Yazdi Ditter).

Halbwachs, M. (1992). *On collective memory.* Chicago: University of Chicago Press (edited, translated, and with an introduction by Lewis A. Coser).

Handler, R. (1994). Is "identity" a useful cross-cultural construct? In J.R. Gillis, ed., *Commemorations: The politics of national identity.* Princeton: Princeton University Press, pp. 27–40.

Heller, M. (1988). *Cogs in the wheel: The formation of Soviet man.* New York: Knopf.

Heller, M. & Nekrich, A. (1986). *Utopia in power: The history of the Soviet Union from 1917 to the present.* New York: Summit Books (translated by Phyllis B. Carlos).

Hinsz, V.B., Tindale, R.S., & Vollrath, D.A. (1997). The emerging conceptualization of group as information processes. *Psychological Bulletin,* 121 (1), pp. 43–64.

Hirsch, E.D. (1988). *Cultural literacy: What every American needs to know.* New York: Vintage.

Hobsbawm, E. & Ranger, T. (1983). *The invention of tradition.* Cambridge: Cambridge University Press.

Holquist, M. (1981). The politics of representation. In S. Greenblatt, ed., *Allegory in representation: Selected papers from the English Institute.* Baltimore: Johns Hopkins University Press, pp. 163–183.

Holquist, M. and C. Emerson (1981). Glossary for M.M. Bakhtin, *The dialogic imagination: Four essays by M.M. Bakhtin.* Austin: University of Texas Press (edited by M. Holquist; translated by C. Emerson and M. Holquist).

Hroch, M. (1985). *Social preconditions of national revival in Europe: A comparative analysis of the social composition of patriotic groups among the smaller European nations.* New York: Cambridge University Press (translated by Ben Fowkes).

Husband, W.B. (1991). Secondary school history texts in the USSR: Revising the Soviet past, 1985–1989. *The Russian Review,* vol. 50, October 1991, pp. 458–480.

Hutchins, E. (1995). *Cognition in the wild.* Cambridge, MA: The MIT Press.

Ivanova, E. (1994). The relationship between types of thinking and the ways of remembering. *Journal of Russian and East European Psychology,* no. 2, pp. 33–49.

Ivanova, E. (1999). Personal communication, September 26,1999.

Jakobson, R. & Bogatyrev, P. (1971). On the boundary between studies of folklore and literature. In L. Matejka and K. Pomorska, eds, *Readings in Russian poetics: Formalist and structuralist views.* Cambridge, MIT Press, pp. 91–93.

James, W. (1890). *The principles of psychology.* New York: Dover.

Kammen, M. (1993). *Mystic chords of memory: The transformation of tradition in American culture.* New York: Vintage Books.

Kermode, F. (1967). *The sense of an ending: Studies in the theory of fiction.* New York: Oxford University Press.

Khubova, D., Ivankiev, A. & Sharova, T. (1992). After glasnost: Oral history in the Soviet Union. In L. Passerini, ed., *International yearbook of oral history and life stories, Vol. 1: Memory and totalitarianism.* Oxford: Oxford University Press, pp. 89–101.

Kima, M.P. (1976). *Velikaya otechestvennaya voina Sovetskogo Soyuza. 1941–1945 godov. Spetsial'nyi seminar po istorii SSSR* [The great patriotic war of the Soviet Union. 1941–1945. Special seminar on the history of the USSR]. Moscow: Prosveshchenie.

King, D. (1997) *The commissar vanishes: The falsification of photographs and art in Stalin's Russia.* New York: Metropolitan Books (preface by Stephen F. Cohen; photographs from the David King collection).

Klein, K.L. (2000). On the emergence of *memory* in historical discourse. *Representations,* 69, Winter 2000, pp. 127–150.

Korablëv, Yu.I, Fedosov, I.A. & Borisov, Yu.S. (1989). *Istoriya SSSR. Uchebnik dlya desyatogo klassa srednei shkoly* [History of the USSR. Textbook for the tenth grade of middle school]. Moscow: Prosveshchenie.

Krivoguz, I.M., Pritsker, D.P., & Stetskevich, S.M. (1964). *Noveishaya istoriya (1917– 1945gg.). Uchebnoe posobie dlya srednei shkoly* [Contemporary history (1917–1945). Textbook for middle school]. Moscow: Prosveshchenie.

Krystal, J. (1990). Animal models for Post-Traumatic Stress Disorder. In E.L. Giller, Jr., ed., *Biological assessment and treatment of Post-Traumatic Stress Disorder.* Washington, D.C.: American Psychiatric Press.

Kvakin, A.V. (1998). Stalinskii mif o "vnutrennem vrage" i poisk "vnutrennego vraga" v beloi emigratsii [The Stalinist myth of the "internal enemy" and the search for the "internal enemy" in the White emigration]. *Istoricheskaya psikhologiya stalinizma i ee sud'ba. Tezisy mezhdunarodnoi nauchnoi mezhdistsiplinarnoi konferentsii. Sankt-Peterburg, 19–21 maya 1998* [The historical psychology of Stalinism and its fate. Theses from an international scientific interdisciplinary conference. Saint Petersburg, May 19–21,1998]. Sankt-Peterburg: Minerva-2, pp. 39–42.

Langer, S.K. (1949). On Cassirer's theory of language and myth. In P.A. Schilpp, ed., *The philosophy of Ernst Cassirer*. Evanston, IL: Library of Living Philosophers. pp. 381–400.

Leont'ev, A.N. (1981). The problem of activity in psychology. In J.V. Wertsch, ed., *The concept of activity in Soviet psychology*. Armonk, NY: M.E. Sharpe.

Lieven, D. (2000). *Empire: The Russian empire and its rivals*. New Haven: Yale University Press.

Linenthal, E.T. (1996). Anatomy of a controversy. In Linenthal, E.T. & Engelhardt, T. eds. (1996). *History wars: The Enola Gay and other battles for America's past*. New York: Metropolitan Books, pp. 9–62.

Linenthal, E.T. & Engelhardt, T. eds. (1996). *History wars: The Enola Gay and other battles for America's past*. New York: Metropolitan Books.

Lotman, Yu.M. (1988). Text within a text. *Soviet Psychology*. 1988, vol. XXVI, no. 3, pp. 32–51.

Lotman, Yu.M. (1990). *Universe of the mind: A semiotic theory of culture*. Bloomington: Indiana University Press (translated by Ann Shukman).

Lotman, Yu.M. & Uspenskii, B.A. (1985). Binary models in the dynamics of Russian culture (to the end of the eighteenth century). In A.D. Nakhimovsky & A.S. Nakhimovsky, eds., *The semiotics of Russian cultural history. Essays by Iurii M. Lotman, Lidiia Ia. Ginsburg, Boris A. Uspenskii*. Ithaca: Cornell University Press (pp. 30–66).

Lowenthal, D. (1994). Identity, heritage, and history. In J.R. Gillis, ed., *Commemorations: The politics of national identity*. Princeton: Princeton University Press, pp. 41–57.

Lucy, J.A. (1992). *Language diversity and thought: A reformulation of the linguistic relativity hypothesis*. Cambridge: Cambridge University Press.

Lucy, J.A. & Wertsch, J.V. (1987). Vygotsky and Whorf: A comparative analysis. In M. Hickmann, ed., *Social and functional approaches to language and thought*. New York: Academic Press, pp. 67–86.

Luria, A.R. (1928). The problem of the cultural development of the child. *Journal of Genetic Psychology*, 35, pp. 493–506.

Luria, A.R. (1979). *The making of mind: A personal account of Soviet psychology*. Cambridge, MA: Harvard University Press (edited by Michael & Sheila Cole).

MacIntyre, A. (1984). *After virtue: A study in moral theory*. Notre Dame, Indiana: University of Notre Dame Press.

Mannheim, K. (1952). The problem of generations. Chapter VII in K. Mannheim, *Essays on the sociology of knowledge*. London: Routledge & Kegan Paul Ltd., pp. 276–320 (edited by Paul Kecskemeti).

Markowitz, F. (2000). *Coming of age in post-Soviet Russia*. Urbana: University of Illinois Press.

Mendeloff, D. (1996). The re-centering of Russian education. *ISRE Newsletter on East European, Eurasian and Russian education*, 5(2), pp. 15–20.

Mendeloff, D. (1997). Nationalism and history textbooks in post-Soviet Russia: The case of the "Great Patriotic War." Paper presented at the 29th National

Convention of the American Association for the Advancement of Slavic Studies, Seattle, November, 1997.

Merridale, C. (2000). *Night of stone: Death and memory in twentieth-century Russia.* New York: Viking.

Middleton, D. & Edwards, D. (1990a). Conversational remembering: A social psychological approach. In D. Middleton & D. Edwards (1990), eds., *Collective remembering.* London: Sage Publications, pp. 23–45.

Middleton, D. & Edwards, D. (1990), eds., *Collective remembering.* London: Sage Publications.

Mink, L.O. (1978). Narrative form as a cognitive instrument. In R.H. Canary and H. Kozicki, eds., *The writing of history: Literary form and historical understanding.* Madison: University of Wisconsin Press, pp. 129–149.

Mink, L.O. (1981). Everyman his or her own annalist. In W.J.T. Mitchell, ed., *On narrative.* Chicago: University of Chicago Press, pp. 233–239.

Nash, G.B., Crabtree, C., & Dunn, R.E. (1997). *History on trial: Culture wars and the teaching of the past.* New York: Alfred A. Knopf.

Neisser, U. (1967). *Cognitive psychology.* New York: Appleton-Century-Crofts.

Nora, P. (1989). Between memory and history: *Les lieux de mémoire. Representations,* Spring, 1989, vol. 26, pp. 7–25.

Novick, P. (1988). *That noble dream: The "objectivity question" and the American historical profession.* Cambridge: Cambridge University Press.

Novick, P. (1996). Personal communication with E.T. Linenthal. Cited in Linenthal, 1996, p. 28.

Novick, P. (1999). *The Holocaust in American life.* Boston: Houghton Mifflin Company.

Olnick, J.K. (1999). Collective memory: The two cultures. *Sociological Theory,* vol. 17, no. 3, pp. 333–348.

Olson, D.R. (1994). *The world on paper: The conceptual and cognitive implications of writing and reading.* Cambridge: Cambridge University Press.

Orwell, G. (1949). *Nineteen eighty-four.* New York: Harcourt, Brace & World.

Ostrovskii, A.V. & Utkin, A.I. (1995). *Istoriya Rossii. XX vek. 11 klass. Uchebnik dlya obshcheobrazovatel'nykh uchebnykh zavedenii* [The history of Russia. XX century. 11th grade. A textbook for general educational academic institutions]. Moscow: Izdatel'skii dom Drofa.

Passerini, L. (1992). Introduction. In L. Passerini, ed., *International yearbook of oral history and life stories, Vol. 1: Memory and totalitarianism.* Oxford: Oxford University Press, pp. 1–19.

Pasternak, B. (1981). *Doctor Zhivago.* New York: Balantine Books.

Pennebaker, J.W., Paez, D., B. Rimé, eds,. (1997). *Collective memory of political events: Social psychological perspectives.* Mahwah, NJ: Lawrence Erlbaum Associates.

Pillemer, D.B. & White, S.H. (1989). Childhood events recalled by children and adults. *Advances in Child Development and Behavior,* 21, pp. 297–340.

Propp, V. (1968). *Morphology of the folktale.* Austin: University of Texas Press (translated by Laurence Scott).

Proust, M. (1982). *Remembrance of things past.* New York: Random House (translated by C. K. Scott-Moncrieff and Terence Kilmartin).

Radzinsky, E. (1996). *Stalin.* New York: Doubleday (translated by H.T. Willetts).

Raeff, M. (1966). *Origins of the Russian intelligentsia: The eighteenth-century nobility.* New York: Harcourt, Brace & World.

Reddy, M.J. (1979). The conduit metaphor: A case of frame conflict in our language about language. In A. Ortony, ed., *Metaphor and thought*. Cambridge: Cambridge University Press.

Remnick, D. (1993). *Lenin's tomb: The last days of the Soviet empire*. New York: Random House.

Ricoeur, P. (1984–86). *Time and narrative*, 2 vols. Chicago: University of Chicago Press (translated by Kathleen McLaughlin and David Pellauer).

Roediger, H.L. (1996). Memory illusions. *Journal of Memory and Language*, 35, pp. 76–100.

Roediger, H.L., & Goff, L.M. (1998). Memory. In W. Bechtel & G. Graham, eds., *A companion to cognitive science*. Oxford: Blackwell, pp. 250–264.

Roediger, H.L., & McDermott, K.B. (2000). Distortions of memory. In E. Tulving & F.I.M. Craik, eds., *The Oxford handbook of memory*. Oxford: Oxford University Press, pp. 149–162.

Rosa, A. (1996). Bartlett's psycho-anthropological project. *Culture and Psychology*, 2(2), pp. 355–378.

Ross, M. (1989). Relation of implicit theories to the construction of personal histories. *Psychological Review*, vol. 96, no. 2, pp. 341–357.

Ryle, G. (1949). *The concept of mind*. London: Barnes and Noble Books/Harper Row.

Sacks, O. (1990). *The man who mistook his wife for a hat and other clinical tales*. New York: HarperPerennial.

Schacter, D.L., ed., (1995). *Memory distortion: How minds, brains, and societies reconstruct the past*. Cambridge, MA: Harvard University Press.

Schacter, D. L. (1996). *Searching for memory: The brain, the mind, and the past*. New York: Basic Books.

Schafer, R. Narration in the psychoanalytic dialogue. In W.J.T. Mitchell, ed., *On narrative*. Chicago: University of Chicago Press, pp. 25–49.

Schlesinger, Jr., A.M. (1992). *The disuniting of America: Reflections on a multicultural society*. New York: Norton.

Scholes, R. & Kellogg, R. (1966). *The nature of narrative*. Oxford: Oxford University Press.

Schudson, M. (1990). Ronald Reagan misremembered. In D. Middleton & D. Edwards, eds., *Collective remembering*. London: Sage Publications, pp. 108–119.

Schudson, M. (1992). *Watergate in American memory: How we remember, forget, and reconstruct the past*. New York: Basic Books.

Schudson, M. (1995). Dynamics of distortion in collective memory. In D.L. Schacter, ed., *Memory distortion: How minds, brains, and societies reconstruct the past*. Cambridge, MA: Harvard University Press, pp. 346–364.

Schuman, H., Belli, R.F., & Bischoping, K. (1997). The generational basis of historical knowledge. In J.W. Pennebaker, D. Paez, & B. Rimé, eds., *Collective memory of political events: Social psychological processes*. Mahwah, NJ: Lawrence Erlbaum Associates Publishers, pp. 47–77.

Schuman, H. & Scott, J. (1989). Generations and collective memories. *American Sociological Review*, 54, pp. 359–381.

Schwartz, B. (1990). The reconstruction of Abraham Lincoln. In D. Middleton & D. Edwards, eds., *Collective remembering*. London: Sage Publications, pp. 81–107.

Seixas, P. (2000). Schweigen! die Kinder! or, does postmodern history have a place in the schools? In P.N. Sterns, P. Seixas, & S. Wineburg, eds., *Knowing, teaching, and learning history: National and international perspectives*. New York: New York University Press, pp. 20–37.

Sherry, P. (1996). Patriotic orthodoxy and American decline. In E.T. Linenthal & T. Engelhardt, eds, *History wars: The Enola Gay and other battles for the American past*. New York: Metropolitan Books, pp. 97–114.

Shirer, W. (1991). *Rise and Fall of the Third Reich: A History of Nazi Germany*. New York: Fawcett.

Shlapentokh, V. (1996). Early feudalism – The best parallel for contemporary Russia. *Europe-Asia Studies*, vol. 48, no. 3, pp. 393–411.

Smirnov, G. (1973). *Soviet man: The making of a socialist type of personality*. Moscow: Progress.

Smith, A.D. (1991). *National identity*. Reno: University of Nevada Press.

Smith, B.H. (1981). Narrative versions, narrative theories. In W.J.T. Mitchell, ed., *On narrative*. Chicago: University of Chicago Press, pp. 209–232.

Solzhenitsyn, A.I. (1976). *Lenin in Zurich*. New York: Farrar, Straus and Giroux (translated by H.T. Willetts).

Stishov, M.I. (1976). *Velikaya otechestvennaya voina Sovetskogo Soyuza. 1941–1945 godov. Spetsial'nyi seminar po istorii SSSR* [The great patriotic war of the Soviet Union. 1941–1945. Special seminar on the history of the USSR]. Moscow: Uchpedgiz.

Stock, B. (1983). *The implications of literacy: Written language and models of interpretation in the eleventh and twelfth centuries*. Princeton: Princeton University Press.

Stock, B. (1990). *Listening for the text: On the uses of the past*. Philadelphia: University of Pennsylvania Press.

Suny, R.G. (1998). *The Soviet Experiment: Russia, the USSR, and the successor states*. Oxford: Oxford University Press.

Taylor, C. (1989). *Sources of the self: The making of modern identity*. Cambridge, MA: Harvard University Press.

Thelen, D. (1989). Memory and American history. *Journal of American History*, 75, pp. 1117–1129.

Tulving, E. (1972). Episodic and semantic memory. In E. Tulving & W. Donaldson, eds., *Organization of memory*. New York: Academic Press, pp. 381–403.

Tulving, E. (1983). *Elements of episodic memory. Canadian Psychologist*, 26, pp. 1–12.

Tulving, E. & Thompson, D.M. (1973). Encoding specificity and retrieval processes in episodic memory. *Psychological Review*, 80, p. 352–373.

Tulviste, P. & J.V. Wertsch (1994). Official and unofficial histories: The case of Estonia. *Journal of Narrative and Life History*, 4(4), pp. 311–329.

Tumarkin, N. (1994). *The living and the dead: The rise and fall of the cult of World War II in Russia*. New York: Basic Books.

Tyack, D. (1999). Monuments between covers: The politics of textbooks. *American Behavioral Scientist*, vol. 42, no. 6, March, 1999, pp. 922–932.

Tyack, D. (2000). Patriotic literacy: History textbooks in the nineteenth century. Unpublished manuscript. Stanford University.

Uspenskii, B.A. (1973). *A poetics of composition: The structure of the artistic text and typology of a compositional form*. Berkeley: University of California Press (translated by Valentina Zavarin and Susan Wittig).

van der Kolk, B.A. & van der Hart, O. (1995). The intrusive past: The flexibility of memory and the engraving of trauma. In C. Caruth, ed., *Trauma: Explorations in memory*. Baltimore: The Johns Hopkins University Press, pp. 158–182.

Vygotsky, L.S. (1978). *Mind in society: The development of higher psychological processes*. Cambridge, MA: Harvard University Press (edited by M. Cole, V. John-Steiner, S. Scribner, and E. Souberman).

Vygotsky, L.S. (1981). The genesis of higher mental functions. In J.V. Wertsch, ed., *The concept of activity in Soviet psychology*. Armonk, NY: M.E. Sharpe, pp. 144–188.

Vygotsky, L.S. (1987). *The collected works of L.S. Vygotsky. Volume 1. Problems of general psychology. Including the volume Thinking and Speech*. New York: Plenum (edited and translated by N. Minick).

Weiner, A. (1996). The making of a dominant myth. The Second World War and the construction of political identities with the Soviet polity. *The Russian Review*, 55, pp. 638–660.

Weldon, M.S. (2001). Remembering as a social process. In D.L. Medin, ed., *The psychology of learning and motivation*. San Diego: Academic Press. pp. 67–120.

Weldon, M.S. & Bellinger, K.D. (1997). Collective memory: Collaborative and individual processes in remembering. *Journal of Experimental Psychology: Learning, Memory, & Cognition*, 23, pp. 1160–1175.

Wertsch, J.V. (1985). *Vygotsky and the social formation of mind*. Cambridge, MA: Harvard University Press.

Wertsch, J.V. (1991). *Voices of the mind: A sociocultural approach to mediated action*. Cambridge, MA: Harvard University Press.

Wertsch, J.V. (1993). Commentary on J.A. Lawrence & J. Valsiner. "Conceptual roots of internalization: From transmission to transformation." *Human Development*, 1993, 36, 3, pp. 168–171.

Wertsch, J.V. (1994). Struggling with the past: Some dynamics of historical representation. In M. Carretero & J.F. Voss, eds., *Cognitive and instructional processes in history and the social sciences*, pp. 323–338.

Wertsch, J.V. et al. (1997). Memory, history, and identity in the former Soviet Union. Final report to the National Council on Eurasian and East European Research. Washington, D.C.

Wertsch, J.V. (1998). *Mind as action*. New York: Oxford University Press.

Wertsch, J.V. & O'Connor, K. (1994). Multivoicedness in historical representation: American college students' accounts of the origins of the U.S. *Journal of Narrative and Life History*, 4(4), pp. 295–310.

White, G.M. (1997). Museum, memorial, shrine: National narrative in national spaces. Theme issue. "Public history and national narrative," *Museum Anthropology*, 21(1), pp. 8–27.

White, H. (1981a). The narrativization of real events. In W.J.T. Mitchell, ed., *On narrative*. Chicago: University of Chicago Press, pp. 249–254.

White, H. (1981b). The value of narrativity in the representation of reality. In W.J.T. Mitchell, ed., *On narrative*. Chicago: University of Chicago Press, pp. 1–23.

White, H. (1987). *The content of the form: Narrative discourse and historical representation*. Baltimore: The Johns Hopkins University Press.

Whorf, B.L. (1956). *Language, thought, and reality: Selected writings of Benjamin Lee Whorf*. Cambridge, MA: MIT Press (edited by J. Carroll).

Wills, J.S. (1994). Popular culture, curriculum, and historical representation: The situation of Native Americans in American education history and the perpetuation of stereotypes. *Journal of Narrative and Life History*, 4(4), pp. 277–294.

Wineburg, S.S. (1991). On the reading of historical texts: Notes on the breach between school and academy. *American Educational Research Journal*, Fall, 1991, vol. 28, no. 3, pp. 495–519.

Wineburg, S.S. (2001). *Historical thinking and other unnatural acts: Charting the future of teaching the past*. Philadelphia: Temple University Press.

Winter, J. (1995). *Sites of memory, sites of mourning: The Great War in European cultural history*. Cambridge: Cambridge University Press.

Yates, F.A. (1966). *The art of memory*. Chicago: University of Chicago Press.

Young, J.E. (1988). *Writing and rewriting the Holocaust: Narrative and the consequence of interpretation*. Bloomington: Indiana University Press.

Young, J.E. (2000). *At memory's edge: After-images of the Holocaust in contemporary arts and architecture*. New Haven: Yale University Press.

Zamora, L.P. (1998). *The usable past: The imagination of history in recent fiction of the Americas*. Cambridge: Cambridge University Press.

Zharova, L.N. & Mishina, I.A. (1992). *Istoriya otechestva. 1900–1940. Uchebnaya kniga dlya starshikh klassov srednykh uchebnykh savedenii* [History of the fatherland. 1900–1940. Educational book for senior students of middle educational institutions]. Moscow: Prosveshchenie.

Zinchenko, P.I. (1981). Involuntary memory and the goal-directed nature of activity. In J.V. Wertsch, ed., *The concept of activity in Soviet psychology*. Armonk, NY: M.E. Sharpe, pp. 300–340.

Index